EVERY MOVIE IS A MIRACLE

EVERY MOVIE IS A MIRACLE

A Colloquy Between
Leonard Maltin
and Nat Segaloff

Sticking Place Books
New York

ISBN 979-8-89976-003-7

CONTENTS

To my granddaughter Daisy,
who brightens my life
Leonard

For Liane Brandon
My friend, my teacher, my hero
Nat

Leonard Maltin, Los Angeles, 2025
Photograph by Jessie Maltin

INTRODUCTION

Though the comparison would make him blush, Leonard Maltin is America's Kevin Brownlow. For more than half a century—ever since he was a precocious 13-year-old—he has leveraged film fandom into a career that includes more than fifteen books as author, ten as editor, thousands of reviews and interviews, teaching, lectures, video commentaries, television specials, and inspiring and nurturing two generations of blossoming film scholars. In this regard he is a popularizer as well as a historian, a savvy communicator who has the ability to transmit his excitement about movies on both a scholarly and a fan level without one passion tainting the other. He is also a collector, filling shelves and cabinets with memorabilia reaching back a century giving a tangible, tactile sense of the growth of the film industry. His collection of toys, models, tickets, fanzines, publicity, and untold merchandise is both impressive and evocative. Moreover, he knows the provenance of every item and remembers what he had to go through to acquire it.

Maltin's success is as much the result of timing as it is of competence. Coming of age just as movies were transitioning from simple entertainment to becoming the signal art form of the baby boom generation, he began as a fan and has never lost his enthusiasm. He is even a brand name; for forty-five years, whenever someone said, "Hand me the Maltin," they were referring to *Leonard Maltin's Movie & Video Guide*, the bible of some 16,000 capsule reviews whose hefty 1632-page paperback volume (in its final edition in 2015) sat atop most TV sets. It also settled its share of bar bets and inspired the "Leonard Maltin game," about which more later.

What's astonishing about the *Movie & Video Guide*—indeed, what's striking about Maltin himself—is that he was already a seasoned film scholar when he began editing it at the age of 17. Starting when he was barely a teenager, young Leonard began attending screenings and interviewing personalities, not as a celebrity-chaser but as a nascent historian. In addition to his youthful zeal, he was blessed by two factors: he had easy access to New York City, and it was an era when many of the people who had built the American film industry were still alive and able to tell their stories to this curious, well-informed kid.

And he was indeed a kid. He produced his first periodical with a friend when they were in the fifth grade. At age 13, he became a contributor to fan periodicals, and started his own called *Profile*, an omnibus celebrity newsletter. Persistence and an encyclopedic knowledge of movies propelled him since then into the forefront of American film scholars.

Although he became most widely known when he joined *Entertainment Tonight* in May 1982 (the show business TV newsmagazine began broadcasting the previous year) and stayed there for three decades, he was already the respected author of seven influential film history books, including *Behind the Camera* (1971), *The Disney Films* (1973), *Our Gang: The Life and Times of the Little Rascals* (1977, with Richard W. Bann), and *The Great Movie Comedians* (1978).

It was that last title that brought us together, that and a phone call from our mutual friend Gary H. Grossman. At the time of its publication, I was the movie "tipster" on Boston's *Evening Magazine,* a TV show elsewhere known as *P.M. Magazine.* Leonard's publisher, Crown Books, sent him on a press tour (they did that in those days), and I was asked to interview him. I had, of course, heard of Leonard for years (we were about the same age and shared many interests), so I was pleased to finally meet him and to produce the segment. For the outro, I appeared on camera while the show's co-host, Marty Sender, asked Leonard about the essence of screen comedy. The two of them agreed that the basic gag was somebody getting a pie in the face, at which point both Marty and Leonard pied me. It was a memorable (albeit sloppy) way to start a friendship that has lasted fifty years,* the permutations of which are reflected in the exchanges that follow. What we discovered in holding these conversations is that the same people fed our devotion to motion pictures while we were growing up, except we knew them at different times and in different ways.

---

* Naturally, this being television, I got hate mail for "wasting precious food." The pies had been shaving cream, but station management told me it was useless to respond to self-righteous viewers.

Leonard has achieved the impossible status in Hollywood of being widely known, well liked, and highly respected. As this comprehensive interview reveals, he has not slowed down his activities in the age of social media. He reviews movies and books for his website (www.leonardmaltin.com), which he runs with his daughter, Jessie. He teaches at the University of Southern California, is on the board of the National Film Preservation Foundation, and is a sought-after interview subject for documentaries.

Maltin's position in film scholarship is unique. Like other cinema historians, he began his career before the internet and did his research by going archive to archive, examining traditional collections of personal papers and contemporary publications. His highly visible role on television made him the beneficiary—though sometimes the target—of film company publicists seeking coverage for their clients. He used this access to serve two masters: *Entertainment Tonight* for the puffy PR questions, and then the more serious, historically valuable questions for himself. His full transcripts, carefully filed, form a personal data bank as he continues to write, lecture, and consult.

Leonard Michael Maltin was born in New York in 1950 and named after his paternal grandfather, Leo. His family has been in the United States for three generations; his great-grandparents arrived from a corner of the Austro-Hungarian empire that was either Poland or Russia, depending upon which army had most recently invaded it. His father, Aaron Isaac Maltin (1915–2002), a lawyer, was a special hearings officer for the Immigration and Naturalization Service and, after retirement, became an immigration lawyer. Jacqueline Gould Maltin, Leonard's mother (1923–2012), was a singer and entertainer. In 1954, the year after Leonard's brother Bernard ("Bud") was born, the Maltins moved from Manhattan to Teaneck, New Jersey where Leonard graduated from Teaneck High School in 1968 and commuted to New York University where he studied journalism. He got his degree in 1972, by which time he was already publishing more than his professors were.

Like all freelancers, even those who hold long-term positions, Maltin has gone where the work is. Although these dates are noted in the text, a timeline here might be helpful:[*]

December 18, 1950: born in New York City

1954: Moves to Teaneck, New Jersey

---

[*] See the appendix for Leonard's C.V.

1962: Publishes first periodical, *The Bergen Bulletin*

1966: Takes over and publishes *Film Fan Monthly*

Fall 1968: Enters New York University

September 1969: *Leonard Maltin's TV Movies* first published

March 15, 1975: Marries Alice Tlusty

May 1982: Tapes first review for *Entertainment Tonight*

May 1982–November 1983: Commutes between New York and L.A.

November 2, 1983: The Maltins move to Los Angeles

June 16, 1986: Jessie Maltin born

March, 2012: Leaves *Entertainment Tonight* after 30 years

In addition to thirty years on *Entertainment Tonight*, Maltin has been a consistent presence on Turner Classic Movies and has written freelance for the *Los Angeles Times*, *The New York Times* (about which there's a story that follows), The *Times* of London, *Smithsonian* magazine, *TV Guide*, *Esquire*, *The Village Voice*, and *American Film* magazine. He was the *Playboy* film critic for six years. He has been guest curator at the Museum of Modern Art film department, and created, hosted, and co-produced the Walt Disney Treasures DVD compendiums, and written, produced, and hosted many video commentary tracks and special features. In 2006, he was named by the Librarian of Congress to join the Board of Directors for the National Film Preservation Foundation and was for several decades a voting member of the National Film Registry.

In 2021, Maltin published a memoir, *Starstruck: My Unlikely Road to Hollywood* (GoodKnight Books). In 2022, after contributing to their events and archives for decades, he was invited to join the Academy of Motion Picture Arts and Sciences as a member-at-large. He lives in a classically styled house in Sherman Oaks, California with Alice, Jessie and her husband Scott Hadfield; their granddaughter Daisy Bea Hadfield; and two small dogs, Logan and Mabel, who pass judgment on everyone who visits.

Inasmuch as the Author and Maltin have known each other for nearly half a century—a staggering realization any way you look at it—what follows is more of a conversation than an interview. These exchanges were conducted in Maltin's home office in Sherman Oaks, California, between August 14 and December 31, 2024, with addenda during the editing process. At times Alice Maltin will recount key moments in her and Leonard's adventures as one of Hollywood's most enduring couples.

Nat Segaloff
Los Angeles

A FAN'S NOTES

Nat Segaloff: Before we talk Hollywood, let's talk family. Where does Leonard Maltin come from?

Leonard Maltin: Years ago, I sat my parents down and did an oral history on 8mm video. When Jessie* was a month from being born, I asked the engineers at *Entertainment Tonight* what form of home video should I use to chronicle my soon-to-be daughter? (Actually, we didn't know it was going to be a daughter. We wanted to be surprised.) At the time, they said 8mm video is the way to go. It was the equivalent of Betamax, and it had the same unfortunate fate as Betamax, so now I have to get those tapes transferred to another format. But happily I have the memories of my father and my mother on record, where they talk about their family and their upbringing, their parents.

Segaloff: Your Jewish family was completely assimilated when you were born?

Maltin: Completely. That surprised Alice, because she grew up in an all-Jewish neighborhood in the Bronx, Pelham Parkway. She says she saw people with tattoos on their arms [from the concentration camps] and a lot of Bolsheviks. She was involved in local politics and when she was doing pamphleteering, she'd get angry responses in heavily-accented English, or in Yiddish. They spoke Yiddish, but my parents did not speak Yiddish. They were that American.

Segaloff: My family came over in the 1880s from Russia and Germany, and as far as we knew we were untouched by the Holocaust; we had no known family back there.

Maltin: I'm probably the same because that never came up. I remember a schoolmate of mine had an aunt or a grandmother who had a tattoo. That's the only time I ever saw that firsthand as a kid. Years and years later, I had a survivor as a guest in my class at USC because I showed James M. Moll's Oscar-winning documentary *The Last Days*† (1998). The director came and brought with him a woman named Renee Firestone, a name I'll never forget. She was a wonderful guest, and she felt, as many survivors do, that it was her mandate to tell her story to younger people, to silence the deniers and to remind people of the events. At the end of the class, students surged forward

---

* Jessie Maltin was born June 16, 1986.
† *The Last Days*, one producer of which was Steven Spielberg, is about five Jews who survived Auschwitz in the last days of Nazi Germany while the Reich was accelerating exterminations.

to touch her. They just wanted to have contact. Some of them wanted to chat with her, shake her hand or whatever, but they wanted to have some connection with her.

Segaloff: What else can you tell me about your father?

Maltin: His older brother, whom he adored, was named Bernard, and my kid brother was named after him. That's Bud, Buddy. I never knew my uncle Bernie because he died when I was a year and a half old. There was a photo of infant me with Uncle Bernie. He was a studio pianist in New York, a working pianist who also wrote songs. No big hits, but some modest successes here and there. His songs were recorded in the Thirties by "Fats" Waller and Ruth Etting and Ozzie Nelson with Harriet Hilliard. My father inherited his ASCAP estate, so growing up I was always keenly aware of the importance of airplay. One of his songs, which was called "Finesse," had lyrics put to it and became a song called "Hanging Around with You," which Dean Martin recorded in the early Fifties. Unfortunately, that cut was never reissued. When I started taking piano lessons, my father's great, great dream and goal was for me to be able to play some of Bernie's piano pieces. About once a year, Lawrence Welk performed one of his songs on his network television show. And Captain Kangaroo did a mime act to another, a novelty song he wrote called "Professor Spoons" on the CBS Television Network. The network play boosted his ASCAP ratings for that quarter, and it was always a big day in our household when one of Uncle Bernie's songs got played.

Segaloff: You wrote that your father read two daily newspapers and also subscribed to *Variety*.

Maltin: I can't make a broad statement, but I guess his brother is why he had interest in show business in general. My mother had been a professional singer and entertainer in her teens. She played nightclubs, singing and playing the accordion. Her stage name was "Jacquelina." It might've been Spanish, might've been Greek, might've been French, might've been Italian; she learned one song in each of those languages so that she could try to pass herself off. She had a look that could have been any of those. But she didn't have an encore for any of those languages.

Segaloff: You wrote that she was in *Carousel* on Broadway.[*]

---

[*] The Rodgers and Hammerstein musical based on Ferenc Molnár's

Maltin: Yes. She joined the chorus of *Carousel* after it had been playing, I think, for almost a year, and she was in it for the better part of a year. She talked about standing in the wings watching John Raitt perform "Soliloquy" night after night after night; it never got old for her. She said it was always thrilling to watch him do that. She also was on *Arthur Godfrey's Talent Scouts*—the radio version of that show in about 1949, I think. *Talent Scouts* was not an amateur show; it was a show where you had up-and-coming professionals who would be brought on as the supposed protégée of some established guest star who was the talent scout. The prize was determined by audience response on the applause meter. As she told the story, the fix was in for Vic Damone to win that week, but she got as much applause as he did. The prize was a full week of appearances on Arthur Godfrey's daily morning show (*Arthur Godfrey Time*) on CBS, so they each got a week on the show. Nothing came of it. It didn't lead to other things because, I'm quoting her, she was too stupid to understand that she was supposed to laugh at everything Arthur said. She didn't know how to play the game. That proved to be a career dead end. We had an acetate recording of that episode of *Talent Scouts* that I wish I could find.

Segaloff: What was your address when you lived in Manhattan?

Maltin: 201 West 77th Street.* I lived there until I was four years old. Another person in that building was Gene Barry. It amazes me that I have very definite and very clear memories of living there and of being in that neighborhood. There was a local fruit seller, an old Italian man named Dominic, a name I'd never encountered before. When he sold you apples and such, they came in little tissues. There was a fire station on the block that may have been decommissioned, but it was still there. It is still there, I think. And there was a supermarket on Broadway that had been a movie theater because they retained the marquee.

Segaloff: What was the name of your local theater where you first saw movies as a kid?

Maltin: The Teaneck Theater. It's still there on Cedar Lane, the main street of Teaneck.

Liliom played at Broadway's Majestic Theatre from April 19, 1945-May 24, 1947.
* Now The Laney at Amsterdam Avenue.

Segaloff: What was the admission price?

Maltin: I remember going to matinees and paying 35¢, and I remember being huffy about when it raised to 50¢. I do remember those specific prices.

Segaloff: You would go alone?

Maltin: I would usually go with friends to Saturday matinees initially. Then there was that day I told you about, the turning point, when I couldn't find anybody to go to the movies with me, and I went by myself and saw *Dr. Strangelove*. A matinee, and I sat through it twice because the short subject with it was "The Critic," voiced by Mel Brooks and directed by Ernie Pintoff. In order to see "The Critic"—which ran three minutes—a second time, I watched *Dr. Strangelove* a second time.

Segaloff: Don't you feel there's something sinful about coming out of a movie on a weekday into the sunlight?

Maltin: I don't know if it's sinful, but it certainly is jarring. The next town over, Hackensack, got movies before they came to Teaneck, so I would go to Hackensack where there were two theaters right across the street from each other. Why would anybody do that? On one side was the Oritani, reflecting Indian names of the area, and the other side was the Fox. The Fox showed Terrytoons, which I hated. The Oritani showed Warner Bros. cartoons, which I loved. The Teaneck Theater showed whatever it could get.

Segaloff: Do you recall any Saturday matinee experiences, whether they're horror films or beach blanket films or anything, with you and the kids in the audience making noises and doing what we see in a Joe Dante movie?*

Maltin: Not precisely. I have a memory of going to see a film that Alice watched recently on TCM. It's *36 Hours* (1964) with James Garner.† It was a Saturday, and I was with a friend. We were at the Oritani and there were some other boys there who were being disruptive. They had a matron at the theater dressed like a nurse. Idiot that I am, I went and tattled on them

---

* Referring to Dante's 1993 *Matinee*.
† An American soldier (James Garner) with knowledge of the upcoming D-Day invasion is captured by Nazis (Rod Taylor) and duped into believing the war has long since ended, leading him to reveal the plans without a second thought.

to the matron. The matron, God bless her, came down the aisle and said, "Are these the boys?"

Segaloff: Why not set off a flare?

Maltin: When we left the theater, they followed us. I can't speak for my friend, but I was scared because I'm a wimp. I've never engaged in fisticuffs or anything like that. Goodness knows what these guys had in mind, but they knew they were spooking us. There was a public library a block down. We went to the public library, and they followed us into the public library. We left the public library, went back down the block, went another block to the Sears-Roebuck, and went into the clothing area and talked to a salesman there. He said, "Well, I don't know what I can do." I forget if the salesman dialed my folks or whether I had a dime to use for the pay phone, but my parents came to pick us up.

Segaloff: How old were you then?

Maltin: Whenever *36 Hours* came out. [Note: 1964; he was 13.]

Segaloff: That doesn't sound like a kiddie matinee film. I've seen it.

Maltin: No, that was not a kiddie matinee. One time, I wore my Cub Scout uniform to a Halloween kiddie show at the Playhouse on the Mall in Paramus, New Jersey. They said, "You, come on in." Anybody in costume for this Halloween show got in free. They counted my Cub Scout uniform as a costume. The Fox did a summer series, Tuesday matinees, and we got a card. They were going to show the Columbia serial *The Great Adventures of the Wild Bill Hickok* (1938). A terrible serial. Most of the Columbia serials were terrible. The theater handed out a punch card at the beginning of this series. If you saw the first fourteen chapters, you got into the fifteenth one free, but they made the dreadful mistake of showing chapters one and two together that first day. I'm trusting in my memory here, which may or may not pan out, but as I recall, at the end of chapter one, Wild Bill is on a railroad train on a trestle, and somebody has blown up the trestle and the train collapses. Oh, my God, how is Wild Bill going to get out of this? Chapter two begins with a recap and then you cut to him standing up having landed on a rocky plateau. He dusts himself off. That's how he escaped.

Segaloff: You wouldn't have followed the serial like that all the way through.

Maltin: I tried. When *Batman* came on ABC television in 1966, I was in junior high school. It was more than a fad. It was like an explosion of interest. They showed two episodes a week. That's all anybody would talk about the next day at school. That winter break, Columbia dug out the 1943 *Batman* serial. I went to the 8th Street Playhouse in Lower Manhattan and watched all 15 chapters of that terrible serial.

Segaloff: Four and a half hours.

Maltin: With J. Carrol Naish as Dr. Daka, The Yellow Peril. It's full of racist dialogue, which is why they've never re-reissued it. They turned instead to the 1949 serial, which is even worse. Less offensive, but worse.

Segaloff: It was worse. The ads read, "An Evening with Batman and Robin," and boy, did they mean it. You could not get high enough to make it through all of those episodes.

Maltin: They showed every inch of every chapter, so we had the titles at the beginning of every chapter. Around chapter five, some wise-ass said, "Boo," when Lambert Hillyer's name came: Directed by Lambert Hillyer. "Boo." It got a laugh, so chapter six, three other guys said, "Boo." By chapter 10, the whole audience is going, "BOO!!!" Participatory. That was the whole point.

A lot of the films that I saw at Saturday matinees I later came to understand were prints that happened to be sitting in the local exchange office. The science fiction and fantasy films were generally not good, but they were such that a 12- or 13-year-old kid could feel superior to them. The Linwood Theater in Fort Lee showed *The Lost Planet*, another Columbia turkey, and my favorite chapter title is, "Dr. Grood Defies Gravity." Dr. Grood was played by Michael Fox, a character actor who caused Michael J. Fox to have to put his middle initial on his SAG card. We kept repeating our favorite dialogue all week long. "Tim, Ella—Okay, robots, let's go!" Tim and Ella had been taken over by robotic forces.

Segaloff: It's often been debated whether movies lead, follow, or ignore public opinion or trends. How do you stand on that?

Maltin: I think they do both. In a number of notable cases, they lead. They lead in fashion, they lead in use of slang, they lead in popular expressions. They lead in social progress, too, not to put too fine a point on it. Sidney Poitier almost single-handedly altered White people's perceptions of Black people. It had been so rare to see an African American depicted with any form of dignity or humanity up to that time. There were Rex Ingram and James Edwards, there are other examples here and there, but Poitier broke so much ground for so many people. He's the most notable example. An obvious example, but I think, a potent example.

Segaloff: You're right about fashion. People wanted to see what Gloria Swanson was wearing or Ginger Rogers or Joan Crawford.

Maltin: Right. And hairstyles.

Segaloff: Those were pervasive. In fact, wasn't it Veronica Lake during World War II—

Maltin: —Yes, right, with the peek-a-boo hairdo—

Segaloff: —who was persuaded to lift her hair off her face as a safety factor for women working in defence manufacturing plants.

Maltin: I remember when I was growing up, my male role models were Rod Taylor and William Holden. I thought, "That's a guy. That's what a guy ought to be like." I was far from the day when I would have any kind of relations with the opposite sex or be carrying myself like a man, not a boy, but if I could have modeled myself, I would have modeled myself after the general persona that they represented. They were not one-trick ponies; they had range, both of them. Speaking broadly, they made a big impression on me.

Segaloff: Did you ever get to meet either of them?

Maltin: I met William Holden for ten seconds. They had a college screening of *Network,* and he was stuck at the front of the theater, and they had to walk him up the aisle. Alice and I went to the aisle and I stopped him long enough to just shake his hand. He was polite, he was civil. He was a graduate of the studio system. He knew how to behave. He had what my friend calls toilet training.

Segaloff: Were there any actresses that you had a crush on when you were a kid?

Maltin: Oh, lots. I can't remember who got to me when I was that age.

Segaloff: Would they have been like grown-up women or child stars?

Maltin: Well, Cheryl Holdridge in the Mickey Mouse Club, I thought she was really cute and remained cute for a long time. I finally got to meet her and interview her for one of the Disney Treasures DVDs. She was very sweet. I was not one of the boys who were into Annette. She didn't do it for me, but Cheryl did. I also like Darlene Gillespie who starred in —

Segaloff: — *Corky and White Shadow* —

Maltin: — *Corky and White Shadow.*

Segaloff: We are in sync here.

Maltin: She seemed really cool. I almost never saw serious movies when I was growing up. I was only interested in comedy. Same on TV. I did watch Roy Rogers' TV show. I try to explain this to my students that before the MPAA Ratings Board's ultimate breakdown in the late Sixties with *Who's Afraid of Virginia Woolf?* and *Bonnie and Clyde* and everything that followed. It wasn't that I *couldn't* go to see *Peyton Place* or *The Best of Everything.* It's that I had no interest in them. If I had gone to see grownup films like that, I wouldn't have understood them anyway. It would have sailed over my head, all of the adult content. Now I'm in no desirable demographic.

Segaloff: You've gotten lazy and choosy since the pandemic.

Maltin: Yes, because films seem to come and go. Films have become ephemeral in our society, I think. You remember when *Diva** played at the Paris Cinema in Manhattan for over a year? That was a phenomenon then. That was not the exception. That was not the rule. That was the exception to the rule, a film having that kind of staying power. I don't know if anything has staying power now.

---

* Jean-Jacques Bieneix's 1981 French thriller about singing, the mob, and kids. The art film played forever in small theaters.

Segaloff: Only midnight shows if that, and they probably went away with the pandemic.

Maltin: Since the pandemic they've made it so easy to stay home. There's every disincentive to go out. First, it was a matter of health, and for some people, a paranoid matter of staying healthy.

Segaloff: The industry was built on the fact that people wanted to get out of the house.

Maltin: Right, and they still do.

Segaloff: But not always to a movie theater.

Maltin: No, they still do. If you have the right movie. Apparently, *Inside Out 2* is the right movie right now.

Segaloff: Look, I remember going to a theater, not just for the movie, but for the theater itself. It was fun. There were certain things that happened, whether it's the buttered popcorn, or the architecture, or the experience of being with people. Showmanship.

Maltin: That's the word that is missing from all evaluations that I've read and heard. The exception is those two great interviews that TCM did with Scorsese and Spielberg, where they talk about double features, and what they saw when they were growing up. Their spiels captured the idea of fun. It was *fun* to go to the movies. It was *fun* even when you came in the middle and stayed through the end of picture A, and the trailers, and the cartoon, and the newsreel, and watched all of picture B, and then watched the beginning of picture A until your father or mother said, "Okay, this is where we came in."

Segaloff: "This is where we came in." That's right.

Maltin: Everybody knows that phrase. It's a generational touchstone. Those words, "this is where we came in."

Segaloff: We've been lucky enough to live in towns that had good theaters. But the number of theaters where you wouldn't want to show even the bar mitzvah movies, let alone a feature film, across the 23,000 screens of America, is insurmountable. That's why George Lucas had the Theater Alignment

Program.* That's why NATO† ultimately fights any kind of improvement. A lot of the theaters in this country are shit-houses, and that takes away from the moviegoing experience.

Maltin: Yes, it does. You don't want to go into a movie theater and have your feet sticking to the floor, or encounter chewing gum on the seat, or strange aromas, or people getting on their phones or texting. I still go to movie theaters as a paying customer. Not often lately, not that often. When I do, it is never on a weekend. Never on a Saturday night, goodness knows. I've had for decades the luxury of being able to go on a Thursday afternoon or a Tuesday evening, and that's when I choose to go. I want there to be somebody in the audience, preferably, but not a crowd, and not a rude crowd.

Segaloff: I worked in movie theaters for four years in college and then five years as a publicist, and I dreaded going into movie theaters for every reason you've just categorized. Years ago, I was speaking with Mel Wintman, who was the head of General Cinema Corporation, the innovator of shopping center theaters. He was in charge of 1,500 screens at the time and I asked him about presentation, about 70mm, about Dolby sound. He said, quote, "Look, if you have the film they want to see, you can show it in the toilet and they'll still come." That, to me, summarized every exhibitor I ever dealt with.‡

Maltin: When I was growing up, there was a theater called the Park Lane in Palisades Park, New Jersey. They went to a $1 price policy in the '70s. Two shows a night, approximately 7:10 and 9:20. Films that had died first-run in Manhattan weeks earlier or months earlier got packed houses at the Park Lane because there was street parking, for starters. It was easy to go to, it only cost a buck; it was an audience that was there because they wanted to be there. They were curious to see the movie. They weren't curious enough to pay $4:50 or drive into Manhattan.

---

* Upset with how poorly films were being presented in American theatres, George Lucas and Lucasfilm embarked on an ambitious program to set standards for sound and projection with the threat that studios would pull films out of theaters that did not comply.
† National Association of Theater Owners.
‡ General Cinema Corporation folded in 2002. Melvin Robert Wintman (1918–2001) was a lawyer who prosecuted war criminals after World War II and went into the exhibition business.

Segaloff: That was what doomed the Jerry Lewis Cinemas, which is that, at a dollar admission, they became financially unattractive for film companies to book. For all the dreams that Jerry had, it was not a workable business model. That's what's happened to exhibition. Sticking to the floors, the overpriced candy. Now, you spend more in the concessions than you do going to the film.

Maltin: Where does that word come from? I'm trying to get to the root of it.

Segaloff: Concessions?

Maltin: Concession.

Segaloff: It started in the circus, didn't it? The concession stand, the concession business. It's where theatres make their money, not from ticket sales.

Maltin: What is being conceded?

Segaloff: Your salary.

Maltin: But why *concessions*? Refreshments, I understand. The slogan was never "The Pause that Concedes."

Segaloff: There must have been something at the dawning of sound. You can imagine in silent movies, people cracking their cellophane wrappers. Then at a certain point, you had to hear the track, and they must have done something about making quieter candy wrappers.

Maltin: Having just watched *Once in a Lifetime*, Jack Oakie's always cracking nuts, and it gets on the soundtrack of the film that he's making. No one knows what it is except Aline MacMahon.

Segaloff: Tell me more about your family.

Maltin: My father put himself through law school during the Depression working as a bagger at a grocery store. He went to Brooklyn Law, and when he got out, his first client was Ray Heatherton, who became known and loved in the New York metropolitan area as the Merry Mailman, the host of a popular children's TV show which was on WOR. He was the father of Joey Heatherton [the actress] and Dick Heatherton, who was a popular FM disc jockey in the Sixties and Seventies.

Segaloff: In 1954 you moved to Teaneck, New Jersey. Do you remember your address there?

Maltin: Oh, memorably. It was 77 Grayson Place. People hummed it to the tune of the popular TV series *77 Sunset Strip*.

Segaloff: What was school like in Teaneck?

Maltin: There was one aptitude test that I had to take, I think it was the language requirement. I'd been taking French. Teaneck decided that they were going to experiment when I was in the first grade and teach French and have the same teacher follow us from first through twelfth grade. I had 12 years of French and I still can't speak it because, in those days, in those unenlightened times, they didn't believe in a conversational language education. It was conjugating verbs and memorizing definitions.

Segaloff: But you couldn't ask for a cup of coffee.

Maltin: Exactly. But I still love the language and it's one of the reasons I love French films. I can understand a little more than the subtitle gives me. I understand certain colloquialisms and things like that, so it makes me feel smarter. [The former CEO of Disney] Michael Eisner said the reason that they opened Disneyland Paris is because he took French in school. He had a relationship to the language.

Segaloff: Most kids have trouble in high school. What about you?

Maltin: I was the oddball who loved movies. In fact, I turned to movies to rescue me whenever I was failing a subject or having trouble with a subject in school. I would go to the teacher or at NYU, the professor, and ask if I could do a paper for extra credit, and usually they said yes. I'd write it about a movie, or something to do with a movie and raised my average to a passing grade. That was my ace in the hole. I was the editor of my junior high school (and then high school) yearbook, which led to my first public-speaking experience. I had given our principal an announcement to read over the p.a. system asking for candid photos. It had elicited no response, so I asked permission to make a brief speech before our next assembly program in the school auditorium. I had never spoken to so many people at once before, and I have a clear memory of looking down and seeing my knees shaking back and forth! I took a deep breath, and said, "As you may remember I put out a call for candid photos to use in our yearbook and I would like to thank every student who responded. (pause) Both of you." With that, I stepped off the podium. It was my first attempt to tell some form of a joke, and it worked. There was a buzz of confusion among the students, who were accustomed to only half-listening to announcements of any kind. There was some delayed laughter. But I scored. Kids were caught off-guard and they liked how I got my message across. I've had occasional moments of nervousness over the years, but I've never had my knees shake like that again.

Segaloff: Let's go into *Film Fan Monthly*, which you took over in 1966, and tell me something about Daryl Davy, who was the fellow who began it.

Maltin: I learned about *Film Fan Monthly* and *The 8mm Collector* in the pages of *Famous Monsters of Filmland*. One month, Forry [Forrest J. Ackerman, the publisher; q.v.] decided to shed a spotlight on fanzines, and he had a guy named Oscar Estes (why do I remember that name?) review/plug five current fanzines, not all of them about film. One was about Edgar Rice Burroughs, one was a science fiction fanzine, and two were for film collectors: *The 8mm Collector* out of Indiana, Pennsylvania, and *Film Fan Monthly* out of Vancouver, Canada. I wrote to both of those editor-publishers and sent a sample column for each one. When they accepted them for publication, *then* I told them I was thirteen. Sam Rubin (Samuel K. Rubin, publisher of *The 8mm Collector*) wrote back on a postcard, "I don't care. I like what you did, send more." Daryl essentially said the same thing and revealed that he was 19. I never met Daryl, sorry to say, and he died young. I got to meet and know Sam. He started Cinecon, and I missed the first Cinecon because I chose not to ride in the back seat of a Volkswagen beetle driven by friends for eight hours to Indiana, Pennsylvania. But I went to Cinecon 2 in Baraboo, Wisconsin, and I was able to do that because I flew, the first time I ever traveled without my parents.*

Segaloff: Were your parents encouraging of you in these early endeavors?

---

* *Film Fan Monthly* lasted nine years before Maltin's academic responsibilities and other writing jobs became overwhelming. During its run he had given opportunities to other writers just as he had been given when he he had been starting.

Maltin: They were. They didn't lead me anywhere or push me anywhere, but they appreciated what I was doing. I remember when the copy of *The 8mm Collector* came in, my byline was "Len Maltin." My father said, "You should use your full name." My mother had a particular aversion to "Lenny" as a nickname. As far as we could figure out, it was because of *Of Mice and Men.**

Segaloff: How many hard drives do you have in your brain? How do you remember all of this?

Maltin: This is what matters to me.

Segaloff: How did you begin researching books when you were the guy doing the original research? There was nothing else to depend on.

Maltin: The first articles I wrote for my mimeographed fanzine *Profile* were about Buster Keaton and Mary Pickford and Douglas Fairbanks. They were not stolen from, but sourced from, existing books that my local library had. They were just my retelling of their careers minus any original critical input.

Segaloff: Had you seen any of their films so that you weren't doing a clip job?

Maltin: No, no, no. I had an 8mm print of *The Mark of Zorro*, which is still one of my favorite Fairbanks films. That was his first swashbuckler. Have I talked about John Griggs already?

Segaloff: No, but I knew him too. John Griggs' Moviedrome was one of my favorite sources.

Maltin: Around the same time that I was discovering *Film Fan Monthly* in Canada and *The 8mm Collector,* I saw these ads for Griggs' Moviedrome in Englewood, New Jersey. That was right next to Teaneck where I lived. I looked him up in the phone book and I called him, and he was very welcoming. He invited me over—and to bring friends if I wanted to— for an evening of silent film, which meant that my parents had to drive me over and drop me off and then pick me up at the end of the evening. I was shown down to his basement where, on the outer wall of his projection booth, he had signatures of luminaries who had been there—Lillian Gish, Buster

---

* John Steinbeck's novella about a feeble-minded man, Lenny, and his protector, George.

Keaton—those are the two I remember. I can't remember if Dorothy Gish was there as well, but Lillian certainly was. He had what was, at the time, one of the finest, if not *the* finest, private collections of silent film prints. And he had scores for most of them on reel-to-reel tape played by various pianists and organists. I don't remember what we saw the first night there, but we started going pretty often on Friday nights or Saturday nights. The more the merrier as far as he was concerned. One night he said to us, "Have you seen *The White Hell of Pitz Palu*?" I said, "What is *The White Hell of Pitz Palu*?" "*You haven't seen* The White Hell of Pitz Palu?"

Segaloff: It sounds like Carl LaFong. Carl LaFong?

Maltin: I said, "no," so he showed it to us. It's an incredible film. Do you know it?

Segaloff: No. What is *The White Hell of Pitz Palu*?

Maltin: It's one of the German mountain films from the Twenties and early Thirties from the Weimar era, directed by Arnold Fanck. We met Luis Trenker, who worked with Fanck, decades later at the Telluride Film Festival* because Bill Everson insisted to Bill and Stella Pence and Tom Luddy, "He's still alive. You've got to bring him here." His leading lady in the film was Leni Riefenstahl.

Segaloff: She made mountain films before she took up documentaries.

Maltin: It's quite a remarkable film. I got to revisit it. Kino Video released a whole bunch of those pictures a decade or more ago. Anyway, we had these wonderful adventures with Mr. Griggs. He was a character. He was a working actor, never a star. When I was trying to explain who he was to people, I would say he played Ralph Kramden's boss on a couple of episodes of *The Honeymooners*. I've since found a couple of stills of him, other stage work that he did. His son Tim went to Yale, but I think his film collection wound up at the Harvard Film Archive. They have all the prints now, not that anybody's looking for 16mm.

---

* Founded in 1974 by Tom Luddy, James Card, and Bill and Stella Pence, the Telluride Film Festival (so named for its location in Telluride Village, Colorado) is a key showplace for new and independent films and filmmakers.

Segaloff: No one knows anything about Griggs other than that he was an actor and had this great collection. He, of course, sold copies of the films. My superb print of *The Last Laugh* came from him. He even purposely said in his little catalog that all of the films are "as best can be determined by the Copyright Office" to be in the public domain. So there was no guilt involved. I certainly didn't see his private collection.

Maltin: You could say I was his protegé and he was one of my mentors, but he was really a very active mentor to me. It was devastating when he had a heart attack.

Segaloff: When was that?

Maltin: When I was thirteen or so. He recovered sufficiently well to invite us back. And the night he invited us back, he had a print that he had borrowed temporarily, of *Mutiny on The Bounty* (1935), which is not a short film. It was on 1600-foot reels. He only had one projector, so it was always a break when he had to rethread the projector. I had to call my mom and say it's going to be a little late tonight. And she said, "Well, we're going to go to sleep, so it's now or never." And I had to say to Mr. Griggs, "We have to go home." "*But you haven't seen the mutiny.*" He was genuinely upset. How could parents be so dense as to rob us of the opportunity of seeing the whole film? Sam Rubin came to visit one weekend, and we took him over to meet John Griggs and either Sam or John—it must have been "Mr. Griggs," I never called him "John"—had us all line up like soldiers to greet Sam. But then he did pass away, much too soon. His previous protegé was David Shepard.* Apparently David didn't know a thing about a silent movie until he met John Griggs.

Segaloff: Good God.

Maltin: Think about that for a minute. Just digest that.

Segaloff: It's a chilling moment when you see how this one man can bring together David Shepard, Leonard Maltin, Sam Rubin, and many other people who became the next genera-

---

* David Shepard (1940–2017) was the legendary film preservationist whose was a major aggregator, collector, and restorer of world film heritage. His holdings are now at the Academy Film Archive as part of the Lobster Film/Film Preservation Associates Collection. His work is inestimable.

tion of film scholars. Did you qualitatively discuss the films after the screenings?

Maltin: We talked about them. I don't think we talked about it in very deep conversation. He was a great admirer, and I inherited from him an admiration for Henry B. Walthall,* and I am now an aficionado. John Griggs has another claim to fame on a sidebar basis: He was an active member of the Player's Club, the actors' organization that's housed at Edwin Booth's former home on Gramercy Park. He used to put on silent film shows there, and you had to be invited to join. I remember he had to sponsor you. He sponsored Peter Coyote. I told Peter that when I first met him many years later.

Segaloff: We should probably segue into William K. Everson. Everson was the major force in my early life as well as yours and, as far as film history, was certainly one of the great film scholars and film promoters. He was also a little eccentric.

Maltin: Bill said that England was made up of two kinds of people: eccentrics and bores.

Segaloff: You must have known him outside of his classes.

Maltin: Oh, I never took a class with him.

Segaloff: So you went over to the apartment?

Maltin: No, I knew him primarily through the Theodore Huff Film Society. And then later The New School where he did Friday night screenings. When Alice and I were getting married, she and I were looking for an apartment on Thanksgiving weekend of '74. We were going to be getting married on the Ides of March 1975. We wound up moving into a brand-new building at 79th and Amsterdam, a half a block from Bill Everson. Some people accused us of doing that to be close to his film collection, which was not true—but it didn't hurt.† One day we ran into him on the street, and he said,

---

* Best known today as "the Little Colonel" in D. W. Griffith's *The Birth of a Nation*, Walthall (1878–1936) was a major leading man who appeared in over three hundred silent films and, in the later years of his life became a reliable character actor.

† Everson lived in a cramped apartment strewn with film cans. The author was once invited by our mutual friend Myron Meisel to a screening in his living room amid the wonderful clutter. A signed Christmas card from D. W. Griffith stood framed atop a bookcase (Everson's son was named Griffey after D. W., and Bambi his daughter). It was to be a

"Have you heard about *Strictly Dishonorable**?" The Regency, which was then a revival house on Broadway and 67th Street, had been sent the wrong print by MGM. Instead of getting the remake with Ezio Pinza, they sent the Preston Sturges original, which nobody had seen since 1931, the Universal picture, and so we all got to go. But that was by passing on the sidewalk that I got that information from Bill. We used to see his son Griffey skateboarding with his friends when we'd walk our dogs at night. I'm still in touch with Bambi.

Segaloff: What sort of early writing enterprises did you have besides mimeographed fanzines?

Maltin: I called myself Research Unlimited. What research could I do? The foremost Laurel and Hardy collector in the country, Mike Polacek, was from Huntington, West Virginia. I had met him; he'd come up and visited my family in Teaneck. He wrote and said, "I've been trying to find out the name of the guy, the heavy-lidded, shady looking guy who has bit parts in six Laurel and Hardy films. I've asked Stan," meaning Stan Laurel, "and he can't remember." So one Saturday, my good friend Louis Black and I were making our rounds in New York, which usually involved stopping at Entertainment Films,† 850 Seventh Avenue, just to pass the time and say hello to its proprietors. And there was Bill Everson chatting with them. I was introduced, got my invitation to come to the Huff Society for the first time, and I said, "I've got a guy trying to find the name of the heavy-lidded, shady looking fellow…" And Bill said, "Oh, you mean Leo Willis?" Just like that. That gave me my first coup answering a research query accurately, all because of Bill Everson and the chance of meeting him. Then that Monday night in a rented room off Union Square with folding chairs, I saw Al Jolson in *The Singing Fool*. That was the first screening I attended at the Huff Society with my mother, who drove me. She loved movies and she had a

---

triple feature of Hawks' *A Girl in Every Port*, Ford's *Arrowsmith*, and McCarey's 1939 *Love Affair*, none of which was easily available at the time. Everson sat with us through the Hawks, after which he said, "No, I still don't like it very much," and left the living room. I wish I had spent the evening talking with him instead of watching his collection. I moved from New York shortly afterward and never saw him again.

* *Strictly Dishonorable* (1931). John M. Stahl directed an early Preston Sturges script (based on his Broadway play) for Universal of a love triangle among a male singer, a female singer, and her fiancé. In 1951 MGM remade it and suppressed the original version so as not to have competition.

† A leading seller of 8mm copies of classic films.

good time. I met the denizens of the Huff Society who were an odd group, and I say it endearingly, because most of them were endearingly odd. Some of them were not lovably odd, but some were endearing. One of them was a guy who had a windbreaker that kept moving. He had a rhesus monkey with him, and the theory we all had was that since the monkey watched the film, Bill let him stay.

One night he was showing a Republic picture from 1937 called *The Wrong Road* where Richard Cromwell is an innocent victim of circumstance and is being hounded by the police, led by Lionel Atwill. At the end of the film, Helen Mack says to Cromwell, "I'm tired of running. I'm tired of always looking over our shoulder. I want to be free. I want to be able to laugh. I want to be able to smile again." And from behind a tree, Lionel Atwill comes out and says, "You kids can start laughing right now" because he's found out that Cromwell was innocent. That's the end of the picture. Lights come up, and I say to no one in particular, "You kids can start laughing right now." And a guy behind me says, "I started laughing when I sold the print to Bill." That was my introduction to Herb Graff, who would go on to be Alice's and my matchmaker. Herb lived in Brooklyn, and he drove a car, so he often took Bill places or accompanied him places. Bill did not drive, which was a good thing for humanity in general. Sometimes Bill would fall asleep in the back seat and be doing something with his fingers as he dozed. When I heard someone question him about it, he said he was focusing the projector.

Segaloff: This is the early-to-middle Sixties, right? This was just before film became the language of the baby boom generation, just as Instamatic cameras and Super-8 were being introduced, so you were ahead of the curve in a different way. Film wasn't a novelty to you; it was a way of life. It was an area of study.

Maltin: I didn't think of it that way. I just loved movies, and I fell in love with movie history.

Segaloff: Did you ever have the desire to make movies?

Maltin: When I was a kid, yes. When I was in junior high school, I made movies with some friends with a friend's father's 8mm silent Kodak movie camera. The problem was that the films I envisioned in my head were like real movies. As I came to learn, you can do wonderful things with an 8mm silent movie and a blank slate, but only if you can scale your thinking to the capabilities and limitations of that medium.

I judged a couple of film festivals. If you have imagination and some skills, you can do great stuff but it's not going to look like a Hal Roach comedy. I did it through high school.

Segaloff: Did you have a group of friends you would work with and go out and do costumes and make up stuff and all that?

Maltin: We weren't that ambitious, but we did some stuff. I was trying to do slapstick pie in the face comedy and such. It just became too frustrating. I learned that editing is crucial, I learned that pretty early. We did some very rudimentary animation—like a cutout character walking across a background—and we experienced firsthand how labor-intensive that is, but what fun it is to get the result. To get the result of course, in those days, you had to bring it to the local pharmacy who sent it out to Kodak, who sent it back to you days later.

Segaloff: Were you the director?

Maltin: Yes.

Segaloff: Writer?

Maltin: Yes.

Segaloff: Producer?

Maltin: Yes.

Segaloff: Caterer?

Maltin: No, I don't think I catered. It was also a way to meet girls.

Segaloff: Okay. A man with a movie camera and girls.

Maltin: It gave me an excuse to talk to them.

Segaloff: "Would you be in my movie?"

Maltin: Yes.

Segaloff: Better than etchings?

Maltin: At that age, yes, at that time and at that age.

BREAKING IN

Segaloff: You attended New York University at a turbulent time.

Maltin: I entered NYU the fall of '68 and commuted from Teaneck. That spring was the Paris riots, and then a take-over of the campus of Columbia University. They invaded different halls and departments and burned papers. When I went to NYU for orientation a few days before classes began, it was a jarring experience because the student council, which ran the orientation, had been taken over by the SDS,* so it was weird. I was naïve and apolitical, very unworldly, and suddenly people were talking about how could NYU invest in Union Carbide? Everything about it was radical and I was so far from radical. That was an unusual transition.

Segaloff: Were you allowed to major in your freshman year at NYU or did you have to wait until you were a junior to be able to major in journalism?

Maltin: I think I was able to do it in my freshman year. The best part is that they let me cherry-pick film courses, not to audit them, but for credit. I applied to two colleges—you know what kids go through today—I applied to Columbia and NYU and was interviewed by both. Columbia said no and NYU said yes. At the time, NYU did not have an under-graduate film studies major. They had an undergraduate film-making program in place, but not for film studies. That's why I decided to major in journalism, which was a good choice, especially since they let me take some film courses.

Segaloff: But you had already been published by then. You were running *Film Fan Monthly* (q.v.)—

Maltin:—oh yeah—

Segaloff:—so it would kind of silly to make you take the core courses if you were already a recognized publisher and writer.

Maltin: I don't know about "recognized," but the first edition of the *Movie Guide*† came out during my freshman year, 1969 (q.v.).‡

---

* Students for a Democratic Society, a left-wing campus-based polit-ical organization, formed in 1961 in Michigan by, among others Alan Haber and Tom Hayden.

† a.k.a. *TV Movies*, New York: Signet Books, January 1, 1969. 536 pages, about which more later.

‡ *Leonard Maltin's Movie & TV Guide* was originally published

Segaloff: This must have embarrassed the professors who were struggling to publish so they could keep their tenure, and here you were turning out manuscripts left and right.

Maltin: The best part was that, over those four years, all the courses were taught by working journalists in New York. Oh man, it was wonderful. I was exposed to all sorts of interesting people. I remember there was one course called "Magazine Making and Editing." Every week the professor had a guest lecturer come in, and it was fascinating to me to hear them talk about the same problems and challenges that I was facing with *Film Fan Monthly*: deadlines, circulation, whatever it was.

Segaloff: Bringing the actual living working world into the classroom is something you were doing yourself years later at the New School for Social Research and now do at USC.

Maltin: I took a class with Clive Barnes.* He was no longer the all-powerful theater critic of *The New York Times*, who supposedly could open or close a show with one wave of his hand. We heard his side of all that, which was really interesting. He said, "I didn't ask for that power. I took a job. I was doing my job." And when producers would say to him, "Do you know the lives of seventy-five people depend on what you're writing?" he said, "Well, am I really responsible to those seventy-five people or to the thousands of people who are reading this review, trying to decide whether it's worth their time and money to come and see the play?" The *Times* would try to meet them halfway. They said, "Print two reviews" so one critic wouldn't dominate the *Times'* opinion… so they had Walter Kerr on Sundays.† And then what? What if Walter disliked it, too?

Segaloff: Well then, make a better play.

Maltin: Exactly. Exactly.

Segaloff: Did this shape your thinking? I remember years and years ago you told me you were uncomfortable being a critic. I think this was right before you became a critic. Did

in 1969 by New American Library as *TV Movies*. It was revised in 1974, 1978, 1980, 1982, 1984, 1986, 1987, and published annually 1988 through 2014 when it was discontinued with the dominance of IMDb and other sources.

* Lead theatre critic for *The New York Times*.

† The equally powerful former lead theatre critic for *The New York Times*.

this sensitivity or even hypersensitivity to the working people who were trying to do something affect you?

Maltin: No, I don't think so. It was at NYU that I wrote my first movie reviews, other than the little capsule paragraphs for the *Movie Guide*. I wrote my first journalistic reviews for what was then called the *Washington Square Journal*. We were a professional-level newspaper published Monday through Thursday, four days a week. Within a year I was promoted to entertainment editor, supervising the other people who were writing the music reviews. The guy who became my best man, as I was at *his* wedding, Dennis Fine, who died very young — a massive heart attack — was into music. He went every weekend to the Fillmore East, and I remember him coming in and talking about this guy, Elton John, how fantastic he was, that kind of thing. I cut classes regularly to just hang out in the newspaper office. It was so exhilarating. And pretty soon I was promoted to Entertainment Editor, which meant that one night a week I had to go to the print shop and supervise the page makeup of the paper. What a glorious experience it was to work with linotype operators, whose jobs would soon be eliminated by new technology. I'll always be grateful for that experience.

Segaloff: It was said that a journalism student could either have their name on the masthead or on a diploma, but seldom both. That was your calling?

Maltin: I don't know if I knew it entirely then, but it was great. Down the hall from where we were was WNYU, the college radio station, which was only available if you were in an NYU dorm.

Segaloff: Oh yeah. The carrier wave station at 640 and 1240 AM, and to get it you had to hook your antenna up to a radiator. I was on one of those at Boston University.

Maltin: We used to joke that, at any given time, there were more people in the studio than were listening to the station, but one of the people who worked there was Martin Brest.[*]

Segaloff: How did you develop your aesthetic of reviewing, since we're clearly talking about when it began?

---

[*] Director of *Going in Style*, *Midnight Run*, *Scent of a Woman*, *Beverly Hills Cop*, and *Meet Joe Black*, among other films.

Maltin: I had some experience because of having to write these bite-sized reviews for the *Guide*. But I guess my biggest influence, bar none, was Bosley Crowther, who is now held up to ridicule and marginalized, to put it mildly, as he was when he cast his negative review for *Bonnie and Clyde* so many years ago, and then doubled down by reiterating his dislike for that film.* He was who I read because my parents subscribed to *The New York Times*; it was on the doorstep every day, and so that's who I was exposed to—followed by Vincent Canby and Roger Greenspun, the unsung, very smart, very savvy second-string critic. He was in second position, but he got to review a lot of the more interesting films, not the mainstream hits, but the offbeat and the indie and the foreign films. The third in line at *The New York Times* was Howard Thompson, who did their very funny one-line notations for movies playing on television. He's the one who, for *Abbott and Costello Go to Mars*, once said, "And about time." He had a kind of a cult following because he came up with *bon mots* like that on a regular basis. In fourth place was a fellow named A. H. Weiler.† They were all there for a long, long time. This all leads to a story. I'm going to try to tell it in the right order.

My great ambition at that time was to get published in the *Sunday New York Times* Arts and Leisure section, which everybody read, or so it seemed. I think I had submitted a couple of proposals that were turned down. Then I took that class with Clive Barnes. The nice thing about all those teachers that I had was that I was selling freelance articles to a handful of magazines, and they would let me turn in a carbon copy (I'm dating myself) for assignments.‡ As you know, some schools say, "No, you do schoolwork now and you do that on your own after you graduate." This was a professional-level department, and they welcomed you pursuing your profession. And I did. Clive asked me to stay after class one day and took an interest in me. He said, "Have you tried pitching an idea to the *Times*?" Seymour Peck was the editor of the Arts and Leisure section. I said, "I have, but I haven't gotten anywhere." He said, "Would you mind if I spoke to him on your behalf?" I said, "No, I'd be thrilled." So he did, which was incredibly kind and generous of him to do. I followed

---

* Chief film critic for *The New York Times* from 1940 to 1967. When he went after *Bonnie and Clyde* (1967), which was being proclaimed not only as a hit but as a game-changing film, he was eased from his post by the end of 1967 for being "out of touch" with young audiences.

† Abraham H. Weiler, 1908–2002.

‡ Meaning that he turned in the typed original to his editor. Photocopies were unheard of at the time.

up with either a phone call or a letter, and it didn't lead to anything. I mean, [Peck] heard me out but wasn't interested in what I was selling. Then I think I wrote a letter to Vincent Canby, and he invited me to have lunch with him in the *Times* dining room when it was still on 43rd Street, its long-time home. I had a lovely lunch with him and his second-stringer Roger Greenspun, and Vincent said, "Have you tried selling a story to Peck?" I said, "I have tried. And Clive Barnes was kind enough to intercede on my behalf, but it didn't work out." He said, "Let me talk to him." So now I had Vincent Canby touting me to the editor of this Sunday paper that I was dying to be published in, to no avail.

The head of the journalism department at NYU, M. L. Stein, was my guidance counselor. I saw him casually here and there, but I had to see him every semester to touch base about what courses I was taking. I had turned in a piece, and he said, "I like that piece you turned in about such-and-such. Would you mind if I showed that to Seymour Peck at the Arts and Leisure section?" I said, "No, I wouldn't mind." And of course it didn't come to pass. At one point I pitched very specifically a piece on Don Siegel, who was really coming into his own at that time, He was making films like *The Beguiled* and *Charley Varrick*. I knew I was going to be interviewing him for the Directors Guild magazine, so I pitched that to Guy Flatley, who was Sy Peck's number two. He said, "Don Siegel, I don't see it." And then *he* did an interview with Don Siegel for the *Sunday New York Times*.

Finally, I did get my byline in that paper in that section. It was in 1974, right after meeting Alice.* And she wasn't impressed—which was devastating because who else would I want to impress? It took what should have been a hugely satisfying moment and undercut it.

Segaloff: Well, it just shows there's no—

Maltin:—business like show business.

Segaloff: How did you get to speak to these famous people when you were so young?

Maltin: Waiting at stage doors to get interviews. When I started my first fanzine, I was still living at home in Teaneck. The next town over was Paramus, where America's first shopping malls, the Garden State Plaza and the Bergen Mall, were located. It was called Bergen County. There was the Play-

---

* Alice Tlusty, about whom more later.

house on the Mall, on the straw hat circuit. My parents met a nice couple who were the publicists for the Playhouse on the Mall, and they said, "Anytime we can do anything to help, just say the word." Well, Chester Morris and Maureen O'Sullivan were coming to town in, I think, *Never Too Late*. I'd love to interview either or both of them, so I sent them a letter. (In those days, I could send a letter to someone knowing that it would get there the next day and they could respond to you on a timely basis.) And the response was, "They're unavailable," "Their time is spoken for," or, "Oh, it's too bad." I forget who the next star was, but by the third time I tried, I got the message: they weren't going to help me. I was muttering about this to someone who said, "Playhouse on the Mall? You can walk backstage. There's no guard there." So I went to see Hans Conried in a show called *Spofford*, which Melvyn Douglas had done on Broadway. At the end of the performance, I knocked on his dressing room door and he answered. I said, as fast as I possibly could, "I'm a great fan, and I publish this magazine, blah, blah, blah, and I'd like to talk to you about your film career." He looked at the magazines and he said, "Young man, we cannot have you living under the delusion that I had anything approaching a film career." I said, "Well, I still would love to talk to you about it." He said, "Come Monday night an hour before curtain and we'll talk." I returned Monday with my tape recorder and sat with him. He did very little prep for his part, very little makeup, a little wardrobe, which he did himself. At ten minutes before curtain, he said, "Come back tomorrow night, let's talk some more." I did three nights running and had the time of my life with him. He was just so amusing. And it kills me because I wasn't interested in old time radio then; I had no interest in radio. And he was one of the most prolific actors in that medium.*

Segaloff: I'm still getting over the fact that you met Uncle Tonoose.

Maltin: Very early in my career, as well as early in my interviewing career, I interviewed Anita Loos. That came about because she published an autobiography called *A Girl Like I*. I got to go to her apartment on West 57th Street. I will never,

---

* It is impossible to count the myriad appearances Hans Conried (1917–1982) made in his career. His TV credits alone exceed two hundred. Many of a certain generation came to know him as the face of the magic mirror on *Disneyland* and would celebrate each time he showed up as Danny Thomas' beloved "Uncle Tonoose" on *Make Room for Daddy*.

ever forget the experience of transcribing that interview, because she spoke in complete sentences, and what's more, complete paragraphs. I've never had that happen before or since.

Segaloff: Who is the first major star—either a recognized star or one whom you regarded as a star—with whom you landed an interview?

Maltin: Eddie Bracken, and it came about because I got to see him and Mike Kellin on Broadway in *The Odd Couple*. They were, I believe, the second cast of the Broadway show, following Art Carney and Walter Matthau. I was by myself, and I was reading my *Playbill*, and in the *Playbill* bio for Eddie Bracken it said he was in the original silent *Our Gang* comedies. Even then, that was a provocative thing to see, and I said, "I've got to interview him." I went to the stage door and, in so doing, developed a lifelong aversion to going to stage doors. I was standing out on West 49th Street. I was a teenager hanging around, and the crusty central casting stage doorman finally said to me, "What are you doing?"

I said, "This is a magazine I publish, and I'd like to interview Mr. Bracken." He said, "Wait here." He went and came back five minutes later. He said, "Mr. Bracken said if you come back after the matinee on Saturday, he'd be happy to talk to you." Well, great. I went home. Now, this is 1966. I don't even remember where or how I acquired some knowledge of his career because there was no such thing as IMDb or the internet, but I at least came up with a list of his films. Thus prepared, which is to say not sufficiently prepared, I went back on Saturday, and he couldn't have been nicer. I didn't know what to ask. I didn't understand how to ask a follow-up question.

Segaloff: Had you seen any of his Preston Sturges films by then?

Maltin: I think I'd seen *Miracle of Morgan's Creek* and fallen in love with it. I had a general idea of his career, but as I say, looking back, I can only blame youth and ignorance. The first thing he copped to was that he was not in *Our Gang*. He was in, he said, a rival series called *The Kiddie Troupers*, which may or may not be accurate, but I gave him the benefit of the doubt. It was harder to give him the benefit of the doubt when he said he created Francis the Talking Mule, of which I could find no evidence. He spun a couple of other tales. The one thing he said was that he liked Preston Sturges very much, but people came to think that that was who he really was, meaning people in the show business, and that he was not "Norval Jones."* I got a publishable interview out of it for *Film Fan Monthly* in its earliest months of existence under my editorship, but I've never reprinted it. It's just not good enough, but it was my first experience, and you've got to start somewhere.

Segaloff: This time when they said, "Come back after the matinee on Saturday," they actually meant it, they weren't just blowing smoke up your byline?

Maltin: No, no, no. He was good to his word.

Segaloff: It sounds as though you were a facile writer right from the start.

Maltin: "Facile" is a good word. Not a lot of depth, but I could sell a subject. But you asked a serious question about my aesthetic, and that derived largely from reading *The New York Times*. I then started reading some other folks. I certainly read whoever was reviewing for *Variety* at the time, and I bought the *Film Culture* issue where Andrew Sarris first published his auteur theory essay in the English language.† I bought that at the New Yorker bookshop, which was just around the corner from the New Yorker theater, my home away from home on Broadway and 89th Street. I'd never read anything like his writing, and I didn't understand why he was so turned off to Billy Wilder and so dismissive of some other filmmakers I liked a lot. But it was challenging and compelling reading, nonetheless.

Segaloff: Were you one of these kids who would watch *Million Dollar Movie*?‡

Maltin: Oh, yeah. Through the week or stay up late. I would set my alarm. There were certain films that never seemed to show

---

* Norval Jones is the character Bracken played in Sturges' *The Miracle of Morgan's Creek*, a hapless nobody who becomes the adoptive father of sextuplets.

† Andrew Sarris, "Notes on the Auteur Theory in 1962," *Film Culture* #27, Winter 1962/63.

‡ Starting on Secaucus, New Jersey/New York TV station WOR (Channel 9) in 1955 and continuing through 1988, this show would run the same movie twice each night for a week, making it theoretically possible to watch it ten times. Many 1960s and '70s filmmakers recall indulging their early interest in film with *Million Dollar Movie*, even though televised prints were in black and white, panned-and-scanned, and were often cut for time.

up at the New Yorker or the Thalia or MoMA (the Museum of Modern Art), my three primary places of discovery, so I had not seen *Twentieth Century*. I set my alarm for 2:15 AM and tried to go to sleep a little earlier than usual. Then I tried not to wake up the household because I didn't have a headset and fell in love with *Twentieth Century*. Then I had to try to wake up and go to school the next day and be functional. I did that for *My Man Godfrey* and *A Message from Garcia*, which is not in the same league as those other two films, but it's still interesting to see. Television was hugely important, as it was to Mr. Scorsese. By the way, had I arrived at NYU just a couple years earlier, I would've had Scorsese as a teacher because my friend Allan Arkush did. He wrote a wonderful article about it, which he let me post on my website.

Segaloff: If you're watching *Twentieth Century* and *My Man Godfrey*, you must have heard about them somewhere and knew to stay up late.

Maltin: The first book that had a real influence on me was Mack Sennett's *King of Comedy*. It's the first book I took out of the local library and read hungrily. Later I found out that it was largely a figment of his imagination, but not completely. He captured the era very well and described life in early Hollywood, the sort of ramshackle, helter-skelter era of moviemaking. I still love that book. Then my folks gave me as a present Arthur Mayer and Richard Griffith's, *The Movies*.* That was a big one because it covered so much ground, with a large number of illustrations. Then *Famous Monsters of Filmland*† opened another door very wide. Then I am going to cite Robert Youngson's film *The Golden Age of Comedy*. And somebody reminded me that they used to show silent comedy shorts on *Howdy Doody*.

Segaloff: Really?

Maltin: Yep.

Segaloff: Wow. I didn't remember that at all.

---

* Richard Griffith and Arthur Mayer, *The Movies*, New York: Simon and Schuster, 1957, rev. 1970.
† Fan magazine extoling horror movies published by Forrest J. Ackerman (1916-2008). Many horror film makers and afficionados of the baby boom era had their early cinema nightmares legitimized by "Forry." *Famous Monsters of Filmland* was published between 1958 and 1983, then reborn 1993 until 2008.

Maltin: Many years later, my friend Herb Graff, who was also my matchmaker [to Alice] purchased a collection of all those shorts, all the 16mm prints they had used on *Howdy Doody*. I inventoried the collection for him and watched every one of them.

Segaloff: You mentioned the Museum of Modern Art before. It has a special place in your youth, doesn't it?

Maltin: In 1935, Iris Barry came to Los Angeles on a Rockefeller expense account and was fêted by the likes of Mary Pickford and Douglas Fairbanks and Charlie Chaplin and Walt Disney. They were honored that their work was being taken seriously and was going to be on permanent display at a museum like other works of art and various media. It was a successful trip, and from that she got many donations of films, which wound up in the circulating library. (Availability in the circulating library was key to people knowing about a film, otherwise it could be forgotten.) It's pure circumstance—I don't know if that's quite the word—that *Million Dollar Legs** is the nonsense comedy of the early '30s that survives, or is noted or footnoted or acknowledged, because it was in their circulating library.

Segaloff: And that's where people saw it.

Maltin: Yes.

Segaloff: That's why *It's a Wonderful Life* is so popular. Movies that are available tend to get remembered over others.

Maltin: My students don't believe that this could have been true: when my friend Louis Black and I used to go to New York on a Saturday for the day, we'd take the bus over the George Washington Bridge, and the subway down to Midtown, and we'd go to the matinee showing at the Museum of Modern Art of say, *King Kong*. There was a sandwich shop on 53rd Street. We'd get a sandwich, and it would be our lunch. We'd walk to the middle of the block, and under the canopy of the entrance to the Museum of Modern Art at 11 West 53rd. Street, try to find a sympathetic looking grownup who would be willing to purchase tickets for us. We were allowed to buy tickets to the museum and see the exhibits, but not to see the

---

* Edward F. Cline, Paramount, 1932, starring Jack Oakie, Andy Clyde, and W.C. Fields. A young woman enters a foot race.

movie. There was a New York state law that said you couldn't sell an admission ticket to a movie to a minor.

Segaloff: What?

Maltin: I cannot describe it any better than that. There's probably some hitch, but the thing is, the ticket to the movie was free. You paid $1.75 to get into the museum. With it, you were entitled to an admission ticket. That was a way to say to the movie studios, "We don't charge for our movies. We show them for free."

Segaloff: Strange. I remember having to join a film society in Washington, D.C., because they were showing films that—there were no ratings then—were considered for adults, and I was sixteen. For private, non-public showings, you could do it.

Maltin: We studied faces. You'd find somebody who looked approachable, and say, "Excuse me, sir. My friend and I want to go to the movie today in the museum, and they won't let us have tickets, but we have the admission price. Would you be good enough to ask for two tickets?" We could always find somebody who would do it for us.

Segaloff: They didn't stop you at the gate when you went into the auditorium?

Maltin: No.

Segaloff: That's wonderful, and totally hypocritical.

Maltin: One time it was raining hard, and we had to do it in the outer lobby, instead of outside on the sidewalk, and approached a nice woman. She said, "Oh, sure, no problem." The ticket seller, though, said, "You know you're responsible for them now?" Ten to fifteen years later, when I worked at MoMA, they were still that way! MoMA had coat-check people who could make you feel belittled. Snobby, snobby, snobby people.

In those early days of my going there, the silent films were accompanied by the wonderful Arthur Kleiner, a Viennese gentleman of the old school and a very florid, wonderful pianist, wonderful accompanist. I never thought I would ever see him again, but we went to the Cinecon 13 that Ron and Chris Hall hosted in Minneapolis in 1978. Mr. Kleiner retired to the Twin Cities, and at our dinner, he was introduced and celebrated, and he sat down at the piano and played a score for a non-existent movie. It was just a series of themes. It was like being on a magic carpet. What a lovely man he was.

When my shorts book came out in 1972, I pitched to Margareta Akermark* at MoMA a series of noontime shows of short subjects, all from my 16mm collection. The late Ricky Scheckman attended all of those. Several people in the New York film buff crowd were very fond of that series. It was from 12:00 to 1:00 PM every Wednesday for four Wednesdays. One week, I carried in my prints at 11:20 in the morning. Margareta was very cross. "The projectionists need time to prepare these. This won't do." I made some friends there. Then, in 1975, programmers Adrienne Mancia (who just died a year or so ago, she lived into her nineties), and Larry Kardish,† who's now retired, approached me. They wanted to do something for the bicentennial in 1976. It seemed that no department of MoMA was going to do anything. They proposed to do a major show of American comedy—something that was uniquely American and then traveled the world. They hired me as guest curator.

It was an unforgettable gig. Ted Perry was the head of the department at the time. Nice man, nice to me. He said, "There's a meeting of the board of directors next week. I'd like you to come up to the Founders Room and just explain the show, pitch the show so that they know what we're doing." "Fine. I have no problem with that." I go up to the Founder's Room, and I'm at the end of a long table with very high-backed chairs, and I'm looking down this row of maybe twenty people with famous last names. I do my song and dance. "We're very excited. It's going to be 450 films. We're going to cover every aspect of comedy, blah, blah, blah. We're getting wonderful response from the studios and distributors, and some of the filmmakers themselves, blah, blah, blah." No reaction, no eye contact. I could have been talking to wax dummies. I've never had that experience before or since. Absolutely no response. Not a nod.

Over eight and a half months, we showed 450 films, shorts and features. That was a big deal and very exciting to work on. I'd never worked in an office before. They gave me a desk. Not my own office, but a desk in an office with some other people there in the film department. Nice folks. I started writing letters to some studios and archives. I had a wish list. I also started learning about rights and who owned what, and

---

* Margareta Akermark (1913–1983) was Curator of MoMA's film collection and encouraged the creation of the circulating library.

† Laurence Kardish (b.1945) programmed and wrote about film for MoMA from 1968 to his retirement in 2012.

who we had to try to talk into what. It was a real education in the nuts and bolts of film exhibition and distribution.

All my problems and headaches came from the archives. I'd been raised to believe that the studios were the enemy. When I was just getting into this field, studios were the ones who were preventing us from seeing that film or wouldn't clear the rights on that film. They were the bad guys. But my problems came from the archives.

Segaloff: How can you explain that? Is there a collecting mentality that affects archivists that studios don't care about?

Maltin: The archives are not run like a business. Not one of them. Which is to their benefit as well as their detriment. For instance, when we got a film in from the George Eastman House, now George Eastman Museum, in Rochester, New York, we had no indication that it had Croatian subtitles. Their answer would be, "Well, we just have the film. We don't have time to prescreen it before sending it off to you. That's why we make no promises about those."

Segaloff: They really are basically aggregators.

Maltin: Yes. Sometimes the film ends weren't taped down properly and would come loose and start to unwind in the case. Unbelievable. For my opening night, there was no money to do anything on this show. Their development department tried very hard to get a sponsor for this bicentennial show. They were surprised at how difficult it was to lure a sponsor for American comedy.

Segaloff: You'd think anybody would want to help, especially those who had films in distribution.

Maltin: No, nobody, except my friend Harvey Chertok. The same man who helped me through the doors of Bonded Film Services.* Harvey was working for Time-Life Television, which had just acquired the Harold Lloyd library for TV. Harvey said, "We'll do a party, and we'll show a Harold Lloyd film that night." I picked one of the lesser-known ones, which is still lesser known, *For Heaven's Sake* (1926). Very funny. An original 35mm print. It was after Lloyd left Hal Roach. The later Harold Lloyd films were distributed by Paramount. Paramount donated that print to the Library of Congress for the AFI collection. David Shepard had negotiated that deal for

---

* Now Bonded Services Group, LLC. (q.v.)

all the Paramount nitrates. I knew because I'd seen it, I knew that Bill Everson had a perfect 16mm print which would have been more than adequate to show. We borrowed it to have a back-up. I couldn't show the Time-Life print because they did an optical reduction of the screen size so it could show in a theater without a 1.33:1 projection setup.* Harvey sent out invitations to this opening night screening party on a straw hat, a die-cut oval piece of paper. How I don't still have one of those to show you, I don't know, but I don't. I invited my new boss, Jeffrey Reiss, from Showtime.† He and his wife came and we had a full house. I think it was a Tuesday night. Bill Perry was with the house pianist at MoMA.

That afternoon, the Library of Congress print hadn't shown up yet. I'm pacing the floor. I'm going down to the loading dock. The guy whose job was getting prints in and out was not a type A. It was just a job; he was not going to have a heart attack over this print not showing up. Then it came like at 5:00 in the afternoon. The film begins, looks great. At one point on the screen it says, "End of Reel 1." Our projectionist is smarter than that; you don't show that when you're playing a silent film. What happened was that somebody had lifted an excerpt from the middle of Reel 1, and instead of putting it back where it belonged, had just spliced it at the end of the reel.

Segaloff: You had the slug, and then you went back to the movie?

Maltin: Out of sequence. I was running up the aisle to go to the projection booth before I figured out that, in all eight reels, somebody had done a compilation of some sort. How could the Library of Congress not have known that this print was screwed up? "We don't have time to pre-screen." The film played great in spite of this because it's so funny. It worked. I got up and gave a little apologetic speech, and then at the party afterwards, people said they didn't know why I had to apologize.

---

* Modern 35mm projector aperture plates use a 1.85:1 aspect ratio that would cut off the top and bottom of films that were originally shot 1.33:1. To accommodate this standardization, some distributors will optically shrink a silent film image so that, when shown 1.85:1, it is uncropped top and bottom but has black bars on the sides, sort of a sideways reverse letterbox. Archives and museums like MoMA are equipped to handle 1.33:1 prints.
† Showtime network was launched in July, 1976 (q.v.).

Segaloff: If you played Bill Everson's print, it would've been wonderful.

Maltin: That's right.

Segaloff: It's remarkable that a film is that strong, despite incoherence.

Maltin: There were other things I learned: The development people were upset that we were showing the films chronologically, because that meant we were starting with primitives. Turn-of-the-century Edison, Biograph and Vitagraph shorts with John Bunny and Flora Finch. They said, "Can't you start with something that has a little more marquee value?" Larry and Adrienne said, "You don't get to interfere with our programming." *The New York Times* that week or the week before had just started a new section of the paper: the *Friday Arts and Leisure* section. That Friday, above the fold, there was a gigantic picture from *Tillie's Punctured Romance* (1914) touting this spectacular new show at MoMA, starting that weekend. *The New York Times* told New York, "You should go see this." New York came. It was a hit the first weekend.

Segaloff: Insane.

Maltin: Along the way, things happened. We had the first screening of Chaplin's *A Woman of Paris*. Just on a whim, I wrote to Sir Charles Chaplin. I heard back from his loyal representative, Rachel Ford, who said, "As it happens, Sir Charles has recently composed a score for the film, and we're preparing the finished print, and we'd be glad to have you show it in December." I got credit like I magically made it appear. Herman Weinberg, who remembered seeing it in the '20s, said that he was almost certain that Chaplin re-sequenced it and made some alterations.

Segaloff: Still, it was a great coup.

Maltin: I showed Hecht and MacArthur's *Once in a Blue Moon* (1935) with Jimmy Savo. Howard da Silva had a small part in it and showed up just to see it and then said a little impromptu hello to people. It was for that show that I went through the entire card file, as you used to have in a library. I went through every card, A to Z, to see exactly what MoMA had. I found Reel 1 of "The Battle of the Century."[*]

---

[*] "The Battle of the Century" (Clyde Bruckman, 1927) is the classic

Segaloff: Wait, back then?

Maltin: Yes.

Segaloff: Yet it's taken how many years to be discovered?

Maltin: All this time. Because Reel 1 doesn't matter. No one cares about Reel 1.

Segaloff: They do now.

Maltin: They do now, right. I couldn't believe my eyes. I ordered them to pull it in from their vaults and screened it, mouth hanging open. That's the reel where you could see Lou Costello as an extra at ringside. There were two films that I showed in that series. One was a very funny Billy Bevan-Mack Sennett short called "The Duck Hunter" (1922) where he winds up in an ostrich farm. Just automatically funny. A wonderful Will Rogers feature from 1921 called *Doubling for Romeo*, both of which have disintegrated, I'm reliably told. They never got around to preserving them. It's just the luck of the draw.

Segaloff: That's probably the same attitude that the museum development department had, which is, "If we haven't heard of it, we don't want it."

Maltin: I also learned a new word from the development department: *vitrine*. You know what a vitrine is?

Segaloff: It sounds like the Canadian dish with gravy.

Maltin: No, Mr. Bones, what is a vitrine? It's a window display case.

Segaloff: Oh, okay. Thank you. Next.

Maltin: The in-house design department was going to create a poster for this show. They chose a famous publicity still of Mae West as the Statue of Liberty. It's American film comedy, September 8th through February 10th, whatever. They went to the bookstore people and said, "We're going to print these up and offer them as an incentive to join the museum. If you

---

Laurel and Hardy pie fight film. It was originally released with a first reel that contained a boxing sequence that was later removed for unknown reasons and presumed lost. Decades later the second reel turned up and has been restored.

take a membership, you get a copy of this swell poster. Would you want to increase the run so you could sell them in the bookstore?" "No, I don't think so." I also had a humbling phone conversation with the manager of the museum bookstore imploring them to carry one of my books.

Anyway, it was a wonderful, terrible, wonderful experience. I wanted to show *Hellzapoppin'* (1941) and I knew that Bill Everson had a print. The film is not in release in the United States. Universal can release it, I think, almost anywhere else in the world, even Canada, but there's some entanglement involving, I think, the estates of Olsen and Johnson. Someone proposed that I write a letter to Alexander H. Cohen, who was then producing a stage show of *Hellzapoppin'* with Jerry Lewis and Lynn Redgrave which was out of town, in Baltimore, someplace like that.* Mr. Cohen wrote back a perfect letter saying, "Insofar as I may have any rights to this film, I have no objection to your showing it." With that, we showed it.

Segaloff: You got a good print.

Maltin: Oh, a 16mm print.

Segaloff: The response of the waxworks at MoMA is the same as any academic environment where they just don't take film seriously. God forbid you were doing comic books. They don't consider it to be publishing if you've only made a movie.

Maltin: The cliche is that the newspaper editor is clearing off his desk at the end of the day, and he opens an envelope and in it are two passes for the Bijou Theater where they're showing that night the first screening of *Ben-Hur*. He says, "You, there, you go write it up." That's how people became film critics. You didn't need any background, any entrance exam, any credentials. It's just a movie. Hey, we've all seen movies. We can write them up.

Segaloff: When we were starting our interest in movies, there were damn few books about film and none about the film business. I'm going to name some now. I know you'll know all of them, but if you can tell me some books that you remember besides the Sennett book. There was Paul Rotha's

---

* *Hellzapoppin'* closed on the road before making it to Broadway in 1976.

The Film Till Now,[*] Arthur Knight's *The Liveliest Art,*[†] which was the only film book for a while.

Maltin: *The Liveliest Art* was a breakthrough book, a game changer. Everybody had to have it. It cost what, 35 cents? And what a wonderful irony that I wound up inheriting Arthur's class at USC decades later.

Segaloff: Ezra Goodman, *The Fifty-Year Decline and Fall of Hollywood.*[‡]

Maltin: I know of it, but I didn't read it.

Segaloff: Siegfried Kracauer's *From Caligari to Hitler.*[§]

Maltin: Oh, this is all too high class for me.

Segaloff: Theodore Huff's Charlie Chaplin book.[¶]

Maltin: Aha! The first book I ever purchased was at the Teaneck Public Library. They were having a book sale, and they were deaccessioning a rebound copy, not original dust jacket or anything, of Theodore Huff's biography of Charlie Chaplin for ten cents. Best ten cents I ever spent. I've always loved books. My library was walking distance of my house, and the librarians in the children's room were awfully nice and very encouraging. Even when I got older, I learned the Dewey Decimal System to figure out where books about film and theater and show business would be.[**] I think I was ten years old when John McCabe's book, *Mr. Laurel and Mr. Hardy,* was published in 1961. I took it home, inhaled it, brought it back, checked it out again. Took it home, inhaled it again,

---

[*] Paul Rotha, *The Film Till Now*, New York: Funk & Wagnalls Company, 1949.

[†] Arthur Knight, *The Liveliest Art*, New York: MacMillan, 1957.

[‡] Ezra Goodman, *The Fifty-Year Decline and Fall of Hollywood*, New York: Simon and Schuster, 1961.

[§] Siegfried Kracauer, *From Caligari to Hitler*, New Jersey: Princeton University Press, 1961.

[¶] Edmund Newell, Jr., (a.k.a. Theodore Huff, 1906–1953) was among the first generation of American film historians. At various times he was associated with the Museum of Modern Art in New York, the National Archives, and the British Film Institute. His 1951 biographical study *Charlie Chaplin* (New York: Harry Schuman, 1951) remains a milestone. The Film Circle, a screening group he co-founded in 1952, was renamed the Theodore Huff Memorial Film Society after his death.

[**] To save you the trouble: 791.437.

checked it out again. It wasn't that it was revelatory, it was that so much of it had not been public knowledge. There was no place to learn the facts, the basics.

Segaloff: There was also something, whether you're talking about that or of Forrest J. Ackerman, that gave approbation to our interests when no mainstream source would ever say, "It's okay to be interested in this, kid." That's extremely, extremely important.

Maltin: The same with Rudi Blesh's book on Keaton.* I have a visual memory that I'm calling up right now of having my copy of that book in a classroom. I guess I had to be in high school by then. These are foundational books. Joe Hyams' *Bogie*. Wonderful book.†

Segaloff: Then there was Daniel Blum's *A Pictorial History of the Silents* and *A Pictorial History of the Talkies*‡ with beautiful, beautiful photo reproduction.

Maltin: Hundreds and hundreds of photographs. A sidebar: When Daniel Blum died, a man named John Willis carried on *Theater World* and *Screen World*, these annual hardcover books. John Willis read up an article about me in the Sunday rotogravure section of the *New York Daily News* and called me on the phone, I was still living at home with my parents, and said, "I have eight- or nine-years' worth of press kits, stills, and such on all the movies released in the U.S. I offered them to Lincoln Center and they didn't want them. Would you want them? Could you make use of them?" I said, "Yes." My dad drove into the city—it may have taken more than one trip—we bought file cabinets to store them all, and that covered the '60s. I think it was from the mid-'60s to the mid-'70s. He called me again for several successive years when he finished, got all the stuff back from the publisher. I had possession of all that material for a long, long time, and made very good use of it, and then donated to USC.

Segaloff: How did you build your book collection? You must have spent a fortune.

---

* Rudi Blesh, *Keaton*, London: Secker and Warburg, 1966.

† Joe Hyams, *Bogie: Humphrey Bogart*, New York: New American Library, 1966

‡ Daniel Blum, *A Pictorial History of the Silent Screen*, New York: Grosset & Dunlap, 1953; *A Pictorial History of the Talkies*, New York: Grosset & Dunlap, 1958. John Kobal took over in subsequent editions.

Maltin: When I took over *Film Fan Monthly* at age fifteen, I learned that I could call a publisher and ask for a review copy, and then review it legitimately in the magazine. I've paid for very few books since then and have built my library, too. My timing was good because that's when a lot of these now standard works were coming into being. I reviewed *Bogie*, I remember. I saw Bob Thomas on *The Today Show* promoting *King Cohn*.* He told these wonderful stories, wonderful anecdotes about Harry Cohn, the despotic head and co-founder of Columbia Pictures. I called Putnam's — again, the nerve! — and asked if it would be possible to interview Bob Thomas while he was in town. They said, "Yes, come to the Oak Room of the Plaza Hotel at four o'clock today. He'll be happy to see you." I did. I wore my only jacket and tie. My mother advised me, I think, that if I wanted to act adult and order a drink that wasn't Coca-Cola, I could try Vermouth.

Segaloff: How old were you here? You weren't eighteen yet.

Maltin: No.

Segaloff: You really shouldn't have been served.

Maltin: No.

Segaloff: Okay, just asking.

Maltin: Bob took a liking to me, and he would call me every time he came to New York. He would always get two seats for a Broadway show. I attended several Neil Simon shows with Bob. *Plaza Suite*, I remember, a couple of them. Then he became the editor of *Action*, the Directors Guild magazine. Anytime he had a New York based story, he would hire me to do it. I had wonderful experiences. I interviewed John Cromwell, H. C. Potter, George Stevens. Then he called and said, "There's a new show starting this fall on PBS called *Sesame Street*. The director's name is Jon Stone. Here's the publicist's name, go hang out for a day or two, and write a story about this upcoming show." I did. I was taken to lunch by Jim Henson and Frank Oz without having a clue who they were and, essentially, who they were to be. We went to an Italian restaurant on the west side near the studio. They couldn't have been nicer. I was in the green room with Joe Raposo,† as they taped the first rendition of "Rubber Duckie."

---

* Bob Thomas, *King Cohn*, New York: Putnam's, 1967.

† Joseph Guilherme Raposo (1937–1989) was the primary composer

Segaloff: Boy. Present at the creation.

Maltin: That's all because of Bob. He also hired me to do filmographies for his *Thalberg* book*, and I think his *Selznick* book.† One day, I was in his hotel room, getting ready to go out to the show, he showed me a very slim portable typewriter. It may have been a prototype or something. Four letters on the keyboard were in red, D, I, T, and S. "What's this?" He said, "Oh, that's a promotional gift from David O. Selznick for *Duel in the Sun*."

He'd been an AP (Associated Press) correspondent since 1945. His father was a publicist before him, so he grew up in and around the business. He went to UCLA. When I first moved out here, he told me, "I don't have any friends in the business. I have lots of acquaintances, business associates, people I know, people I've met." His only friend, he said, was Ken Murray.‡ I got to meet Ken Murray. I went to his house and, on the spur of the moment, he threaded up his projector and showed me *Bill and Coo*, for which he won an Academy Award. They were mutual friends with Billy Gilbert. The first celebrity I met on my first trip to Hollywood was Billy Gilbert. How did I know Billy Gilbert? Principally, from *Andy's Gang*.§

Segaloff: Not from *Laurel and Hardy*?

Maltin: From *Laurel and Hardy* too, but what really got to me was in *Andy's Gang*, when he would try to tell a story, and be interrupted by Froggy the Magic Gremlin. Or he would do his sneezing routine. This was just a speck of activity in his long, long career but it was a big deal to me. When I went to his home in North Hollywood, he'd had a stroke. Physically,

---

for *Sesame Street*. Among his songs are "Bein' Green," "'C' is for Cookie," "Sing," and the *Sesame Street* theme.

* Bob Thomas, *Thalberg: Life and Legend*, New York: Doubleday & Company, 1969.

† Bob Thomas, *Selznick*, New York: Doubleday & Company, 1970.

‡ Producer Ken Murray (1903-1988) gained fame for having taken home movies of absolutely everybody in Hollywood during its golden, silver, and modern eras and showing them as examples of the industry's history. He won a special Academy Award in 1947 for his film, *Bill and Coo*, about two lovelorn parakeets and their animal friends.

§ *Andy's Gang* (NBC, 1955–1960) was a children's show hosted by beloved actor Andy Devine (1905–1977). It was sponsored by Buster Brown shoes. Gilbert played a teacher who made guest appearances. The human hosts' major nuisance was Froggy the Magic Gremlin who would interrupt them and then plunk his magic twanger on their request.

he was fine, but his memory was on again, off again. His wife, Lolly, knew all of his stories. She was essentially his translator. They were very sweet people. He wrote an introduction for my comedy team book as well. They had a big scrapbook, either nine by twelve or eleven by fourteen, of portrait photos. They were signed to him by all the people that he worked with, which is everybody in show business. We turned the page and there was Shirley Temple. "Oh, she was adorable," blah blah blah. Turned the page, there's Eleanor Powell. "Oh, nice, nice. What a talent," blah, blah, blah. Turned the page, there's Glenn Ford, "That son of a bitch. Eleanor Powell was so sweet, and then she had to marry that no good son of a bitch." It was the image that brought that forth. He said Joseph Breen* stopped by their table at lunch one day to tell them that he had just seen *The Great Dictator*, and that one particular scene with Billy was just hilarious and wonderful, and Chaplin cut it from the film. I couldn't have asked for a better kickoff.

Segaloff: It's wonderful that you knew about these people when you were at such a young age. Do you ever stop to think that, in a lot of ways, you're a kind of a pioneer?

Maltin: How so? That I pursued these people before other people did?

Segaloff: Partly that, and also that you have found a way to popularize people who might otherwise be forgotten.

Maltin: I was given the vehicles. I was given the tools. A book on comedy teams with chapters on Clark and McCullough and Wheeler & Woolsey that could be purchased for a dollar and a half at Woolworths, not by mail order from a specialized distributor that you had to know about and have a secret handshake. The corner drugstore, that's where that book was sold.

---

* Joseph Ignatius Breen (1888-1965) headed the Production Code Administration, keeper of the censorious Production Code.

THE COLLECTOR

Segaloff: Clearly, the fates came together with the publishing industry that was seeking to expand. Venues where people actually bought books, and people who actually bought books. You also started collecting films at some point, and not all of them from legitimate sources. By way of full disclosure, that's something we share.

Maltin: I hope the statute of limitations has run out on this. 16mm prints were made largely for television distribution, but also for non-theatrical exhibition. That's why they existed in the first place, but they were not meant to be bought and sold by private collectors. It was, on the whole, a black-gray market. Let's call it a gray market just to be euphemistic. When it came time for me to buy a 16mm projector, I think I turned to my source for all things, William K. Everson, asking, "What kind of projector should I buy?" He said, "You want to buy an old RCA.* Very kind, very tolerant of film, very gentle on film." "Where do I find one?" "Alan Starr on West 44th Street." Alan Starr looked and talked like a Damon Runyon character. He was a guy who sat there and smoked on a stogie with his feet up on an old wooden desk. He would buy projectors from schools and YMCAs, and other places that were unloading them, and from the military, I guess. They were mostly from the '40s. I don't remember how much I paid for it. I wish I did. When I bought it, he said, "I've got a Porky Pig cartoon here for five bucks, you want it?" "Yes." That was the first one. There was of course Blackhawk Films, which was the oldest and most established legitimate dealer in 16mm. They had a license for the Laurel and Hardy Films which was wonderful. I wrote descriptive copy for the Blackhawk Bulletin in exchange for credit at one time.

Segaloff: I must have read your stuff.

Maltin: You did. Not early on; Kent Eastin† did most of that.

---

* The RCA 400 Senior (with a huge speaker in a separate suitcase-sized box) and RCA 400 Junior (with a speaker built into the projector's detachable cover) were durable, quiet, gentle machines that required manual threading. They enjoyed noble service for decades in school audio-visual departments.

† Eastin founded Blackhawk Films in 1927. In 1947, he partnered with Martin Phelan and over the years built a huge company selling legitimate copies of classic films (heavy on railroad films) for nontheatrical use. Their tabloid sales periodical was a trove of historical information as well as advertising.

Segaloff: Didn't Blackhawk also have some of the Paul Killiam stuff?

Maltin: Yes, they did. Then at one time they had the NTA Paramount shorts. NTA (National Telefilm Associates) was a TV distributor that acquired the rights to all the Paramount talking shorts. David Shepard also made a deal with Fox Movietone. They were a little pricey, but obviously from the original negatives, and so Rudy Vallee, Ruth Etting, Eddie Cantor, Burns and Allen, and many others probably wouldn't exist today if they hadn't struck those prints.

Segaloff: As far as the ones that Blackhawk didn't handle, the ones that you and I were involved in, were they sold as service prints?*

Maltin: Well, a guy named Milt Menell worked one floor up from the Willoughby-Peerless Camera Store in New York City, a world-renowned camera shop which had a 16mm counter. I remember seeing a sign saying, "Edgar Kennedy comedies, $9.95." If only I had known, I might have bought one or two. When a laboratory either closed down or took inventory, or saw who wasn't paying their bills for storage, Milt would pay the bill, acquire these prints, and sell them over the counter.

Segaloff: No rights given or implied, if I remember the phrase.

Maltin: One day, I went up there and I got very friendly with one of his functionaries, a guy named Charlie Pavlicek. Sweet, sweet man. He had the entire Hal Roach talkie short subject library. Everything: Charley Chase, Thelma Todd, ZaSu Pitts, Harry Langdon. He would let me borrow six or so of these two-reelers at a time. I watched them all, and that was also for *Movie Comedy Teams* (q.v.). That's how I saw those. Fortuitous timing. Then I got to buy some. I've used my print of Charley Chase and Thelma Todd in "The Pip from Pittsburgh" (1931) in my USC class for the past twenty-six years. It can't be screened anymore; it started showing signs of vinegar syndrome twenty years ago, and I put it in the freezer in our garage. Doing that has enabled me to keep it alive all this time, but it's now starting to show some shrinkage.†

---

* Many 16mm prints that were sent to military bases disappeared on the way back to their studios.
† Acetate prints, unlike nitrate prints, don't combust, but they do shrink as moisture sublimes from the base and begin to smell of vinegar as the cellulose morphs.

One night none of us will ever forget, we were in our house in Toluca Lake and I showed Ruth Etting in "Derby Decade," a really entertaining RKO short in 1934. It already smelled to high heaven, but it didn't seem warped or shrunken. As it ran through the projector, two things happened. It emitted a white ooze, and it changed polarity. It went from positive to negative! That was the last time that print ever saw a projector. Dick Bann was kind enough to take alcohol swabs and clean the gate of the projector and the film path. Whoever dreamed such things could happen to a print?

Segaloff: I've never ever heard it happening and I've handled some weird prints.

Maltin: People say to me, "Well, why don't you have them all preserved?" I say, "They're preserved in the Library of Congress or MGM or Warner Bros. but this is *my* copy." I'll say achingly that I had a wonderful print of Frank Sinatra's "The House I Live In," an original first-generation print, great picture and sound, better quality than any other copy I've seen, including the Sinatra family's copy that they've used in documentaries and such… and it turned vinegar. The shrinkage is just heartbreaking.

Segaloff: You've got me scared because I have a copy at home in a metal can I haven't opened in years. Now I'll open it in the backyard.

Maltin: Whoever dreamt? When I was feeling flush, I would drive to MPE, Motion Picture Enterprises, on the west side of Manhattan and buy ten or fifteen shiny new cans, 400-foot or 800-foot cans, and label them, all stacked up nice. Now it turns out that was the wrong thing to do.

Segaloff: Didn't King Vidor once say, "If it weren't for the film pirates, we wouldn't have any history at all," because the studios destroyed stuff. How much stuff is in the fill dirt at the 405 freeway or in Santa Monica harbor?

Maltin: Speaking of King Vidor, I have a story. Looking back, I marvel at all the opportunities I had. Saul Turell, the cofounder of Janus Films, took a liking to me, which paid off in one of the great experiences of my life. His company distributed *Our Daily Bread* (1934), King Vidor's ode to communal living—not Communism, exactly, but close. Vidor's home base was MGM, and he had delivered their all-time biggest hit, *The Big Parade* (1925). That gave him a golden ticket to make such daring movies as *The Crowd* (1927) and *Hallelujah* (1929), but when it came to *Our Daily Bread*, the idealistic director had to finance it himself. Turell carried it in his catalog for many years and made a point of having lunch with Vidor whenever he was in Los Angeles. One day he mentioned that he had just acquired the television rights to the Hal Roach library. Vidor said he saw Hal "at the track" on a regular basis and urged Saul to put him on film while he was still alive and coherent. The veteran director even offered to conduct the interview himself. Guess who Mr. Turell hired to write a list of questions—and sit in on the filming?

I can't describe what it was like that day when a crew gathered at Mr. Roach's Bel Air home and the camera started rolling. I was in heaven, that's all I know. They proceeded at such a pace that during a lunch break someone on the crew was tasked with purchasing more raw film stock. (Only two years ago I learned that the line producer on that shoot was Mr. Roach's daughter Maria.) Roach tended to lean on a repertoire of anecdotes that played well with audiences, but Vidor was able to spark some stories I hadn't heard before. He also remembered that ZaSu Pitts was named for "the last of Eliza and the first of Susan."

As I flew home the next day my mind was racing. Having recently screened dozens of Hal Roach comedy shorts I could envision how to weave them into the conversation of two Hollywood veterans. All I wanted was a chance to piece that material together.

But here Saul hesitated. He had laid out the cash for the shoot and wasn't eager to spend even more out of his pocket to turn the raw material into a show, most likely for public television. I went to work and established contact with the program director for WGBH, the Boston PBS station where some of the most popular PBS shows originated. Getting this fellow on the phone wasn't easy, but he was intrigued by my pitch and agreed to meet with Saul and me on his next trip to Manhattan.

Unbeknownst to me, Saul had acquired another protégé, a young filmmaker named Jeff Lieberman who had made a modestly successful horror film called *Squirm*, about an army of worms with a taste for human beings. At the meeting that I had initiated and sweated out I came to realize that Saul intended to give my dream job to this guy—and there was nothing I could do to stop it.

Well, that's not entirely true. When I stopped nagging Saul and the elusive executive from WGBH the project died on the vine, from neglect.

That precious footage is still in Janus Films' vault—and I'm still available to edit it should anyone hire me to do it.

HAND ME THE MALTIN

Segaloff: While you were a student at NYU, having entered publishing in your teens with *Profile* and *Film Fan Monthly*, you got a call that made you a professional. Let's talk about the movie guide, and a particular aspect of it, which is how your name has become a brand. When people say, "Hand me the Maltin," I know exactly what they mean. Do you have a sense that you're now part of the culture?

Maltin: The origin of that book was Patrick O'Connor of New American Library saying to me, "Do you know of this Steven Scheuer book called *Movies on TV*"? I said, "Yes, I know it backwards and forwards. I use it every day." He said, "What do you think of it?" I said, "Well, I think it's okay as far as it goes." And he said, "What would you do differently?" And I swear this is true. (Patrick changed his story periodically. It all comes to the same conclusion, but he liked to embellish the detail.) I said, "He only lists two cast names. I've got to have more names than that. I'd put in the director's name and say whether it was made in black and white or color"—this was 1968, so that was still relevant. The local TV stations chopped these films to hell. "I'd give the original running time," and I just rattled all that off. And he said, "Well, how'd you like to do it?" I said, "Do what?" He said, "I'm looking for somebody to do a rival book. You want to do it?" I said, "Yeah, I guess so." I was completely unprepared for this.

Segaloff: How do you start something that massive?

Maltin: A contract still had to be "negotiated." I didn't negotiate anything. We took a nice sum of money he was offering me. But he said, "What are you going to do now?" I said, "I'm going to NYU this fall." He said, "Why? I just gave you a job." I said, "Because I'm supposed to go to college." It never occurred to me not to go to college. That's what you're supposed to do. If the line says, "Stand here," I stand here. I'm a rule follower.

Segaloff: But how do you physically start doing it?

Maltin: He said, "You're going to have to hire people to do this with you. You can't do it alone. Just try to have some money left over when you're done." Well, there was this guy, do you know Jim Parish?*

---

* James Robert Parish is a prolific researcher, editor, and writer of over one hundred film books.

Segaloff: For years. We're close friends.

Maltin: Jim had an office at the time on West 57th Street called Entertainment Copyright and Research, and a woman working with him called Florence Solomon. This became the hangout for wandering film buffs—two large rooms, shelves with *Film Daily* Yearbooks and things like that. That's where I met Joe Dante.* I hired Jim and Florence to essentially do this book. He did me one great service/favor. He said, "The BIB Source book. Did you ever use that?" "No." "It was a trade publication that every TV station had to have, and it was published by the Broadcast Information Bureau in Long Island. It listed every film available to television. Jim noticed that the write-ups were often word for word the same as in the Scheuer book. We don't know who was copying who, but he said, "We'd better be sure we don't even accidentally copy." But for a B or B-plus movie from the Forties where the plotline is, "Man murders his wife and carries her body to San Francisco by freight," how many ways can you say that? "A woman's body turns up in freight San Francisco. It turns out she's been rendered by her husband."

Some months into the process of doing the book. Scheuer got wind of it and called my editor, Patrick O'Connor, and threatened to sue. Patrick called me and I said, "He doesn't have a leg to stand on. First off, we didn't use his list of films as our foundation. We built our own list using *Film Daily* yearbooks." That's why there are virtually no silent films in that first edition. And because I was addicted to movies on television, I knew what was playing and what wasn't. I knew which Thirties movies were in constant rotation and which never seemed to turn up. We built our own catalog, whatever you want to call it, so when I assured Patrick of all that, he breathed a sigh of relief and invited Scheuer to come over. He showed him some of the write-ups, and Scheuer, miffed and upset, stormed out.

Segaloff: This is ironic because you had to call some other people on the carpet in later years when they were using your capsule descriptions from your TV movie book.

Maltin: Larry Jackson† was the one who said the *Sunday Boston Globe* TV pullout section is using the reviews. And we got a check from the *Boston Globe* to settle that. A nice check.

---

* Former editor for Roger Corman who later directed *Gremlins, Matinee*, and other films heavily steeped in movie lore.

† Larry Jackson was chief programmer of the Orson Welles Cinema in Cambridge, Massachusetts and was key in establishing numerous

Segaloff: What are some of the other guidelines O'Connor gave you?

Maltin: He gave me several specific directives. He said to write the reviews in a telegraphic style and not to use too many articles of speech: "Neat melodrama about rumrunners in Florida." It was five years before I got to revise the book, and from that day to forty years after, I unwrote the first edition. The first thing I did was try to find and get rid of descriptions like "seedy meller" (sleazy melodrama) and "oater"* (Western).

Segaloff: Like the trades used to do, aimed at their intended audience.

Maltin: Also, he said, "You've got to have star ratings." I said, "Ah, they're such a drag. They don't really tell you anything." He said, "People love 'em and they love to argue with them." He was right, as I learned again at *Entertainment Tonight* when I did a one-to-ten scale. People loved guessing what my number would be and feeling proud of themselves if they guessed right. But I will tell you that, within ten days' time in New York, decades ago, I ran into two people who stopped me on the street. One of them says, "I use your book all the time." I said, "Thank you." He said, "But you know what I do? I double your star ratings to know if I'm going to agree with them or not." And I met another guy who said, "You know what I do? I cut your ratings in half, and then I know if I'm going to agree with what you said about the movie."

Segaloff: I hated star ratings and when I was reviewing for *The Boston Herald*, which was a Murdoch paper, they insisted on star ratings. What I did insist on, however, and I actually got them to change their format, was adding the name of the writer to the credit block, which they hadn't been doing. In your case, you added the name of the director.

Maltin: That was a big deal at the time. In later years I said, "OK, any film that gets a three and a half or four-star review, we should name the writer, so we're crediting the writer when we really like a movie." I also expanded the reviews, especially

---

specialty films, including *The Harder They Come*. He later entered film acquisition and distribution and worked with Orson Welles himself on *The Other Side of the Wind* (2018).

* *Variety*-ese for a Western. Horses eat oats, get it?

for significant films. They were so short and so telegraphic at first. It served a purpose; there were 8,000 mini reviews, and they really *were* mini reviews. But when I was unshackled from that directive, I took advantage of it.

Segaloff: Among you and others who contributed to the book, had at least *someone* seen every film?

Maltin: That was the theory.

Segaloff: What was the practice?

Maltin: The practice was yes. I kept up with movies. I mean, I read the trades, as we say, in those days, and if I got a great review from one of my contributors of a movie that I'd read nothing but lousy things about, I either reassigned it or made myself the arbiter. I'd go and see it and be the tiebreaker.

Segaloff: Toward the end of the *Movie Guide* adventure, you told me something which I found interesting and tragic at the same time: you had pushed the limit of the perfect binding of a paperback book,* so you had to start cutting titles out, which is why I guess you went from 17,000 to 16,000 toward the end. How did you decide what titles to remove?

Maltin: First, we got rid of all the made-for-TV movies. We had been including made-for-TV movies for a number of years, and they were all written and researched by Alvin H. Marill, who was the acknowledged chronicler of made-for-TV movies. He later published several books, including a five-volume encyclopedia.† That was the first thing to go. Then, because I had my feelers out and I was aware of what tended to show up on cable and what showed up on local television, I got rid of a lot of early talkies before TCM came along and before really obscure movies had been rescued on DVD or VHS. In the early days, we had had Lex Barker films from West Germany, all sorts of flotsam. That's a good way to describe it.

Segaloff: I cannot imagine having to go through galleys on that book. It must have been crushing.

---

* In a "perfect binding" one edge of the stacked pages is glued together like a pad of paper, rather than being held by traditional folding and stitching.
† *Movies Made for Television: 1964-2004*, Volumes 1-5, Foreword by Leonard Maltin. Scarecrow Press, 2005.

Maltin: You're not going to believe this, but it's true. We would take a copy of the current edition and cut up all 10,000 reviews, and using a glue stick, put each one on an individual piece of 8½ by 11 paper. Then if somebody had corrected the running time, using the ballpoint pen, we'd put a line through 86 minutes, and then write in the margin, 87 minutes. Or if we were adding a cast name—Eddie "Rochester" Anderson—draw a little caret where it should go. People said, "Can't you just do this on a computer?" I said, "You show me a faster way to do this, and I'll do it." There was no faster way to do it. It was absurdly Do-It-Yourself.

Segaloff: And then you had to go to the typesetter, right, with a filing drawer full of sheets of paper.

Maltin: *I* didn't have to go to the typesetter.

Segaloff: How did you and Patrick get along during what was obviously a complex production period?

Maltin: Patrick told me that I was only allowed one complaint call a month. ("It's not in the window of Doubledays on Fifth Avenue." "I know, I heard it already.") At one time I was told that seventy percent of all book sales in the United States occurred on Fifth Avenue: Scribner's, two Doubleday stores, four Barnes & Nobles. And that was my education. It was also sold in other stores that were not as diligent as keeping their shelves stocked. There was a mess of a bookstore on the east side of Times Square toward Broadway, a big barn of a place. I went there and found where they had the rack of movie-related books. Not too many, but there I found my book. The wire metal shelving would hold, I think, four or five deep of my book. There on the floor was the shipping box that they came in with more copies. Every time I went to Manhattan or was going to be in the neighborhood, I'd stop in and see, and for a long time they had sold out the four or five, and the rest were still sitting in the box on the floor, so *I* restocked the shelves. I restocked my own book on the shelf until one day the box was empty and the rack was empty. Then I had to muster up all my chutzpah and go to the front desk and ask the guy behind the counter, "Do you have a book called *TV Movies*?" "If we do, it'll be over there." I walk over there, pretend to look, come back, "Well, then we don't have it." "Well, could you order it?" "Well, yes." The education of an author. That's what I call it.

Segaloff: True or false, if you go into a bookstore and you autograph your new book, they can't return it, they have to sell it.

Maltin: I think that's fiction. But it's a good excuse. I've used it. It's all a learning process. Related to that, the smartest thing I ever heard an author do was Jacqueline Susann, author of *Valley of the Dolls*, who used to go to a bookstore when she was traveling and find her book and purchase several copies of her own book and autograph them to the manager and all the people who worked in the bookstore. If you don't think that doesn't mean she got special treatment and featured prominence in the front of the store, you're crazy. Isn't that ingenious?

Segaloff: At what point did the large print edition start coming out? I remember buying that. It was very impressive.

Maltin: It was to me, too. Then that too evolved because in time, the tail wagged the dog: the large format edition, which was under the banner of Plume, sold the majority of copies, and the old-fashioned paperback became secondary.

Segaloff: What kind of personal changes did you go through when all of this good stuff fell upon you?

Maltin: It changed over the years. The first chance I had to revise the book and update it was in 1974, which is the year I met Alice. She came in at the tail end of that process, but then when we did it again in 1978, four years later, she was an active participant and we decided that what we were going to do was take a copy of the book and cut up all the entries, and for each entry, we would glue stick it to an eight and a half by eleven piece of paper as we had done originally. Then new entries would be typed.

The other thing that was completely inconsistent then was computer usage. I was not on a computer yet, and we had different typefaces, different font sizes. One of my contributors could only do single-spaced. It was very haphazard. It began to overtake our lives. The normal gestation for a book is about the same as a baby, nine months or so. More, if it's a heavily illustrated or designed book, a volume to go on a coffee table; less if it's just type. But for the purpose of being an annual book, we had to solve several riddles about how we were going to try to remain as current as possible. Most studios wouldn't show you a film until two weeks before it opened. The production manager at Penguin, this is just fool luck, was a fan of the book, and so was the copy editor. One of them stayed at the company for a long, long time. The copy editor changed at a couple of different points, but they went the extra mile, beyond the prescribed protocol of how to get a book produced on a timely basis for me to be able to get releases from early spring, let's say, or mid-spring into a book that was coming out in the fall.

Segaloff: There was also a window in those days between when a film was released on home video or on the TV.

Maltin: We ignored that. We just wanted to have it listed. What we eventually did was submit it to typeset in January and they sent galleys for proofreading. Then when they had to paginate those galleys, we devised a list of upcoming releases through May 31st, and they left twelve lines. For several years, it took time to figure out how many lines would be ideal. Sometimes they put in slugs. If the review turned up short and we did it eight lines, they put in slugs. We had quite an operation going. The hitch was that the release schedules changed. Sometimes we had to fill that space with something, so I put in a really obscure old movie or something that used to be in the book that I had to take out. The one that really zapped it to us was when they changed the name of the movie from *Flight 93* to *United 93*. We had left fifteen lines open in the "F" section and no space open in the "U" section.

Segaloff: Did you say, "*United Flight 93* — see *Flight 93*"?

Maltin: No. I shortened a couple of reviews on that page, took out a cast name or two. By the time that book was finished, there were no widows. The first thing we did to save space or to acquire space was to get rid of widows.

Segaloff: You better explain what a widow is.

Maltin: A widow is a line of type or a paragraph, usually, with only one short word on the last line leaving a lot of space open. There's no space open anymore.

Segaloff: I don't think people realize how tough it is to write that concisely and still have a worthwhile user experience.

Maltin: I remember we were about to take a trip once. My longtime assistant Cathleen Anderson, who died very young, was devoted to this book, and she could handle my being away for a little while and keep the pot boiling. But every now and then, she'd have to call me wherever I was, and we had to invent things over the phone. In that way it did intrude on our lives during springtime when the deadline was lurking.

Segaloff: People don't understand.

Maltin: No, no one does. Nor should they. Nor should they have to. Of course, I had by then amassed a wonderful cadre of contributors who had specialties. Bill Warren handled all the genre pictures: horror, sci-fi, fantasy. That was his domain, and I trusted his judgment in that area. Pete Hammond, with whom I worked at *Entertainment Tonight*, saw a lot of obscure stuff. He said I gave him the worst movies to review. Our daughter Jessie said that too when she started contributing. She says she was the Rob Schneider specialist.

Segaloff: Oh, poor thing.

Maltin: Luke Sader, who I also worked with at *E.T.*, had a great eye, good proofreading eye, and he was also very good at looking at a cast list and saying, "Oh, you ought to mention so-and-so. They're on a new sitcom." It was really useful to get not just a cast list but a *smart* cast list. I saved certain reviews for my old buddy, Mike Clark, whom I miss terribly. Terribly. Not that we got to see each other very often, since he barely ever came out here, but every now and then, on a book tour, I would get to go to Washington, D.C. and we could see each other for a little bit. Mike used to room with Adam Reilly. Do you know Adam Reilly? Adam wound up in Denver programming repertory cinema there. Mike was an NYU grad student when I met him, and we hit it off. He was a Dean and Jerry fanatic. There was a time at *E.T.* (we got our job roughly the same time) when I said, "It would be easier for me to pitch a story to you, plant it in *USA Today*, and then show it to my boss to get it on the air." They wouldn't trust anything they didn't already know or wasn't already acknowledged."*

Segaloff: The first edition of the *Movie Guide* came out in 1969, right? That's an extraordinarily short window for a book like that.

---

* The Author (Nat) worked in television at the same time and I recall my executive producer saying, "We should do that story. It's getting a lot of coverage." He couldn't understand my belief as a competitive journalist that we should be breaking stories, not waiting until someone else got there first.

Maltin: Yes, it was, and that's when I learned a useful lesson, to put it mildly. The production manager at NAL gave the manuscript to two different proofreaders: to a proofreader and a proofreader/movie genius. I never found out who—I think I know who it was, but I never found out for sure—who made endless amendments and corrections. He saved my tush and made it a better book. When it first came out, all I could see were mistakes or mistakes of omission. They stood out like neon on the page to me. I'd gone through the galleys, and I found that to be true for many years. You can look at it and look at it and look at it and, the minute it's in print...

Segaloff: That's the curse of the writer. You open the box of authors' copies* and the first page you turn to has a mistake.

Maltin: But it taught me a valuable lesson. When we finally got up to speed doing the book annually, as we did from the mid-Eighties onward, every review passed under several pairs of eyes (can an eye be well-informed?) and that made a huge difference. Somebody knows something that somebody else may not know. I got a twenty-one-page, single-spaced letter from a guy named Bill Warren, when I was still living in New York, filled with corrections and also what I'd call complaints. He was an expert in the areas of fantasy, science-fiction, and horror. I incorporated all of his corrections the next year. He lived here in L.A. and, after doing a second round the following year, I hired him, put him on the team, and he was a valuable contributor for many years.

Segaloff: Okay, at this point you've become established as a writer. Now we need to revisit Herb Graff as your match-maker to get to when you met your wife, Alice. You spoke in Herb's course, and Alice complimented you at the end of your talk. Is this one of those things where she was the student and then sought you out afterwards?

Maltin: More or less. She always loved movies. Her whole family loved movies so much that she says they always used to stay and read the credits. They were really into that. And Herb, who by day was a *shmatte*† salesman, and a successful one, was also a 16mm film collector and friend of Bill Everson's. His course at NYU extension was significantly less expensive to take than Professor Richard Brown's at the New

---

* Including this one, no doubt.
† *Shmatte* is the Yiddish word for rag and is used as a self-deprecating way of saying that one is in the clothing business.

School.* She took Herb's class, and Herb had a guest lecturer, a friend who every week came and did a spiel. I did my spiel on the history of animation and afterwards she came over to me to chat me up and, apparently, I was cold. I was unresponsive, so she figured either I was gay or I was spoken for. Neither of those things was true; I was just too stupid to recognize somebody that I should have paid more attention to. Then, at the end of that semester, Alice said to Herb, "I love all this, but I'm just a working stiff. I don't have a lot of money. How can I see more of these wonderful films?" He said, "I'm going to introduce you to a guy who watches movies for a living." That was John Cocchi.† He was an incredible film savant. I was going to say expert, but more of a savant. He worked for *Box Office* magazine, which was one of the trade magazines that was just barely hanging on. John was a regular at the Theodore Huff Film Society. Herb invited Alice to meet him one night at the Huff, which had by then moved to the School of Visual Arts on East 23rd Street. I arrived as Herb was leaving, and he said, "I don't feel well. I'm going home. Look out for Alice. Alice Tlusty. You remember her? You've met her in my class." I said, "I don't really remember." He said, "You'll spot her. She's blonde." There were no other heterosexual women coming that night, and it's an amphitheater room, and I was sitting toward the back. I saw her come in and I waved, and she waved back. We spent our first night together watching two silent films under the aegis of William K. Everson: Maurice Tourneur's *The Whip*, 1917, and Paul Bern's *Open all Night*, 1924, with Adolphe Menjou and Raymond Griffith. We were, I think, the only social success to come out of the Huff Society in its long and checkered history.

---

* The New School is a wide-ranging progressive academic institution founded in 1919 as The New School for Social Research. It is presently accredited and affiliated with MSCHE (The Middle States Commission on Higher Education). Richard Brown is one of their primary film professors.

† John Cocchi (1929-2014) had an obsessive knowledge of films and was a consultant to the American Film Institute when they assembled their catalogue of American films. He also advised American Movie Classics at the start of that cable channels run and provided rare prints to the Cooperative Film Society in New York.

A COLLABORATIVE MARRIAGE

The Maltins—Leonard and Alice—are a business partnership as well as a couple. In an industry where marriages are often as permanent as an echo, theirs has survived half a century. Their early years were a struggle, both financially and in an effort to become parents. Typically, they met through a kind of Kismet.

Alice Maltin: I took this class at New York University evening extension. As I always say, I took *it* as opposed to Professor Richard Brown's class at the New School because I couldn't afford that one, but I could afford this one. I just loved it. My whole family, we're all film buffs. We really are, but we didn't know you could be a film buff. We didn't know there was such a thing. We would just stay and watch the credits, and everybody would laugh at us. They yelled, "Who's the second unit director?" We took a lot of abuse, my mother, my father, my brother. I loved the class. Herb Graff brought in various friends whom I didn't know then, and it was called Film Genres. One time, he brought his friend Leonard Maltin, who had already written several books, and I thought he was adorable. I just did, and I tried to pick him up at the end of class. Frankly, he was a bit aloof, and I said to myself, "Well, either he's gay or he has a girlfriend," because I was a cute thing. I really was. Seven years older than him, but still a cute thing.

I worked in a restaurant called the Running Footman on East 63rd Street where I saw a lot of very famous people. Michael Pearman, who started Michael's Pub on East 48th, was the owner. There were fifty-three backers, all movie people—Kirk Douglas, you just name it, producers, directors. I actually met Cary Grant at the restaurant. Mr. Pearman introduced me—I know I'm going off track, but he introduced me. I'm taking lunchtime cash, and he said, "Ms. Alice, this is Mr. Grant. Mr. Grant, this is Ms. Alice," that's what they always called me. I couldn't say a word. Grant obviously was used to this. He was very kind and very sweet, and I thought, "Holy shit, I just met Gary Grant." Also, Mr. Pearman had friends. Douglas Fairbanks Jr. was his good friend, and David Niven. I saw them having a wild lunch, laughing like crazy.

I touched showbiz. I loved it. I said, "Look, I have no money, and I love movies." Herb said, "I'll take you to a place where you'll see rare old films, and I'll introduce you to a guy who watches movies for a living." This was John Cocchi of *Box Office Magazine.* John was an Italian, from Brooklyn. I'm a Jew from the Bronx. He was really sweet, and I did get to see different movies. Herb took me to see this movie, and I kept thinking about Leonard, of course. Then Herb invited me to the Laurel and Hardy *Sons of the Desert* dinner and the Theodore Huff Society.

Maltin: Then he didn't feel well; he went home early that night. As I was arriving, he was leaving, he said, "Remember that girl, Alice, from my class?" I said, "No." He said, "You'll recognize her, just look out for her." I said, "Fine." It was an amphitheater room. I was sitting toward the top, but when she came in, the entry was at the bottom of the steps, and you came up. She stood out because she was a female.

Alice: And I was pretty.

Maltin: Oh, you were the whole package.

Alice: Smart, that's what I was told.

Segaloff: What makes Leonard appeal to you?

Alice: He appealed because he was adorable. He was very knowledgeable. We sat together through two silent movies. I loved it. I wasn't pretending, "Oh, I think I'll sit through two silent movies." It was wonderful. Then he said he would call me. But he didn't call me. He didn't call me! Then, at the Laurel and Hardy *Sons of the Desert* dinner where John Cocchi took me, there was Leonard across the room. I said to myself—this was May of 1974—"I want him for Christmas." I really did. I said that to myself. He went off in the summertime.

Maltin: I went to the Annecy Animation Festival. When I came home, I called her.

Alice: We saw each other July 1st. Then he went off. I saw him again two weeks later. That was really it. It was funny because I had a best friend married to a lawyer. Successful. Two kids. Mind you, I was thirty years old. I would say, "How do you know when you meet the right person?" She always said to me, "You'll know." When I met him, it felt different. He was just so cute.

Segaloff: Was the age difference a significant part at any point in your relationship?

Alice: No, it really wasn't, although we wanted to have a baby right away, but we had problems. I told him about the second or third date, I said, "I'm older than you." He said, "Yes, I thought so." He said, "How old are you?" I said, "I'm 30. I'm going to be 31 soon, next month." He said, "Oh, okay."

Segaloff: What was the wedding like? [March 15, 1975]

Alice: Oh, it was a Jewish wedding. My father was a window cleaner from the Bronx and all he wanted to do was to give me a beautiful wedding. I too was very much into all that stuff. I had been to all my cousins' weddings. I had to catch that damn bouquet.

Maltin: She comes from a very big family. They had family circle meetings.

Alice: And a lot of cousins.

Maltin: And getaway weekends together, and all that. I was on the tail end of that. That was my only time in the Catskills. We went to a Catskills weekend with more cousins than I could count. The truth is, I didn't want a big wedding, but I couldn't deny her parents this joy that they were going to have.

Maltin: We courted during July 1974. On the second or third date—

Alice: —we just knew it—

Maltin: We just knew we were going to get married.

Alice: I came home. I said to my mother, "Mom, there's this guy." My parents were sleeping. I woke them up. I said, "Mom, there's this guy. It's very different. I feel very different with him, Mom." My mother's like, "Huh?" She's containing herself.

Segaloff: You were thirty.

Alice: Thirty? Yes, right. A loser. Get the loser daughter married.

Maltin: My parents did not feel—

Alice: No, they were not that happy, because I was from the Bronx with a window cleaner father. They wanted—and I understand this for their prince—a doctor's daughter from a wealthy suburb. Why would they want a window cleaner's daughter from the Bronx, who really had no career? I was a secretary. I was an assistant. I just worked to make money for my car and for my therapy which, as far as they knew, meant you were nuts. They were not fans of psychoanalysis, let's put it that way. It was a disaster for them. We moved very quickly.

Maltin: We would have gotten married immediately. We would have done it right away. End of the summer.

Alice: We got engaged on Labor Day weekend. We went to the Cinecon in New Haven, Connecticut and we got engaged. We never really discussed these things. It was sort of like, "Okay, I need a ring." "Okay, we'll get a ring." That kind of thing.

Maltin: Because my parents were upset, I was upset at their upset-ness. I had never rebelled. I never had a teenage phase, as many do. This was the first time that we weren't in harmony. I was still living at home. I said to Alice, "I can't just do this. I've got to give them time to get used to the idea because I'm not changing my mind but we're getting married. They've got to make their peace with it." We put it off. When we were thinking about when we could do it, there's a thing in the Jewish calendar.

Alice: You're not supposed to get married for seven weeks.* It's right around spring. More than that, when we were at the hotel in New Haven, one day I got to meet Jeanine Basinger. You really want your friends to like who you choose. I met her in the hallway, and I said, "You're Jeanine Basinger." She said, "You're Alice." She embraced me. No questions asked. Her attitude was, "If he chose me, I had to be the right person." That's the faith that she had.

Segaloff: What happened when you physically met each other's parents?

Alice: His parents said to Jeanine, because they so respected her, "Talk him out of it. He's with this girl. He doesn't work anymore. He's just with this girl." Jeanine said, "Leonard is like a champion ice skater. All his life he's been skating. Now he's fallen in love. He'll go back to skating." That was her attitude. They wanted her to talk him out of me. Really. She said, "Alice will leave Leonard sooner than Leonard will leave Alice." It was very hard for me. I'm not a secure person. I know I appear that way, but to have his parents let me know—! That night when we came back from New Haven and were engaged, it was not a happy scene in his house.

---

* Weddings are forbidden under Jewish lore during the seven-week Omer period between Passover and Shavuot.

Segaloff: You were there for it?

Alice: Yes, I was there. I didn't know what to say. My parents are ecstatic, and his parents are miserable. That was really hard. The parents tried to accept each other.

Segaloff: That's a nice gesture.

Maltin: It was a very difficult period. Very, very.

Alice: Not a happy time for us.

Maltin: They did put on a great wedding. There were two hundred people at this temple in Harrison, New York. Everyone had a good time, except my parents and, to an extent, me. That was a rocky start, but we loved each other.

Alice: Yes, we did.

Maltin: We made each other happy.

Alice: I was a virgin, but I drifted. We spent a couple of weekends in Connecticut before we were married. There was the Silvermine Tavern in Norwalk. My father's a very old-fashioned man, and maybe a month before the wedding, we're at the Silvermine Tavern, and my car broke down. I had to ask my father to come get us. I thought, "Oh, Jesus, he's not going to like this." He comes in. My father's a strong man. He comes in. No problem. Nothing. It's like nothing. It's like Uber. He's picking up the luggage, getting it in the car, and not saying anything, everything is fine because he loved Leonard. He and Leonard would talk about old movies for hours. Leonard was my gift to my father in the three years that he survived after our marriage, really. He's so beautiful.

Segaloff: After you moved out here, your mother Judy came to live with you, right?

Alice: My mother lived in Florida, which is what you do when you become a widow.

Maltin: We got married in 1975, the Ides of March 1975. Six months later, her father had a heart attack.

Alice: In Europe. Walked around with a heart attack. When we picked my father up at the airport, I took one look at him and took him right to the hospital.

Maltin: Came home, and we inherited the rescue dog, Pippin, that Alice and her folks had taken in. I was not a dog person but when he had his heart attack, we were forced to take over the custody of this little dog. I became a dog person because this little guy was so easy to get along with. He was quiet. He was smart. He was no trouble. Then there was another dog that, a year or two later.

Alice: We lived at 79th and Amsterdam, and the park was just a block away. This dog followed me home from the park. I couldn't get rid of him. He was skinny.

Maltin: Undernourished but a cute dog.

Alice: Kind of like a Basenji. He had Basenji qualities.

Maltin: You named him Simon Charley Chase. Charley for short. Alice said, "One dog, two dogs, what's the difference?"

Segaloff: The life of a freelancer is perilous. Alice, how did you and Leonard work together to become a team?

Maltin: There's a very specific day.

Alice: I worked for Bantam Books, which published the Scheuer book (q.v.). That was pretty funny.

Maltin: Charlie Chaplin died Christmas Day, 1976. I got a call from *the Soho Weekly News* asking if I would write a piece in remembrance, an appreciation. Sure. "We'll send a messenger to pick it up." No faxes yet. "We'll pay you $175." "Fine. I'd do that." I had a whole bunch of freelance gigs that month. We thought we were doing well. We were paying $415 a month for our three-and-a-half-room apartment in this brand-new building. But nobody was paying me. That was January, and I'm owed a lot of money, but no one's paying up. What did Alice do at Bantam Books? She worked in the credit department.

Alice: I was the secretary to the credit manager. Life is funny, isn't it?

Maltin: I worked at home in our apartment. There were no walls, Alice heard me trying to talk to the editor who commissioned this piece about getting paid. When I got off the phone, she said, "That's not what you do. What you say is blah, blah, blah." You said, "Blah, blah, blah."

Alice: He got mad at me.

Maltin: I got very defensive. Finally, I said, "You're so smart. Why don't you do it?" Pause. Beat. Yes. Why *don't* you do it?

Alice: I got money out of people who never gave money. I do it very nicely. There are ways of getting money without anybody being upset, knowing what to say. I did it.

Segaloff: For all the freelancers reading this, how did you do it?

Alice: Very simply. You call people and you say, "Okay, so you owe this." They'll never tell you why they can't pay you. I wish they would, because I'd be understanding. You say, "Oh, okay. Can you pay a little of it?" "Yes, we could probably. You wouldn't want $50." I'd say, "Yes, I'll take the $50. When can I expect the rest?" They'd say, "Probably in two weeks." I said, "I'll call you in two weeks." That's how you get your money. It always worked. Nobody was angry, except for the one time we actually had to file. This was an education.

Maltin: I got a call out of the blue from *Museum Magazine*. Nice, slick magazine. I went to have a meeting with the two editors. "We're going to do a piece on animation art." Good gig, $500. I did it, turned it in. I wasn't smart. I signed the piece of paper that I'd be paid on publication rather than being paid on receipt of the article. Several months passed; it had a long lead time. When the issue came out, I forget how, we found they had left Manhattan. Now they're up in Westchester County. Not a good sign.

Alice: I talk, I ask, and I'm not getting anywhere with them. Finally, I decided I had to take this to small claims court. They think by moving somewhere that I don't have a car and I can't drive up to that courthouse and file a claim? I filed the claim. They make you fill in a court date. I said to the woman, "My husband is commuting to L.A., I don't know when he'll be back." She said, "Honey, don't worry. The day before your court date this guy's going to settle." I said, "Really?" She said, "That's what happens." That's what happened. I said to the guy, "Listen"—and of course, I wanted a check that was a real check—"Why didn't you tell me you were having problems, because I could have worked with you." Nah, he wasn't interested in that. The clerk said to me, "Don't worry. It'll be fine." It was.

Maltin: I don't know if anybody else who freelanced for that issue ever got paid. That was the turning point, though. That day that Alice was coaching me, and I realized she could just do it better than I could.

ENTERTAINMENT TONIGHT

From 1982 to 2012, Leonard was the critic and film history expert on the syndicated show business newsmagazine, Entertainment Tonight. *Over a remarkable thirty years, he reviewed films, conducted interviews (with both stars and filmmakers, famous and obscure), and contributed tribute and historic features. Because his E.T.* stint overlapped so many of his other activities, it will be helpful to see how he went from being a fan and historian to a celebrity in his own light.*

Segaloff: How did you acclimate to *Entertainment Tonight*? I'm interested in how you grew as a television producer and as a television personality working with the show. Did they just set you down with a Teleprompter at first, and then did you later move to writing and producing?

Maltin: The call came from Bruce Cook. Alice answered the phone. They wanted to speak to me about employment. She said, "Yours or his?" Bruce said, "His." Alice said, "I'll put you right through."

When they brought me out here, I didn't know what it was for. I made the incorrect assumption that they wanted me to do feature stories about Hollywood history because that's my area of expertise. When I was shown into the office of Jim Bellows, the legendary newspaper editor who had just been hired by Barry Diller, he said, "Well, you know, we brought you out here to do reviews, so could you tape two reviews for us tomorrow morning, first thing?" I tell the story to my class every semester. At that moment, I swear my thoughts went soaring back to all the stories I'd read about the silent era when, first thing in the morning, the assistant director would go to the front gate and there'd be a little crowd there, and he'd say, "You, can you ride a horse?" If you wanted to make five bucks, you said yes, otherwise you'd only make three for milling around in the background. So I said, "Yes, sir." He assigned me a producer, a wonderful guy named Steve Paskay, and Steve walked me through the procedure of writing an introductory paragraph and then picking a clip from the handout reel—3/4-inch tape in those days—and then continuing the clip or showing another clip with some voice-over and then returning to me on camera to wrap up the review. I got the hang of it pretty quickly. I had seen two films that were just on the verge of being released. One of them was at the Santa Fe Film Festival where Miklos Rózsa had been a guest, and they showed *Dead Men Don't Wear*

---

* *Entertainment Tonight* debuted in April 1981. Its similar title to Steven Spielberg's massive hit *E.T.: The Extra-Terrestrial*, which opened in June 1982, didn't hurt establishing it, either.

Plaid. That was one of the films I'd seen that was about to come out. The other one, I think, was *Annie*. I'm pretty sure it was *Annie*, because I was on the press list in New York, so I got to go to screenings. Those are the reviews I did the next morning in Merv Griffin's studio at 1428 Vine Street in Hollywood. Vin Di Bona was the line producer on the show, he was relatively new.* They'd been through five producers in the first season, and they'd been through almost as many stations in L.A. finding the right time slot. At that time, they were on KTLA at 4:30 in the afternoon and midnight, twice a day. I finished taping those two reviews and they were all amazed that I was able to not only read the prompter, but then when they wanted to do the shot over my shoulder to watch a non-existent screen so they could matte in the clip later, I was able to do that. Apparently, they auditioned someone else who couldn't master that.

Segaloff: But you'd been doing public speaking, you'd been on television.

Maltin: I had never addressed the camera. I'd been on television as a guest.

Segaloff: Including for me on Boston's *Evening Magazine*.

Leonard taped his audition May 27, 1982 and commuted between Manhattan and Los Angeles for the next year and a half while he and Alice tried to get pregnant. (By then, they'd had three miscarriages).

Maltin: We moved out to Los Angeles on November 2, 1983. I know very precisely, and our dogs came with us. They spent their sunset years sitting by a pool.

Segaloff: Did you acclimate to TV?

Maltin: I'd never written for the ear or addressed the camera. I look at those early reviews and they seem very stiff, but I think I got away with it because I was writing and delivering my own copy.

Segaloff: Who typed it up? Who put it on the Prompter?

---

* Vin Di Bona later created and produced *America's Funniest Home Videos* beginning in 2001.

Maltin: I typed it on an IBM Selectric and someone else retyped it on Prompter. They used to have carbon paper.

Segaloff: Did you have to join the Writers Guild?

Maltin: No. The Writers Guild allows you to write for yourself.

Segaloff: How long was it before you got into producing packages [feature stories]?

Maltin: They wouldn't let me for a long time and they didn't want me to, but I kept sort of nudging in that direction. Within a year, I was fooling around with feature pieces and I fell in love with video editing. I couldn't sit at the console, but I sat with the video editor.

Segaloff: You did your edit plans* and then you worked on it with the editor, or did you wing it from the footage?

Maltin: Both. I learned very quickly that the better prepared I was, the smoother the session went. But I also learned that if I did the whole thing on paper, it didn't allow for accidents and surprises that could give a piece life.

Segaloff: After you did interviews, did somebody give you a transcript with time code and that sort of thing?

Maltin: I transcribed them.

Segaloff: You transcribed yourself? You're my hero.

Maltin: I have all my transcripts in the garage. On paper. I don't have all my video. I have a tiny fraction of my video because I found it's very difficult to archive yourself, it's time consuming and, well, it's hard to do.

Segaloff: And somebody's always walking past the dubbing room making wisecracks about your ego.

Maltin: But I compiled some best of reels in different moments, so I had those.

Segaloff: You were on for how many years?

---

* An edit plan is a after-script that tells the editor where to find and place video that has been shot.

Maltin: Thirty.

Segaloff: What was it like when you began there?

Maltin: We started off working in Merv Griffin's building on Vine Street, which was a maze of corridors and offices. It was never meant to house one show or one entity. It was added onto. It had been a radio studio.

Segaloff: A warren as opposed to a newsroom.

Maltin: Yes. We were there for the first year that I worked at the show. Then we moved to the Paramount lot (5555 Melrose Avenue, Hollywood). A couple of weeks before we were going to make the move, I said to Jeanne Wolf, or she said to me, "Want to go over and get a sneak peek of what it's going to look like?" I said, "Yes." We got a pass to drive onto the lot and went to the Mae West building and climbed to the second floor. (P.S. I suggested that our business card say, "Mae West building, second floor, come up and see us sometime." No one took me up on that.) We went upstairs and it was all new. New fabric-covered cubicles, new desks, new chairs. We looked: Where are all the reporters? Where are we going to work? Couldn't find it. Finally, we walked down one hallway, all the way down. It seemed like a long walk from the newsroom where they had a news desk that was Action Central, where the monitors were. We walked down this hall and then there was a sign that said "talent." We looked and it was one room with four desks on each side. It looked like a microcosm of the shot in *The Apartment*, of those mind-numbing rows of desks. We said, "Oh, no." No partitions, no privacy. Just the opposite. There were eight of us at the time, eight on-air people. I said, "We ought to name it." Scott Osborne was sitting next to me. I knew Scott because he had been on WCBS-TV in New York. He was the exception to the rule; he did not work his way up from market to market; he started at the top and then moved around. I was not a TV animal. I had no experience and no credentials as a TV journalist or a TV reporter or whatever. Anyway, I said, "Let's call it 'the exile room.'" Scott said, "No, no, no. When they're running you out of town, the thing to do is grab a baton, run to the front and lead the parade with a big smile." We decided to call it "The Talent Oasis." We had the art department make a sign and we called it "The Talent Oasis." We moved one desk to the wall, and we tried to break it up a bit. Miraculously, we all got along really well and were able to conduct our lives and our business without intruding on each other. I don't know how we did that. It was seldom that all eight of us were there at once.

Segaloff: It wasn't like the criminal courts room in *The Front Page* where you were all fighting each other for the same story, was it?

Maltin: Oh, no. Nothing business-wise. I'm just talking about, "Your wife is calling because you missed a lunch date," just personal stuff. Talking to your agent or blowing off steam because you didn't like the way they cut your piece, those things, the day-to-day stuff. Jeanne was a bombastic person-ality and a small tornado of energy. She always had an assistant and an intern—at least two people working with her and for her. I learned a lot from her. We're still friends. People would say to me, "How can you work, how can you concentrate with all that going on?" I said, "I used to be able to read on the subway, too. I just compartmentalize." One of the things I learned from her is she had every interview transcribed.

Segaloff: Which you also did.

Maltin: Learning from her.

Segaloff: I understand why you would do that because you're a historian, but why would Jeanne do it?

Maltin: For reference. If a follow-up story needed to be done, she wanted to call on some element or component from some-thing she had already—

Segaloff: These were all printed, so it wasn't that you could call up a Word document and do a Word search.

Maltin: No, this is all pre-computer. There was a woman on the staff at *E.T.* who was our human computer. If you went to her and said, "I need a shot of Joan Collins. I'm referencing celebrity culture, and we need a B-roll shot of Joan Collins." She'd say, "We just shot her at an opening of a wine store on Melrose a week ago Tuesday" and you'd call up that tape from the tape vault, which was in the basement of the building. Then they went to file cards, and then eventually went to computer. I interviewed Sir David Lean on several occasions, and three days afterwards, I asked for the tape, which had been filed, and they couldn't find it because the intern who had filed it filed it under "Sir."

Segaloff: When it came to clearances, did the show have a blanket permission arrangement for stills and clips with all the studios?

Maltin: No.

Segaloff: You had to bargain every one of them?

Maltin: Everything had to be cleared. This was before anyone had taken up the Fair Use doctrine.[*] There was no such thing. We were told, if I was going to use an episode of *The Twilight Zone*, better to use a 1959 episode than a 1962 episode, because SAG residuals were due for any appearance after 1960. They had to go to CBS and get the actors' clearance. Every actor had to be cleared. The woman whose job it was not only had to work under the gun but had incredible resilience and determination. I heard her on the phone cajoling agents who would then call their client. It was just stupefying what hoops we had to go through. They did a weekend show about the year 1969, and I used stunts from whatever James Bond film came out that year, because we didn't have to clear British actors who were not members of SAG, or stunt people who were not members of SAG.

A guy who was a scam artist got away with a ruse involving music, not film clips. There was a terrible, disreputable show that Paramount did, a nightly show, called *Hard Copy*. They did a needle drop[†] of Laurel and Hardy music, a British band leader who did it before the Beau Hunks[‡] did it right. This guy did a pretty good imitation or replication of some of that music. He purported to own the rights. He pulled a Raymond Rohauer:[§] "I'm going to sue you for everything you're worth," blah, blah, blah. Paramount took it seriously.

One of my jobs was doing pre-obits or shelf obits.[¶] I used needle drops all the time of that whole line of recreated film music by Franz Waxman's son, George Waxman. I used all

[*] The Copyright Act of 1976 allows unlicensed use of copyrighted material under certain circumstances. See https://www.copyright.gov/fair-use/

[†] An excerpt of previously recorded music.

[‡] A Dutch band that performs cover recordings with documentary accuracy. Their name comes from the title of the 1931 Laurel and Hardy comedy set in the Foreign Legion.

[§] Raymond Rohauer (1924-1987) was a highly litigious collector, restorer, and distributor of classic films who never passed up an opportunity to claim ownership of titles that were in the public domain.

[¶] Completed obituary videos produced in advance and kept on hand for when an elderly or ailing celebrity dies.

the great masters—Steiner, Korngold—to score my pieces. The ruling came through: no more needle drops, only mediocre production music.* I was doing a shelf obit of Bob Hope. I said, "You mean I can't use 'Thanks for the Memory'"? "No." I said, "Every other obit on television show is going to be dripping with "'Thanks for the Memory' because it's his signature song. The lawyer said, 'No, sorry.' As I was dejectedly walking back to the edit bay, a light bulb went on. I went back. I said, "Even if it's a Famous Music-published song or theme?"† He said, "Oh. Well, I guess that's okay then." Paramount owned Famous Music, one of the leading music publishers in the world.

Segaloff: I assume the same thing happened with stills.

Maltin: They decided that stills, and especially posters, including lobby cards, were advertising material, as were book covers and magazine covers.

Segaloff: What were some of the uncomfortable situations you encountered on *Entertainment Tonight*?

Maltin: I think I may be the first or possibly only film critic to work at a movie studio. I mean, I had an office. I was on the Paramount studio lot for twenty-four years. Frank Nugent‡ had been *The New York Times* critic. He became a screenwriter, but he didn't hold both jobs simultaneously. Roger Ebert found himself working for a newspaper that was acquired by Rupert Murdoch when Murdoch bought 20th Century Fox. He technically was working for the *Sun-Times*.

Segaloff: Pauline Kael worked for Paramount for a time. Warren Beatty had them give her a sinecure to neutralize her. But you never walked both sides of the street at the same time.

Maltin: I had been there a matter of weeks when I reviewed *Grease 2*. I heard the phone ring in the newsroom, and one of

---

* Production music is best described as canned music with no royalty entanglement.

† Famous Music Publishing was the music publishing company owned by Paramount for whom Bob Hope had been under contract when he recorded what became his signature song, "Thanks for the Memory," in *The Big Broadcast of 1938*. In May 2007 Famous Music was sold to Sony.

‡ Frank Nugent (1908-1965) wrote, among other films, *The Quiet Man* and *The Searchers*. He was brought to Hollywood from the *Times* by Darryl F. Zanuck and had an affinity for John Ford.

the producers—in fact, the guy who had made the call to hire me—picked up the phone. I heard one half of the conversation, but it was somebody at Paramount, the movie studio, calling somebody at a Paramount television show saying, "How can you have this guy throwing bricks at one of our pictures?" My producer said, "Well," he said, "we've hired him as a critic, and that's his opinion. We're not going to interfere with it. That's just the way it is." I was delighted and mildly shocked. Of course, it helped that *nobody* liked *Grease 2.* Had I been expressing a maverick opinion or a minority opinion, that might have colored that conversation differently, but it was a welcome boost of confidence and a nice show of integrity.

Segaloff: Is that the only instance that you know of when somebody connected with a film called to complain about anything you'd said about it?

Maltin: I reviewed *Rhinestone* and decided, because I liked Dolly Parton—who doesn't like Dolly Parton?—and I liked Sylvester Stallone, I decided not to take any cheap shots. There were very punny critics on TV especially. There were people who then, I guess as now, wanted to make their bones by seeing how many wisecracks they can put into a review of an overstuffed Hollywood movie. I took what I thought was the high road, and—while giving it a bad review—said, "It's a shame to waste the talents of these two charismatic people in such a mediocre film." The following week, my colleague, Jeanne Wolf, was covering a premiere for *E.T.,* and she saw Stallone and said, "Sly, come over and say hello." He said, "Oh, I dunno if I'd like to talk to you, Jeanne. After what that man said about our movie. I don't mind constructive criticism, but that guy was *vicious,*" which taught me an early lesson: You can't win.

The worst? Burt Reynolds got a bee in his bonnet that I had it in for him in some way, or that I was gunning for him in some way, and it wasn't true. It simply wasn't true. He was making films at that time like *Cannonball Run 3* and *Stroker Ace* that warranted negative reviews, in my opinion. He really went on a rampage. Paramount did a pilot for a primetime interview show à la Barbara Walters with the Canadian comedian and sometimes-filmmaker David Steinberg. One of the segments was David interviewing Burt Reynolds. They had worked together on *Paternity.* David Steinberg directed that film. How did I learn about this? One day, I'm walking down a corridor at *E.T.,* and one of our camera guys said, "You've got a big fan in Burt Reynolds." I said, "What do you mean?"

He said, "You'll find out soon enough." He had shot the piece. Someone else told me about it before it aired. Then I went to NATPE and ran into one of our vice presidents, a guy named Randy Reiss. I said, "On a Paramount show, you're going to let this guy rip me a new one?" He said, "Are you kidding? It makes him look like two cents and you come out smelling like a rose." I said, "You really think so?" He said, "Yes." I said, "Okay."

I adopted that attitude, but I didn't count on how my parents or my friends would respond if they chanced to see it, which they did. My father nearly kicked in the TV set, apparently, and a friend of mine in Minneapolis said, "How could he get away with that?" They were appalled. I shrugged it off, but they were appalled.

A little time went by, and I was covering the Golden Boot Awards for *E.T.* as I did for many years. In the green room before the event began, in walked Burt and Loni Anderson, and they were asked if they would be willing to come on camera separately and talk about the event. "Sure." As our camera guy is hoisting this camera onto his shoulder, Burt says to me, "I ought to slug you, but there's ladies present." I said, "What?" He said it again. I looked him straight in the eye, and I said, "I have never said an unkind word about you, ever. About some of your films, yes, but never about you." He said, "Oh, so it's not personal then," in a mocking tone of voice. I said, "No, it's not." He then gave me a wonderful series of sound bites about why he loves Westerns. More time goes by, and I joined the advisory board for the Golden Boot Awards. We'd meet in a conference room at the Motion Picture Television Fund Foundation, which was in Studio City in an office building, around a big horseshoe desk with lots of chairs. We did this early in the morning. Who walks in late? Burt Reynolds, and he sits down right next to me. At the end of the meeting, he said, "We should get together and have lunch sometime. I love talking about Old Hollywood, and I know you love it, too." I decided he was like the drunk in *City Lights* who, when drunk, was Charlie Chaplin's best friend, and when he sobered up in the morning, had no use for him. That was my relationship with Burt Reynolds.

Segaloff: We're not saying Burt was drunk, we're saying that he was mercurial.

Maltin: *Mercurial* is a good word.

Segaloff: Your appearances on the show dropped over time, didn't they?

Maltin: I was barely on the last five years or so.

Segaloff: Thirty years is a hell of a run, but it wasn't all baby ducks and unicorns, was it? Tell me about the business end of your *E.T.* adventure. Didn't they begin messing with you even before you were hired?

Maltin: When I did the audition, Vin Di Bona said, "If it was up to me, I'd hire you right now, but it's not up to me. We have to hear from the Paramount brass, but I know they want to have a critic on the air and they're not going to drag this out too long." That was Thursday of Memorial Day weekend. I flew home that afternoon. The next day, Friday, Alice and I flew to Columbus for the first time to attend the Cinevent, and on Saturday I was in the dealer's room looking at stills and lobby cards. And someone said to me, "Hey, you were good on TV last night." "What?" "Yeah." *E.T.* had run one of my audition pieces without telling me! I had signed an AFTRA release so that I could get paid, so it was completely within their rights to run that piece, but they could have told me.

Segaloff: Television is the communications medium that doesn't communicate with itself.

Maltin: I always said, "Somebody has to be the last to know." But I was delighted. I got 500 bucks. Didn't get that for a lot of articles I wrote. Then they ran the *second* piece without telling me. I had obtained the services of a really good entertainment lawyer a year earlier when I was involved with a project that didn't come to pass. He was representing me and Paramount was not offering anything. They wanted me to sign a contract that gave me no advantage at all, paying me what they were already paying me and having exclusive use of my services for thirteen weeks, and then the option of renewing. There was no incentive to sign it. One day they said on a Friday, "Sign this or don't come in Monday." I called my lawyer and I said, "What do we do?" He said, "Well, if you want to play chicken, you can do it, but only if you're willing to lose. Do you want this job?" I said, "Yeah." He said, "Well then, you can't play chicken. We sign the contract." So we did. When it came time to renew, the Paramount business affairs people were really nasty. They took the Nikita Khruschev approach to negotiation.* "We will bury you."

---

* The Russian style of negotiating is essentially not to negotiate: take it or leave it.

To make a long story very short, the week before our daughter was born, my lawyer, Les Abell, was getting nowhere with Paramount, and I said to him one day, "What would you think if I hired one of those cutthroat agents to deal with these guys?" He said, "I think you should do it." That shows what a good guy he was. He wasn't threatened by that. So I asked everybody on the talent staff, would you recommend your agent? They all said no. I finally wound up with a man named Richard Leibner who was something of a legend in the TV world. Richard just passed away several months ago. He represented Dan Rather and Diane Sawyer and Andy Rooney—and the weatherman in Topeka, Kansas. He built a thriving agency populating TV newsrooms, big and small, and for the small, the object was always to move to a larger market. They didn't call it city; they call it a market. They're all numbered: Topeka to St. Paul is an upward move, St. Paul to Des Moines, a lateral move, whatever. I was the exception to the rule. I started on a national show. I met Richard on a trip to New York, and we shook hands and we signed a contract, and he represented me from that day on. There was one year he got Dan Rather a million dollar deal and me a $10 raise per piece.

Segaloff: And obviously it worked; Paramount agreed.

Maltin: No.

Segaloff: *No?*

Maltin: It was always a fight. Always. It was always adversarial and nasty. One day my then-producer, Jim Van Messel, not a warm and fuzzy guy, told me that he told business affairs to knock it off, which was an unusual moment of candor for him. He was saying he liked what I was doing and to leave me alone and make a deal.

Segaloff: There was also a weekend edition of *Entertainment Tonight* where you worked with Gary H. Grossman[*] who is now a best-selling author of thrillers. I knew him when he was working for newspapers, before he produced shows. How did you get to know Gary?

---

[*] Former television reporter for *The Boston Herald*, author of Saturday Morning TV, producer at *Entertainment Tonight* and later partner with *E.T.*'s Robb Weller in the company Weller/Grossman Productions. He is the author of the ongoing *Executive* thrillers: *Executive Actions, Executive Force, Executive Treason*, etc. (Diversion Books).

Maltin: He submitted the *Superman** book proposal to me when I was editing books for Popular Library+ [in the 1970s]. I think he was visiting New York, and I remember him coming to our apartment and we hit it off, and I was able to sell the book to Patrick O'Connor,† and then we worked together on the book. When I came out to do my audition for *E.T.,* I called him up and had dinner. And then, wonder of wonders, he got hired at *E.T.* by Vin Di Bona. That was lovely because Gary got control of the weekend edition, so I could do all sorts of fun pieces for him.

A week before our daughter was born, I got a call from my agent in New York. He said, "Are you sitting down?" I said, "Alright, I am now." He said, "They're not picking up your contract." I said, "But things are finally going right!" I'd won over three producers in a row. Each producer they hired wanted to hire their guy, which is common in business, as it is in television. You want to surround yourself with people you are friendly with, or used to. At *E.T.,* first it was George Merlis, a man with a volatile temper, who once dislodged a phone from the wall and threw it at our post-production supervisor. George had been executive producer of *Good Morning America*, so he was used to Joel Siegel. He wanted me to be more like Joel Siegel.

Alice and I were about to go on the splurgiest vacation of our lives to Hawaii, our first trip to Hawaii when we hit three islands in ten days. We were also trying to have a baby, and we didn't want to be apart that much because, back in New York, I worked at home in our apartment, so we were together all the time. Now that I was commuting and the commuting was getting more hectic, she'd be at home and when I'd get back from a trip, I wanted to do nothing. She was ready to out and do things. That's why she came out with some frequency. She was having lunch one Friday with our head of talent at the time, and our head of talent was friendly with George. She'd worked with him before, and she said suddenly as lunch was winding down. "I can't not tell you this: George is going to fire Leonard."

And Alice said, "*What?*" The head of talent said, "I'm not supposed to know. He's going to fire Leonard." Alice came back to the studio and told me. I said, "They're not going to kill our vacation. I have nothing to gain by staying here." But I went to Gary and I said, "If you hear anything, this is where we're going to be staying." This is before cell phones, of course. He called in the middle of the week to say that he'd

---

* *Superman Serial to Cereal*, New York: Popular Library, 1977.
† Leonard's *TV Movie Guide* editor at New American Library (q.v._

been part of a meeting with the Paramount people about the next month coming up, and George had suggested a promotion or something for summer movies involving me. What had happened was that he'd gotten used to me. He wound up being a booster. Then *he* got fired. Before he got fired, though, he brought in his number-two man from *GMA*, Jack Reilly. They fired George on a Friday. Some people cheered. He was not universally liked, to put it mildly. Jack Reilly was a Joel Siegel guy too. It was really unnerving; I thought I was doing a good job. My colleagues seemed to like what I did, and not only didn't the boss like what I was doing, but they had the Paramount goon-of-the-moment who was talking, not necessarily about focus groups, but about "do more of this, do less of that." They always wanted me to either hate a movie or love a movie. I couldn't be anywhere in between. I said, "Most movies I don't hate and I don't love; most movies are okay or pretty good or almost good, but not good enough."

A couple of years pass, and the storm settles. Jack Reilly stays and he's on board. He's been supportive of me, but I get this call from my agent that they're not going to pick up my contract. I go to see Jack and he says, "Not my call, it's Paramount. I'm really sorry. But you know who doesn't have to know this?" I said, "Who?" He said, "Alice." He knew that she was about to give birth. He said, "Don't tell her." I said, "Really?" He said, "I'm a father of three. Don't tell her. She doesn't need to hear this now." And I went to Gary. Gary said, "Don't tell Alice." So the one person I needed to talk to I couldn't talk to; I followed their advice and didn't talk to her. Jessie was born June 16, 1986 and they kept her in the hospital. It was a C-section. They kept her in the hospital an extra couple of days, and I'm using the pay phone in the hallway to talk to my agent in New York to try to make sense of what we were going to do next. Then my agent's assistant gets Alice on the phone trying to find me and Alice, who has now given birth, is recuperating, and Alice says, "Aren't we supposed to be getting an option pickup around now?" And Nancy says, "You'd better talk to Leonard about that." That's how she found out.

By the way, Jessie shares a birthday with Stan Laurel. And when she was born, Lois Laurel sent her a check that Stan had written to his daughter's nanny in June of 1930. It's a wonderful keepsake.

I was out of work. I had no experience as a television producer. I went to see Michael King of the King Brothers. I met them because they inherited the Little Rascals. Their father, Charlie King, somehow or other, had obtained the rights to the Little Rascals for TV. He was a character and he worked out of a post office box in New Jersey.

Segaloff: And you knew him from the book?

Maltin: I knew them because Michael called me one day and said, "Leonard, we didn't have a list of the films we own until we got your book." I went down to visit them in Berkeley Heights, New Jersey, and they were very nice, the three brothers. That's how I knew them. So I went to see Michael about employment ideas. He said, "You should talk to Alan Landsburg. Alan Landsburg's about to do a new half hour *Photoplay* show" with Dan Lewis. I went to see Landsburg, but there was nothing there for me. I went to see Bill Mechanic, who had been part of the Barry Diller administration at Paramount, who was now at Disney. He followed Michael Eisner to Disney. I had some contacts, some doors were open, but there was no prospect of a job.

Segaloff: But wait, you didn't leave *E.T.* What happened after they were about to can you that kept you there?

Maltin: At the end of thirteen weeks, I had been up for a twenty-six-week renewal. What they wanted to do was turn it into two thirteen-week options. And Richard, my agent, said, "This was right back where you started. You can't have thirteen weeks to shop for a replacement unless Leonard has the same ability to find a new job and get out of this at thirteen weeks." The Paramount lawyer said, "Well, Paramount feels—" My agent said, "Do the right thing," and they agreed. At the end of thirteen weeks, they hadn't found anybody, so they said, essentially, "Well, we might as well sign you again." By that time, I had come to understand that there was no job waiting in the wings and there was no place for pride in all of this. I said to myself, "Just sign, keep the job." So I did. This was over summer 1986.

Around Labor Day, Herb Graff heard a rumor that I was going to be replaced by a woman named Katie Kelly, who was on WNBC in New York. She had gray hair, prematurely gray hair, curly, and she wore a big bow tie. It was kind of a character and she did fun, human interest entertainment stories. She was telling people she was going to come out to LA and take over my job. As it happened, the day she made her debut on *E.T.* was the day I was also on the show doing Cary Grant's obit, for which I wrote and produced the piece. It was also the first day that Dave Nuell was there from WRC-TV scouting his new job as our Executive Producer. Dave took an instant liking to me and an instant dislike to Katie Kelly. He took me, clasped my shoulder and said, "That's a really nice piece today. I look forward to working with you." She was gone within two months, and I stayed on. I mean, you can't predict or chart these kinds of things.

Segaloff: Once you became "Leonard Maltin," what did it feel like being the person that other people wanted to talk to, instead of you wanting to talk to them?

Maltin: Disbelief. Of course, the most satisfying phone call I've ever had with any publisher when my then editor, Arnold Dolin, called me at my desk at *Entertainment Tonight* and said, "We've just had our fall sales meeting and we'd like to make two changes to the book, if it's okay with you." I said, "What are they?" He said, "We'd like to put your name above the title and your photo on the cover." I said, "It's okay with me." It was a sublime turn of events that I could never have masterminded or expected in any way. That was the turning point in the book's recognition because now it was not buried in the back of the store. What's more, that's when we started doing it annually, in the mid-'80s because of home video.

Segaloff: That's when you became a brand name.

Maltin: That's when I became a brand name on a hot TV show. Those things all happened in concert with each other. Now a store knew that they could expect to sell twelve copies, let's say. Instead of ordering by three by rote, as they would on an unknown title, they knew that they were going to sell five or ten or twelve or thirty-two, or however many, of that book by the movie guy.

Segaloff: On *E.T.* you must have been pitched to cover things. I know you would have to pitch the producer on doing stuff, but did people pitch you to cover their clients or did they go into the assignment editor or whoever your employer was?

Maltin: Both. Both. For six years I worked under Dave Nuell and Jim Van Messel, two of the strangest individuals I've ever met in my life, but they were a good team. They were brought in from station WRC in Washington, D.C., the NBC affiliate there. They were each strange in different ways, but they made a good team. They complemented each other and they gave me carte blanche. I had a piece on the air every Monday night, and sometimes they didn't even know what I was going to be doing. I did a piece about the British comedy star

Lupino Lane, and my hook was that *Me and My Girl* was then playing on Broadway with Jim Dale. I got the New York office to interview Jim Dale, because.* I could do that, and he had a little rag doll of Lupino Lane in his dressing room. I was allowed to spend a thousand dollars to buy a clip from MCA Universal from Lubitsch's *The Love Parade* (1929),† and then I added to that a silent comedy clip, which was in the public domain, which I'd gotten from a friend. They liked it so much, they said, "Lose the Jim Dale interview." I said, "No, no, no." They didn't care that it would anger a publicist and be unfair to a Broadway star and all that. So he stayed in the piece. I got to interview Michael Powell as the man who made the most beautiful Technicolor movies of all time.

Segaloff: Was this when Powell was working with Coppola?

Maltin: Yes. I think I got dubs from Criterion, and my producers loved looking at the footage and the sound bites were acceptable to them. I tackled amazing, wonderful subjects that you wouldn't think would get on national television. That was just a golden period. But it had to come to an end sometime. And it did. When Dave left to start *Access Hollywood*‡ and Jim decided to appoint a troika of our segment producers to essentially be the new line producers of the show. He took me to lunch. At that time I was doing a Monday piece, a video piece on Wednesdays and a weekend show piece. On Wednesdays I would take a new VHS release and then show clips from four other movies that's had something in common with it—other circus movies—

Segaloff:—your basic theme piece—

Maltin:—Yes. When I would go to the VSDA, the Video Software Dealers Association convention, mom and pop video store owners said, "Whatever you recommend on Wednesday night flies off the shelf on Thursday." Well, that was great. Jim took me to lunch and he said, "Don't wait for the other shoe to drop. Everything's fine." I said, "Oh, good." He said, "But I don't want you doing pieces every Monday." I said, "Why not?" He said, "We want people tuning in every night to see if you have a piece on." I said, "But people know that I'm going

---

* Lupino Lane drew fame for introducing "The Lambeth Walk" in *For Me and My Girl* in 1939. Robert Lindsay opened the London revival of the show in 1984 and took it to Broadway in 1986. Jim Dale replaced Lindsay on Broadway in 1989.

† Lane was third lead in Ernst Lubitsch's early musical film.

‡ A syndicated NBC show begun on September 9, 1996.

to be there." "That's just it. We want to have people tuning in consistently." This was his logic, which made no sense to me. "And I don't want you to do the video piece anymore." I said, "But the video store owners—" He felt everything was too rote. And the result of that was that the next piece that I prepared sat on the shelf for three weeks unused because it had no timeliness to it. I didn't do timely pieces. This is when I was no longer doing reviews. I was doing only feature pieces and interviews.

Segaloff: Did they sit on stories until they were no longer timely?

Maltin: I got the only interview with André Previn; again, through the New York office, for the first home video release of *My Fair Lady*, and Warner Bros. said they'd give me an exclusive for two days. But *E.T.* didn't feel there was an imperative for them to run it, so they didn't; "Who is this André guy?" After a month or so of that, I went to Jim and closed the door behind me. I said, "Jim, I can't get anything on the show." "It's a transitional period. I know there are bumps in the road, but it'll all smoothed over. It's going to be okay." "You really think so?" "Yeah, I do." "Okay." But my segments just sat on the shelf and never got on the air. I got so depressed that I stopped going in. There was no purpose for me going into the office. I called the Warner Bros. publicist, who felt betrayed, and said, "They lied to me, and now I cannot make any promise to you or any other publicist, and I really apologize." She accepted the apology. That was a dark, dark period and was only relieved when they started sending me out on more interviews.

Segaloff: After thirty years it ended. What was it like? I don't expect Paramount gave you a gold watch.

Maltin: My last four years at *E.T.* were strange. During that time, we moved from our longtime home at Paramount to the CBS Radford lot where people were spread throughout several buildings. I found it very disconcerting, and it did nothing for camaraderie, which was the last thing on my boss' agenda. The show itself had changed from covering entertainment news to keeping up with the Kardashians et al. When my contract ran out, there was no goodbye, on or off the air. Like General MacArthur I just faded away.

WHAT HAVE YOU LEARNED, DOROTHY?

Segaloff: Let's talk about your technique. When you do an interview with someone you don't know, how important is the first question? How do you break the code?

Maltin: I learned an important lesson from Larry King.* This is well into my own television career with *Entertainment Tonight* and elsewhere. When he was with CNN he used to do a one-hour show that ran late on Saturday nights where he did people who weren't headline-makers. Debbie Reynolds was a guest one night, I remember, and Michael Crawford was a guest this one night that I'm going to speak of. He would do a whole career review with them. As you know, Larry King always said, "I do no prep." He was always very nice to me. I don't want to be snide. I was on his *Coast to Coast* radio show more than once when I passed through D.C. on book tours. In fact, one unforgettable night he fell asleep— *dozed* perhaps is the better word—while a call-in listener was talking. It wasn't a conversation with me, it was with one of the other guests that night. But I was fascinated to see how and if he would wake up, and he was a pro. He woke up when he had to wake up and then moved on. I watched him with Michael Crawford, and having done no prep, he said, "How'd you get started?" And Michael Crawford said, "Well—," and he told the story of how he got started. I said, "Here I work myself into a pretzel trying to come up with some original, provocative, interesting way to ask question one and get off on the right foot, and Larry just says, 'So how'd you arrive here? What's your story?' And it still echoes in my head that sometimes basic and fundamental is not a bad way to start

Segaloff: There's a story you told me years ago, and that you put in the book, involving Jackie Cooper, the former child star, later a television producer and director. It says a lot about Hollywood.

Maltin: I used to go fairly often to the NATPE (National Association of Television Program Executives, a trade group) convention, the syndicated television convention, which was held in different cities every year. One year it was in San Fran-

---

* Larry King (1933-2021) was a ubiquitous air personality who was reputed to have logged more on-air time than anyone else in history. His life was also filled with marital and legal adventures. Those wishing a concise portrait of King are referred to "Larry King: Talk of Fame" produced by Nat Segaloff for A&E's *Biography* series. King was famous for winging his interviews and never doing research under the belief that his naïve questions would be what his audience wanted to know, too.

cisco, and we flew home from San Francisco to Burbank, a short one-hour hop. Jackie Cooper and his wife were on the plane, and I struck up a conversation with him in the waiting area, and he was very approachable and very nice. And either I said to him, or he said to me, let's break bread sometime. Let's have lunch. I took his phone number but then got really busy. I can't remember why, but I wasn't able to follow through on that for several months. By the time I called him, he remembered my name and who I was. He took me to an Italian restaurant on Melrose that he liked, and we had an absolutely delightful lunch. I did not have a tape recorder going. I sort of wish I did, but I didn't. He gave me all these wonderful stories about what a son of a bitch Fritz Lang was to him on *The Return of Frank James*. And toward the end of our lunch, he said, "So," and patted the table, "Tell me why you wanted to have lunch." And I said, "Just to do what we're doing, talking about your life, telling stories." He said, "Oh, well, fine." He wasn't upset. He didn't feel he'd been swindled in any way, but he assumed there was an agenda. My only agenda was talking to him and hearing his stories.

Segaloff: This leads us into the etiquette and the protocol of working in Hollywood.

Maltin: I can tell a parallel story. About a year or so before I came out here in spring of 1982 to do my audition for *Entertainment Tonight*, an old friend of mine named Richard Maynard, who taught screenwriting at the New School, called me up. Richard was a brilliant guy. He had degrees in both English and history, and he understood what made movies tick. You could name any film—and he'd seen lots of films—and he'd say, "Oh, it's the Orpheus story, except they switched this, and they made that guy his uncle instead of his aunt." He got it. He understood the core of most movies. He said, "You and I should try to write a movie because we've seen so much. We've absorbed so much. We should be able to craft one ourselves." I said, "Okay, I'm willing. I'm willing to try." We spent several months doing that, working on what turned out to be a treatment for a feature film and a treatment for a sitcom, which we thought had an interesting twist to it. And I'd never felt that kind of satisfaction before. I was flexing muscles that I'd not used since creative writing class in junior high school. And boy, was that fun, especially with a partner who was so sharp.

Meanwhile, he had made some inroads pitching and selling a historically based mini-series to Chuck Fries and also—I don't remember if they were working together on this or not—Herbert B Leonard.* Richard and I had these two ideas, and he was starting to make some trips to L.A. to try to further his nascent career as a writer-producer for television. Then I started making trips from New York to L.A. and we coordinated, and took three or four meetings to do our pitch. I was not connected out here at all, but I knew one or two people. He knew two or three people. It was not like a scene from Robert Altman's *The Player*. We didn't meet people who were pretentious or duplicitous or snarky or ignorant. All the people we met were smart. They'd actually read our proposals and could converse about them intelligently. And I thought, "Do you mean that everybody who has made movies has gone through this?" After four or five meetings I said, "I can't do this. I come from publishing where if it's a magazine they say, 'give me a thousand words by Tuesday and we'll pay you $350 or if it's a book publisher, 'I'll bring it up at the next editorial board meeting and we'll come back and say either 'it's not for us' or 'we'd like to publish this.'" Every meeting had a conclusion or the promise of a conclusion. These meetings were just filling up space on their desk calendar. The one that really surprised me was with someone I'd met when I worked for Alan King† in New York, Alan King and his then partner, Rupert Hitzig.

One of the meetings was with Peter Grad, who I'd met in New York through his wife Laurie Burrows Grad, Abe Burrows'‡ daughter. I remember picking up the phone at *Entertainment Tonight* and calling, because I had just read that Peter was now VP of Comedy Development at 20th Century Fox Television. When I called him, he'd already seen me on *Entertainment Tonight*. He said, "Congratulations, what a great gig" and all that. I said, "Well, yeah, I'm very lucky." I said, "I'd love to come over and see you." He said, "Great. How about next Monday at two?" "Wonderful. Be there." When I arrived, he had his lieutenant with him and someone else. *He knew I was there to sell him something.* How did he know? I never said a word, and he didn't know of me as a

---

* Charles "Chuck" Fries (1928-2021) was a major producer and distributor of television programming. Herbert B. "Bert" Leonard (1922-2006) was co-creator, with Stirling Silliphant, of *Route 66* and other television series.
† Alan King (Irwin Allen Kniberg, 1927-2004) was best known as a stand-up comedian who specialized in outrage, but also acted, wrote, produced, and hosted the New York Friars Club.
‡ Abe Burrows (1910-1985) was a major writer, mostly of comedy, including *Guys and Dolls, Solid Gold Cadillac,* and *How to Succeed in Business Without Really Trying.*

potential writer or a creative, as they say. He just knew that I was not there to shoot the breeze.

Segaloff: Maybe he'd been speaking to Jackie Cooper.

Maltin: That just fascinated me.

Segaloff: There are signals. There're pheromones. You are well-known, so you can probably walk up to Tom Hanks or somebody and say hi. But the average person, what's the etiquette for walking up to a celebrity in public in Los Angeles?

Maltin: I don't know. I mean, because I do it. I once met Will Smith in a restaurant. That was a memorable evening. I had met him before. I don't remember if I interviewed him or not, but I met him. But when we walked into Nobu in Malibu I didn't see him and his wife Jada sitting at their table, but our dining companions did. "Did you see Will Smith and Jada Pinkett sitting over there?" I said, "No." And Alice said, "Go over and say hello." And I said, "No, I don't want to do that. I feel funny doing that." If we had seen each other and nodded, I would've felt I was within propriety, whatever that would be. I didn't want to be a bumpkin to interrupt his dinner with his wife in a public place. Then a waiter came over to our table bearing four martinis saying, "These are from my customer over there, Mr. Smith. And he says to tell you that *The Pursuit of Happyness* opens December fourth.'" That's when I felt we could, and should, go over and say, "Thank you for the drinks." And he was laughing, and he said, "I once read that Elizabeth Taylor used to do that anytime she saw a columnist or a reporter in a restaurant or bar, and I've always wanted to do it." I gave him his opportunity to do that.

Segaloff: When you found that you had become known well enough that you could pick up the phone and meet people, what inspired you to meet one person over another?

Maltin: It's not as simple as that. When we were still living in New York, I was trying to write a story for *The New York Times* Arts and Leisure about movie studio logos, which I used to call trademarks. And I wanted a quote from producer Robert Evans about using the old Paramount black and white logo on *Chinatown*. I even think it's in the 1:33 ratio, if I recall correctly. I called Paramount, asked for his office, and said, "Hi, this is Leonard Maltin. I'm writing an article for *The New York Times*." The only time I think I've ever done that, hyping my status. And he got on the phone and was happy to give me a quotable answer. That's what a credential will do for you. With *Entertainment Tonight*, the show was so successful and so popular that there were very few doors that wouldn't open.

Segaloff: But before this, when you were just a snot-nosed kid, a pisher, how did you connect with people?

Maltin: I used to go to the Teaneck Public Library that had a periodical in the reference room called *Current Biography*. They were monthly publications, and they would put it into a binder every year. For most of the profiles, they would have an address where you could contact the person. Sometimes it was their agent, sometimes it was their publicist, sometimes it was their lawyer, sometimes it was a business office of some sort, and sometimes it was their home address. That's how I looked up Burgess Meredith and found that he had a home in Pound Ridge, New York. I wrote to him and he answered, and I had a wonderful afternoon with him. I learned pretty quickly that the best way to reach someone was if you could talk to them or someone very close to them and not go through agents, managers, lawyers, or reps. Publicists sometimes respond because that's their job. Some of them seem not to understand that, and agents almost never do because there's nothing in it for them.

Segaloff: You mentioned the Manhattan phone book too.

Maltin: Remarkably, people were listed there, including Rube Goldberg.* I looked in the book and there were two Reuben Goldbergs. One of them seemed to be in Harlem at 115th Street or something, and one of them on East 40-something street. I reasoned that he would probably be the more likely Rube Goldberg that I was interested in. I called, and a man picked up the phone, and I said, in a fumbling way, "Am I speaking to Rube Goldberg, the famous cartoonist?" He said, "Yes." I said, "Well, my name is Leonard Maltin, and I publish a magazine called *Profile*, and I wonder if I could come and interview you sometime." He said, "Sure," and made a date. I went to his studio, where he was then sculpting and doing the most wonderful sculptures, which he worked in clay and

---

* Reuben Garrett Lucius Goldberg (Rube Goldberg, 1883-1970) was a cartoonist who specialized in drawing elaborate mechanical devices that were designed to do extremely simple or useless things. The term "Rube Goldberg device" refers to such unnecessarily complex creations.

then had them cast in bronze. Boy, do I think every time I tell this to somebody I say, "…and I didn't bring a camera."

Segaloff: That's the next question: pictures of you with people. They're all over Facebook now, but did you slavishly get pictures of yourself with these celebrities? Or were you more interested in just getting the story?

Maltin: It depends. There was a period when I decided that, instead of getting autographs, I wanted anecdotes. When I came out here to L.A. for the Cinecon in 1980 and met Jack Oakie, I said, "Tell me about working with Charlie Chaplin." And he said, "Well, I'll tell you." He says, "Charlie Chaplin calls me on the phone and says, 'I want you to play Mussolini in this movie I'm making, *The Great Dictator*.' And I said, 'Charlie, Mussolini's Eye-talian. I'm Scotch Irish.' And he said, 'What's funny about Italian playing Mussolini?' And I said, 'All right, I'm your man.'" I got that great story, which was better than getting an autograph. But I like getting signatures on books because there's a tradition there. It's not frivolous.

My great friend Clive Hirschhorn* was a big book collector and was very assiduous about getting those inscriptions, told me that Woody Allen signed, so the first time I met Woody Allen, I was not hesitant to hand him a copy of *Without Feathers* ask him to sign it—and tell him my name, taking no chances.

Segaloff: You don't really have to announce yourself that often, do you?

Maltin: Well, no, I do. I don't assume everybody knows me.

Segaloff: If it helps, Warren Beatty also does it. You're in good company.

Maltin: Phil Donahue interviewed Katharine Hepburn and then gave over his copy of her new book, and she didn't remember who he was, and he was able to laugh at it. He showed the tape of her awkwardly asking him his name.

Segaloff: Would you consider yourself a good writer back then?

---

* Clive Hirschhorn (b.1940) is a South African writer transplanted to England who has written multiple books and worked in television and newspapers.

Maltin: I was… okay. I can read some of my early stuff and not always be embarrassed. I'll tell you what's embarrassing. Karen Everson, Bill's widow, found a letter that I wrote to Bill shortly after meeting him, so I was maybe fourteen years old. It's a single-spaced, typed letter full of opinions. I wrote this chatty, unsolicited letter because I wanted to be in touch with him and ingratiate myself with him. It reeks of chutzpah. I said I found *Metropolis** boring, partly because I watched it at silent speed on my family's Bell & Howell projector, and that's something no one should have to endure. I'm very fond of *Metropolis* now.

Segaloff: It took me years to make it all the way through. Was there a point at which you realized that you were a good writer, that you liked writing?

Maltin: My first ambition was to be a cartoonist—not an animator, but a cartoonist, selling panel cartoons to magazines. There was, at the local library, a book called *Drawing and Selling Cartoons* by Jack Markow. He gave you all the instruction you needed and all the procedural protocol: how to always send a self-addressed, stamped envelope for the editors to return the artwork if they weren't going to purchase it. What kind of nib to use with your pen, and what kind of India ink. I followed it faithfully and I submitted some cartoons to *The New Yorker* and the *Saturday Evening Post*. I still have my *Saturday Evening Post* rejection slip. I wasn't good enough. I really wasn't good enough.

Segaloff: Did you realize that, or did somebody actually tell you?

Maltin: I did. I used to draw comic books with a friend of mine, and they were okay for kid stuff, but I sent some samples with a fan letter to Charles M. Schulz because I loved *Peanuts*. He wrote me back the most extraordinary letter. He sent me a signed original. And I was 11 years old.

Segaloff: Did you ever have trouble doing your homework, writing themes, or anything like that?

Maltin: No. I don't recall having any trouble. The trouble I had was in junior high school and high school, when I took my SATs, I scored higher in math than English by a lot. I placed into advanced math and suffered miserably because

---

* Fritz Lang's legendary 1927 science fiction epic.

I was given no choice in the matter. I had my parents call the school superintendent. Nobody would get me out of this math class. The aptitude test that I had said I had the ability to work in what was then called New Math. Do you remember the Tom Lehrer song?[*]

Segaloff: I had to take it New Math in seventh and eighth grades. It was all set theory and base eight. It destroyed any math skills I ever had and any desire to develop them.

Maltin: I had the same teacher for five years. The nicest man you could ever want to meet. He invited us to call him at home at night if we were having trouble working out problems. I failed a take-home open-book test. Can't get much worse than that. They wouldn't let me out of this goddamn class. Science was Greek to me, to use an old-fashioned expression, which I tend to do. But other than that, I did okay in school. I was never an A student. I was a solid B student, except for math and science.

Segaloff: But it got you into NYU.

Maltin: Yeah.

Segaloff: Was there a particular teacher who encouraged you and who made a mark on your life?

Maltin: Yes. Ms. Martini, Ms. Teri Martini. My English and creative writing teacher who I had a mild crush on as well. But it wasn't because she made it easy. Quite the contrary. She was demanding of your work, and you had to produce, but she made you want to do well so, in that sense, she was very motivational.

Segaloff: What about your family? Did they give you encouragement? Did they read your stuff and comment on it?

Maltin: They were encouraging. Consistently encouraging, but I don't remember specifics.

Segaloff: Can we get to Forrest J. Ackerman? He was quite a controversial figure, but people loved him.

---

[*] New Math, forced on American students in the early 1960s, was born of the mistaken belief that comprehension was more importance than competence. Tom Lehrer (b.1928), a math professor and musical satirist, aptly said of New Math that it was more important to know what you're doing than to get the right answer.

Maltin: He wasn't controversial to me when I was a kid. He was a pied piper, but even I, at twelve or thirteen, got a little tired of the magazine being as much about Forry as it was about Boris Karloff and James Whale and Bela Lugosi, all my other favorites. Had I been living here, I'm sure I would've spent more time with him. But as it was, I only met him once or twice, and I only went to Ackermansion once.[*]

Segaloff: He was a popularizer, I think, more than a critic, but there's lots to say about him. You must have been a subscriber to *Famous Monsters of Filmland.*

Maltin: No, I bought it at the candy store, as we called it.

Segaloff: Is that how you learned about horror films?

Maltin: He opened that door wide for me. He printed photos from films I'd never heard of. Introduced me to actors I was unfamiliar with. He really was a pied piper for me.

Segaloff: When he died childless, Joe Dante and I said, "Well, he may not have had kids of his own, but he raised several thousand of us."

Maltin: Yes, he sure did. I went to the Saturn Awards one year.

Segaloff: That was Dr. Reed.[†]

---

[*] Forrest J. (James) Ackerman (1916-2008) was the publisher of the magazine *Famous Monsters of Filmland,* an immensely popular fanzine for young horror and science fiction buffs. Each issue extolled the achievements of people like Boris Karloff, Bela Lugosi, Lon Chaney (Sr. and Jr.), and other icons of the genre. His home, called the Acker-mansion, at 915 South Sherborne Drive in Los Angeles, was a museum of props, costumes, and other memorabilia that he had acquired. He also represented several authors, some of whom, to put it discretely, were unaware that he was representing them in licensing reprints of their stories for publication.

[†] Dr. Donald A. Reed (1935-2001) created the Count Dracula Society — later renamed the Academy of Fantasy, Science Fiction, and Horror Films — in 1962. Each year the AFSFH presented the Saturn awards to notable genre filmmakers. He also created other associations and was a popular presence among devotees. Considered an eccentric by some and a mentor by others, he held weekly screenings at USC, hosted visits by the people who made the films, and brought respect-ability to genres that were on the fringes when he began extoling them. There is a lovely tribute to him on the Saturn Award website: https://www.saturnawards.org/Saturn-Awards-Founder.php.

Maltin: Dr. Donald A. Reed. I came out here after he had peaked, I think. I never went to one of his morning screenings at USC. But I did know him casually, and he invited me to the Saturn Awards, and Alice and I went when it was at the Blossom Room at the Hollywood Roosevelt. One night I ran into, if I can namedrop, Danny Elfman. I said, "Isn't this great?" And he said, "Usually these things are a chore to go to, but look who's here." I said, "Forry Ackerman is here. Have you met him?" He said, "No." I said, "Would you like to?" He said, "Yes!" So I introduced Danny Elfman to Forry Ackerman and made them both very happy.

Segaloff: I worshipped Forry when I was a kid but met only on the phone after I moved to L.A. In addition to the magazine and collecting, he represented authors, sort of, and I tried to license a story through him for Alien Voices.* I could never get him to talk business, and he was kind of in declining health at the time, so that was sad. I heard he sold off some of the stuff in the Ackermansion before he died, but one wonders what happened to the rest.

Maltin: Peter Jackson showed me things he had accumulated for his proposed museum, which I think is still a goal of his. When Alice and I visited New Zealand, we were on a cruise. We were only there for one day in each city, and he's in Wellington. (Aside: I appeared in Peter's faux documentary, *Forgotten Silver*†. One of my great achievements.) This is why I can't be friendly with filmmakers. It's very, very hard to be actual friends with somebody you're going to criticize or have the possibility of criticizing, the Joe Dante story being my ultimate example of that.‡ But I had appeared in *Forgotten Silver*, and he was grateful for that, and I got to interview him on the junkets for *Lord of the Rings*.

---

* A production company formed in 1996 among the author, John de Lancie, and Leonard Nimoy to produce audiobooks of classic science fiction stories performed by *Star Trek* actors.
† Peter Jackson's and Costa Botes' 1995 faux documentary about Colin McKenzie, a Kiwi who invented every film technique years before others did. Leonard was "interviewed" about McKenzie. The film created a scandal when it was televised because, like Orson Welles' 1938 *Invasion from Mars* broadcast, it was done so realistically that viewers thought it was real.
‡ Maltin was not fond of director Joe Dante's 1984 film *Gremlins*, so in *Gremlin's 2* (1990) Dante had Leonard play himself as a critic who gets attacked by the devilish creatures. Coincidentally, the Author gave a lukewarm review to *Gremlins 2*, prompting a call from Dante taking genial offense with me. All sides remain friends.

A week or two later, when I went to the Four Seasons Hotel for the junket on *Invictus*, the Clint Eastwood film about Mandela and the soccer player, with Matt Damon and Morgan Freeman, Jessie tagged along. I was interviewing Matt Damon and Morgan Freeman when Clint sort of burst in and gave me one of the great casual pieces of video that I landed for *E.T..* I was talking to Clint and we were running overtime because Clint was telling a story and taking his time. Suddenly, Matt Damon and Morgan Freeman are standing behind me and they started heckling him. It was a great moment of spontaneity and, luckily, our cameras captured it on video. Then Jessie and I take the elevator down to the lobby and we see one of the publicists, and we say, "How are you doing?" She says, "I'm just here with my client, Peter Jackson" and Peter comes over. I say, "Peter, we're taking this cruise and we're going to be in Wellington just before Christmas. Are you going to be there?" He said, "Yes, contact me and I'd love to see you."

When we were there, he gave us the most wonderful day. He and his wife Fran Walsh could not have been more kind or generous. He showed me some of what he'd accumulated. He has the Lon Chaney makeup kit. He has Ray Harryhausen's stuff. He has one of the armatures from *King Kong*, or maybe it's *Mighty Joe Young,* I'm not sure. It had been up for auction in London the same day that *The Lovely Bones* debuted, and he was much more anxious about the armature, which I got to hold. He does have a lot of stuff, plus his own archive.

Segaloff: Pardon me, but I'm still getting past the phrase, "I was talking to Clint."

You mentioned a while ago that you feel uncomfortable reviewing the films of someone you know. Do you try to avoid certain situations? If you didn't like somebody's film, do you not talk to them? How does that work?

Maltin: I don't pursue any social opportunities. "Let's have a drink." "Let's have a coffee." I don't do it.

Segaloff: Caesar's wife must be beyond reproach.

Maltin: It's just good business.

Segaloff: Have you ever found yourself in a social situation where a filmmaker comes up to you?

Maltin: Not often. One year at the Independent Spirit Awards I fell into conversation with Ramin Bahrani and we hit it off. We enjoyed talking to each other, so we exchanged some emails. I loved his first two films—*Man Push Cart* (2005) and *Chop Shop* (2007). I think they are examples of great moviemaking. His third one *Goodbye Solo* (2008) is also very good. Those all featured non-professional actors. Somehow we fell out of touch with each other. Then I went to Telluride and he was there with his newest film, his first with professional actors, called *At Any Price*, with Zac Efron, Dennis Quaid, Heather Graham, Clancy Brown, and a couple of other folks about the dilemma of the modern farmer. He spent six months in Iowa soaking up stories and atmosphere. I saw it first thing Saturday morning of that weekend in Telluride, and it rang hollow from the first scene on. Everything he captured so beautifully in his first two films was missing from this one. I went directly from that screening to what they call the class photo at Telluride. It's everybody, all the guests there. We saw each other and he said, "I've got a movie here." I said, "I know. I just saw it." And he said, "What'd you think?" I beckoned him over and I said, "I don't want to sandbag you. I don't want to make nice talk here and then say something in print that contradicts that. I had some trouble with the film." He said, "Would you do me a favor? Would you sleep on it? Because that's what Michael Barker did. He didn't like it at first, but he realized that it stayed with him, and that's when he acquired it for Sony Pictures Classics." I said, "OK, I can do that." Then I just got out of there. That's the kind of awkwardness that I don't want to encourage in my life. But I am friendly with Alexander Payne. Fortunately, I've liked all his movies. I even like *Downsizing*, which other people don't.

I have to tell you an experience I just had in Telluride [the Maltins had returned from the Telluride Film Festival a few days before this part of the interview]. In fact, I made a note of it so I wouldn't forget it. When we fly to Telluride, we're on the charter plane with other guests of the festival. Full-size 727, a lot of people. We land in a town called Montrose where we board a fleet of shuttle buses and vans that drive us the remaining hour and a half to Telluride. Sometimes you wind up with an interesting passenger alongside you. Decades ago, I rode that trip with Sam Fuller. I asked him how he happened to cast Colonel Tim McCoy in *Run of the Arrow*. He said, "Oh, I grew up watching Ken Maynard and Tim McCoy and people like that." Sometimes you're sitting next to a budding filmmaker whose work you may see over the course of the weekend. Two weeks ago, Alice and I were sitting across the aisle from a very nice, cultured gentleman and his female partner, who may or may not have been his wife. He apparently had a lot to do with Iranian cinema. His name was Ahmed. I said, "Hello." He said, "Hello." We chatted a little bit and then rested our eyes as we went through the rest of the journey. Later that evening, he came up to me all abashed. He said, "Oh my God, I didn't realize you were Leonard Maltin. I have to explain to you. When I was young, films were outlawed in Iran. We weren't supposed to watch movies. There was a man who came around once a week with a briefcase full of cassette tapes. We could choose three every week and then return them the next week. The only source I had to tell me what film was what was your book. You had such an influence on my film education." He went on and on. It's not the first time I've been told that, but it was the most recent recitation of that kind of saga. It's humbling. By going to the Telluride Film Festival every year alongside a group of other loyalists who always show up, we've made some wonderful friendships. They're unusual friendships because they're renewed once a year. Ken Burns, Alice Waters, Werner Herzog, and the director Peter Sellars.

A couple years ago, I read that Ken was coming to Los Angeles to promote his seven-part country music documentary. His publicist sent screeners, and we didn't think we'd be interested, but it's so good. We emailed back and forth, and Ken said, "I'm coming in on Saturday and starting that night doing something for PBS and all that. You could be my first interview." He gave us an hour at the Autry Museum where they were setting up something. I had a full hour with Ken, who was a great guy and of course a great interviewee.

Last year we had Werner Herzog on our podcast. We got to go to his home and do an episode with him. We had a surprisingly uneventful and normal—or as normal as it's going to be—conversation with this remarkable guy. There was an empty seat next to Werner on the bus that takes us from the airport in Montrose to Telluride, and Alice sat in it and chatted with him. She always joked that he never acknowledged her, never acknowledged her presence till five years ago or something. His present wife is a nice woman named Lena [Pisetski] Herzog. He was explaining to Alice that she wasn't going to be at the festival that year because one of their dogs needed attending to. When we got to town, I sent her an email saying, "Dear Lena, we're all thinking of you. Don't think that your absence is unnoticed here. I hope the dog is doing well." Later that night we were at a restaurant. I was just outside a restaurant, and Werner came by. He hugged and kissed both of us. He was just so touched. He said, "It was so thoughtful of you to do that. It meant a lot to Lena."

Segaloff: When things were going great guns and you could assign yourself, what people did you use that opportunity to speak to whom you always wanted to?

Maltin: Pinky Lee.* I found out that he was living in Park La Brea [a gated community in Los Angeles], and when I was four years old, I thought the sun rose and set on Pinky Lee. First, I asked him if he had any videotape of his show from the Fifties. He said, "Oh yes, yes, I can bring them." I said, "If you bring them over here on Vine Street, we have a tele-cine [film-to-tape transfer unit] right here and we can transfer them, and they'll never leave your sight. "I gave some stuff to Dick Clark [Productions] and they didn't get it back to me." "Pinky, we can." He was so hyper. He came over and brought a shopping bag with four or six tapes, a couple different formats, some VHS, some three-quarter inch, and we made copies. He said, "Alright, so this is the one that Dick Clark took care of." And then, "Where's the Dick Clark tape?" We started getting nervous. "Well, you just had the Dick Clark tape. Where did it go?" "Oh, there, it's, oh, okay, fine."

That afternoon we went to his apartment to shoot the actual interview, and he was very nice. His wife (Bebe Dancis Lee) was nice, and he had his cap, his famous checkered cap. I said, "Pinky, if you look to camera, would you do your song?"† "Sure." He looked into the camera and the years melted away, and I was a kid again, and I remembered why I loved him. It was just a transcendent moment. I saw why his career probably sputtered because he was so hyper, and I saw why he was so popular when he hit his peak.

Segaloff: Since we're talking about interviews, one of the areas I wanted to go into is how you prepare for an interview and how you conduct an interview—the particulars being how you ask what you know the *show* wants, and how you ask what *you* want to know.

---

* Pinky Lee (Pincus Leff, 1907-1993) was a diminutive, manic vaude-villian who made the transition to early television in 1950. He was known for "my checkered hat/And my checkered coat/The funny giggle in my throat/And my silly dance like a billy goat" and thpoke with a bilateral lithp. His catchphrase was "Oooh, you make me so maaaad!" On September 20, 1955, he collapsed on the air from what was later ascribed to illness, but for years the rumor persisted that he'd had a heart attack.

† "Yoo-hoo, it's me; my name is Pinky Lee," etc. Pee-Wee Herman (Paul Reubens) is said to have been influenced by Mr. Lee.

Maltin: That was exactly my M.O. I knew pretty early on what the show wanted in any given situation, whether it was a planned sit-down conversation or a quick sound bite at an event. One year, 1990 it was, Leeza Gibbons, my colleague, got strep throat, and she usually worked arrivals at the Oscars. My boss at the time said to me, "I'm going to send you down to do it." I said, "Why me?" He said, "Well, you've got all these people arriving and we've got to get them over to you, and if they see someone they recognize, they're going to be more likely to come over." I said, "You mean I'm bait?" He said, "Yes." It was at the Shrine.* That's how long ago this was. It was at the Shrine Auditorium, where I learned they have moths the size of Buicks dive-bombing. It was an awful night. I found myself incoherent. I'd always admired Roger Ebert, who used to come into town and work for the ABC affiliate here on Oscar weekend. He would do pre-shows, post-shows and all that. All I could manage was a, "Hey, some night!"

Segaloff: There are special skills to doing stand-up like that. You need what they call "the insincerity of a game show host" or an AM disc jockey.

Maltin: I had my moments that night, but I also had moments I would rather not have had. *E.T.* had a rule which became more strictly enforced as years went by. We had to be the first TV outlet on the line. The photogs had first dibs, and I would be standing usually next to that whole bank of hungry photographers. I'm talking to Francis Ford Coppola and I see Julia Roberts arriving. I know who *E.T.* wants on camera, and it's not Mr. Coppola. I said, "Oh, jeez." Fortunately, she spent some time posing for the photogs, enough time that Mr. Coppola finished his thought, and I could say, "Thank you very much, have fun tonight," and got her. That was a close one.

Segaloff: Did he see your eyes going past him?

Maltin: I don't know. I don't know. At that time, they let *E.T.* staffers wander the carpet and escort people over to where I was. I had no mobility, standing there with a hand mic. I remember going, "Kevin! Kevin! Kevin! Kevin!" because of *Dances with Wolves.* [Kevin Costner]

---

* For many years between 1947 and 2001 the Academy Awards were held at the Los Angeles Shrine Auditorium, which is the headquarters of the Al Malaikah Temple of the Shriners, the American Masonic society. The 1954 *A Star is Born* opens and closes at the Shrine.

Segaloff: When you're doing sit-down interviews where you were the only one there and you don't have to compete with anybody, and you're interviewing somebody from the Golden Age and you know their filmography, at what point did you start going into questions that Leonard Maltin had always wanted to know, and not that *E.T.* cared about?

Maltin: I tried to get rid of the *E.T.* questions first. That was my general operating procedure. Make sure I had what was my job to deliver, and then have fun and satisfy myself. Sometimes those things would coincide, and sometimes they wouldn't. It took me a while to understand why those people were always mildly and sometimes very surprised that I knew what I knew about their work. I realized that, in part, it's not just that I had that knowledge, but I was in sharp contrast to almost everybody else who was interviewing them. On a junket, they met a lot of pinheads who were clueless. I went to New York for the junket for Oliver Stone's *Nixon*, and Anthony Hopkins was the main interviewee. At that time, I think *Access Hollywood* had started, and Arthel Neville was the co-host of the show. After a couple of questions, Hopkins said, "You haven't seen the film, have you, darling?" She said, "Well, I saw the first hour." He stopped for a moment, thought about, "Am I going to get angry? Am I going to end this interview?" Then he said, "All right, let's keep going," and realized it wasn't worth the emotional energy it would have taken to express his frustration. When I got him, we were fine.

Segaloff: Has anybody ever asked you, "Will anybody care about these questions you're asking?"

Maltin: Yes, I did. I got to interview Bruce Bennett.* I was very excited. It was in 1984 because of the Olympics. Herman Brix was an Olympic swimmer, like Johnny Weissmuller and Buster Crabbe before him. I did at least two pieces on Olympians in the movies. The pieces were hosted by Bruce Jenner. I was not there for the shoot, so I never met him. I suggested they shoot it in the Tarzana post office, where there's apparently some memorabilia of Tarzan and Edgar Rice Burroughs. I also never met Vera Hruba Ralston, who lived in Santa Barbara.† We got a good sound bite from her about losing to

---

* Bruce Bennett (1906-2007) gained fame as a star athlete who won the silver medal in shotput for the U.S. at the 1928 Olympic games in Amsterdam. He then began a long career in films including *The Treasure of the Sierre Madre* (1948). He was born Herman Brix.
† Vera Hruba Ralston (1919?-2003) was an Olympic figure skater from Czechoslovakia who became an actress.

Sonja Henie by seconds in the Olympics. That's how blasé I became at times, that I couldn't get myself fired up to make a drive up to meet Vera Hruba Ralston. What an idiot!

Bruce Bennett was smart. He realized when we put in the third 20-minute cassette that I was fishing for stuff about all of his films and all of his colleagues and all of his memories. I was only going to use one or two sound bites in this general piece about Olympians in the movies. He got it. I was a bit abashed and sorry that I didn't get to use more, but glad to have met him and talked to him.

Segaloff: It's basically saying, "Bruce, you're going to die someday, and I want to have your stuff," right?

Maltin: Yes.

Segaloff: Were there any people that you got to when it was too late to get to them, like when they were not all there?

Maltin: Yes. Myrna Loy. That was sad. That was a sad experience because the guy who had helped write her autobiography, James Kotsilibas-Davis, was the interlocutor for arranging this interview for which I was flying to New York. She asked for professional hair and makeup which my boss at the time, who was not an old movie fan, was reluctant to spend on a guest that he didn't care about. Finally, he said, "All right, we'll do it." We shot it in her apartment, I believe. She couldn't have been nicer. Her memory was almost gone but she was gracious. James could prompt her to provide some answers that were kind of stock answers to things, such as her first meeting with William Powell. I got a story out of it. It was a bittersweet experience.

Segaloff: Tell me about Barbara Stanwyck. That's a great story.

Maltin: Yes, that was quite a story. One of the biggest surprises in all my years there was having Dave Nuell and Jim Van Messel, the odd couple, come to me and say, "We're going to do a tribute to Frank Capra on his ninety-first birthday, and we want you to write it, and we're going to get Jimmy Stewart to host it." I said, "Ok, but why the ninety-*first* birthday?" Because they blew it on his ninetieth birthday. They missed their shot. Only later did I find out it was because Tom Capra [Frank's son] was a honcho at NBC News or at the NBC O&Os. I didn't care about that. I was going to get to do this. Then I thought, "Let me see about trying to get Barbara Stanwyck." I called around, and somebody said, "The way you get to Barbara Stanwyck is through Nolan Miller, the costume designer. He is her trusted friend." He was candid with me. He said, "She's self-conscious because she's been getting steroids, and it has made her a little puffy. You wouldn't just want her voice?" I said, "Maybe I *would* just want her voice." He said, "Really?" I said, "Yes." He fed me the idea. He said, "Well, I'll ask her."

Of course, this was in tribute to her favorite director. She said yes. First, I had to pass muster on the phone. We had a phone conversation. I said all the right things, apparently, and meant them, about her work, about my favorite films of hers, and about why I liked her so much in *Meet John Doe* and *The Miracle Woman* and all of these. An appointment was made. I went with the crew, and we didn't shoot it, we simply recorded it. First, I drafted a voiceover for her based on what she had said to me on the phone. I just ghost-wrote a script for her, which she read, and read well. She was willing to do it a couple times. Then I asked her some spontaneous questions, which she felt comfortable enough by then to answer. She had a guy living with her named Larry Kleno who wrote a "films of" type book on her, and he was her major domo at the time. He's the one who told me that she lost so much of her memorabilia in a house fire, and she was lucky that it only burned one area of the house, and that was a total loss. One of the things that she was saddest about was losing her personally inscribed copy of Frank Capra's autobiography, *The Name Above the Title*.

That set me into motion. I called Larry Edmunds bookshop. They still had a hardcover in top condition. I called my good friend, Jeanine Basinger, who was in touch with Mr. Capra, who was then living at La Quinta in the desert and was in touch with his caregiver. I learned that he had good days and not-so-good days. On a good day, it was within reasonable expectation that he might be able to sign this book to Stanwyck, about whom he was so crazy. He did that. FedEx was available to me and made all this possible. Then I had one of our drivers deliver it to her with the note from me. She was surprised and very pleasantly so. That was a joy to be able to do that. I can show you the note that she wrote back: "My friends call me Missy." That was one of the really good experiences. One of the best.

Segaloff: Were there people who died before you could get to them?

Maltin: One day, early on, I was in, I think, Gary Grossman's office and heard somebody say, "All right, Harry Belafonte's dead." I ran out to the news desk. "Harry Belafonte is dead?" "No, we just killed the story we were planning to do tonight on Harry Belafonte." I didn't know the lingo then. I did a story about voice dubbing and doubling. I saw on the schedule they were going to be interviewing Mr. Belafonte in New York. I called the head of the New York office and said, "I want to send you two questions to ask him about *Carmen Jones*."* He was very agreeable, couldn't have been nicer, and said, "My family teases me about this glorious operatic voice coming out of my mouth whenever they see *Carmen Jones*," which was just the sound bite I had hoped to get. I did a piece about a discovery in Texas of 35mm prints of Black movies, movies intended for the Black movie theater circuit. That was my cue to do a story about that. I had our New York office interview Ralph Cooper, who was the longtime host at the Apollo Theater. People knew him because he was a popular figure in Harlem for a generation. He was the leading man in a number of those films. They got to interview him. Then I saw they were going to be interviewing Redd Foxx for some other story and asked whether he had any stories. He said, "You know, when I came out here in the '40s, I went on a talent call for a Tarzan movie. The assistant director said I was too light. I spent a whole week eating milkshakes and cookies and cakes. I went back and tried again. He said, 'Now, you're too light *and* too fat.'" I love that story.

Scott Osborne sat right next to me at the office. One day, he was going to go to talk to Orson Welles at Ma Maison when Orson would lunch there on a daily basis. I was working on my book about radio. I didn't join him because I felt funny tagging along on Scott's shoot. I shouldn't have felt funny; I should have gone. It's Orson Welles! I blew my one chance of talking to Orson Welles, who nevertheless gave Scott two great sound bites that I quoted in my book. He made the point that, unlike television where you had ABC, CBS, and NBC running the show, in radio, the sponsors controlled the programming. There were an infinite number of sponsors. If you could find a compatible one or one that wanted to do something a little more dramatic or different or daring, then you had that door open to you. That was a very good point. After the "War of the Worlds" broadcast, Campbell's Soup became Welles' sponsor. Before that it was a sustaining program, which meant it had no sponsor. Campbell's came

---

* Otto Preminger's 1954 adaptation of Bizet's *Carmen* with Harry Belafonte and Dorothy Dandridge. Although both were popular singers, their voices were deemed unacceptable for the film's operatic range so LaVerne Hutcherson and Marilyn Horne dubbed Belafonte's and Dandridge's songs but not their speaking performances.

in and it became *Campbell's Playhouse*. He then had a bigger budget. He could afford to pay for guest stars. That's how I got Orson Welles in my book, yes. But I should have gone. I did meet him once for all of 10 seconds. We were boarding a plane at the same time at JFK. He was being wheeled down the jetway. We arrived at the door at the same moment. The attendant said to him, "Do you need help getting up, Mr. Welles?" He said, "No, no, I'm fine." He was getting up. We were doing Alphonse and Gaston. He said, "Go ahead." I said, 'No, after *you*, Mr. Welles.'

That book would be much the poorer if not for *E.T.* because I used so many excuses and opportunities, I didn't talk to Don Ameche but *E.T.* did, and I fed them some questions. I seized every opportunity.

Segaloff: Other than perhaps Orson Welles, has anybody ever intimidated you?

Maltin: I've been doing interviews at the Santa Barbara Film Festival for thirty-five years. It's called their Modern Master Award. About six or seven years ago, Roger Durling, who runs that festival, said he wanted to rename it the Maltin Modern Master, which I thought was very flattering. I agreed. I spent anywhere from an hour and a half to two hours on stage with Sean Penn, Anthony Hopkins, Clint Eastwood, Cate Blanchett, Kate Winslet, Glenn Close, George Clooney, Will Smith, James Cameron, and Martin Scorsese. A pretty great roster of people. Two or three years ago, I did Brad Pitt. I was uncharacteristically nervous because I didn't know anything about him, had no sense of what he would be like. That made me nervous. It turns out he was open and funny. I was not at my best that night, but he was great.

Segaloff: Have you ever intimidated anybody? Did you ever find out that you had intimidated anybody? I mean you're Leonard Maltin.

Maltin: I can't answer that. I don't know how to answer that. Some people say that they're nervous meeting me or talking to me.

Segaloff: You're one of the nicest guys in the business. Has that ever stood in your way? If you were more killer, could you have done other things? Not to say you failed.

Maltin: Long before TCM, Ted Turner decided to do a recreation of that famous MGM photo of all the players under contract at the Blossom Room at the Hollywood Roosevelt. I was there with the camera crew, and I got to talk quickly to Keye Luke and Leon Ames and Tony Martin and Cyd Charisse and maybe someone else. I really wanted to get Gene Kelly. Jeanne Wolf had just had an incident where she did a set visit to *North and South** in which he had a small role. She said she tried this approach: She said to him, "Mr. Kelly, I'll go home very disappointed if I don't get to talk to you." He said, "You'll live."

After they shot the picture and everyone was dispersing, I ran into the hallway and caught up with him and said something along the lines of, "You wouldn't want to take a minute and talk to me for *Entertainment Tonight*, would you?" I sort of talked myself out of him doing a quick interview. Subsequently, he did some promotion for *That's Entertainment Part 3* (1994). I got to have my one and only sit-down with him. It wasn't all that long, but it was good. I dodged one bullet. I'd gotten hold of a clip they didn't use in the film of an unfinished number that he shot with Esther Williams for, I think, *Take Me Out to the Ball Game*. We had a monitor set up, and I was ready to press the play button. I said, "I'd like to show you something, Mr. Kelly. See what you think of this." He said, "You're not going to show me that number." I said, "No." I pivoted and we just blew past it.

Segaloff: My bane was Robert Mitchum on a movie set. I was authorized to be there, but the publicist said he couldn't help, so when I introduced myself, he blew me off. I never got to tell him how great an actor I thought he was.

Maltin: We were pitched Mitchum for an HBO special about him in which he participated along with Jane Greer and Jane Russell and some other leading ladies. I went to one of our segment producers who said, "Why on earth would you want to drive up to Santa Barbara when he's done nothing but been rude to us and blown us off?" I said, "I think I can get to him." They gave us the use of a room at the Biltmore, and he dressed up, looked great. Came in, was not outgoing, but was polite. When we sat down, I said, "I'm watching a movie from MGM called *The Human Comedy*, which stars Mickey Rooney. There's a scene where three soldiers are walking along the street at night, and they come upon this young boy and his sister, they have a conversation, and it's you, and Barry Nelson, and I think Don DeFore. What do you remember of that or what does that evoke, what kind of memory?" He

---

* Television mini-series, 1985.

says, "First," he said, "we shot it in the daytime, but they had this giant tarpaulin covering that part of the back lot." It was moviemaking the way they used to do it at a studio. It obviously was a happy memory for him, and I passed the test. He was really a good interview. I lucked out.

Segaloff: You didn't remind him about his breaking up the brick of grass during the *Ryan's Daughter* junket.

Maltin: No, I did not. I did not evoke that story. Isn't that a great story?

Segaloff: It's a wonderful story (q.v.).

Maltin: He was promoting *War and Remembrance*. One of our early reporters at *E.T.* was talking to him on the junket. In the early days, especially, they always had additional questions to the point of being a pain in the ass. "Turn to the camera and tell your favorite Mother's Day memory."

Segaloff: They would save it to use in the future?

Maltin: Right. She had to ask him if he would ever do commercials because Olivier had just done his first TV commercial. Steve McQueen was doing commercials, but only shown in Japan, that kind of thing. Mitchum had a glass, a tumbler, I don't know what his drink of choice was, but it was a tumbler full. She said, "Would you ever do a commercial like that?" He said, "No, no way. No fucking way."

Segaloff: Then later he did the commercials for the beef industry.*

Maltin: Yes, of course. I was very lucky at *E.T.* that they rarely gave me drudge work and go out and shoot something I wasn't interested in. One exception was the night I covered the NAACP Image Awards, which were in Pasadena at the Pasadena Civic Auditorium. It was the only time I've ever had to interview a succession of people without knowing who they were. Some of them were on soap operas. Some of them were on shows that I didn't watch. Again, I was right next to the photogs, and in some cases, they helped me, but in a lot of cases, I didn't know. I knew who Laurence Fishburne was. I told the story to someone who asked me, "Well, what'd you say? What'd you do?" I said, "Who are you looking forward

---

* "Beef: It's what's for dinner."

to seeing tonight? Are you rooting for anyone in particular? Some night, huh?"

Segaloff: Usually, there's a publicist whispering in their ear saying, "This is Leonard Maltin from *Entertainment Tonight*," but you had nobody who was prompting you at that point, did you?

Maltin: No. My director was useless.

Segaloff: I didn't know these things happened.

Maltin: One of the assignments I got that I didn't care about was to interview John Cusack and James Spader, for the movie *True Colors* in 1991. I was so indifferent about doing this. It was at my home away from home, the Four Seasons Hotel on Doheny Drive in Beverly Hills. I said, "My car knows the way." I confess, and this is very unprofessional of me, but I didn't do my homework, but I had the printed press kit, press notes, and at red lights I was reading the bios of these two guys. It said that James Spader grew up in and around North Andover, Massachusetts. When he came into the room and sat down and said hello, I said, 'What's your favorite flavor of ice cream at Bentsen's?' He said, "How do you know about Bentsen's?" which was an outdoor family-run ice cream stand, only open during the summer. I said, "Well, my wife and I spent a lot of time up there. We had a friend who worked at a boys' prep school." He said, "Which one?" I said, "The Brooks School." He said, "I went to the Brooks School." He said, "Who was your friend?" I said, "Mike King." "*Mike King?*" Art teacher and a dorm master. Well, it's like we were old friends. We had a wonderful conversation. I was very impressed with him. He worked in a TV movie with Mitchum. He told a wonderful story about the time they were doing a shot in which he was sitting next to Mitchum in the cab of a flatbed truck. Mitchum had to drive it around a curve of a street and come to a stop and then they had dialogue. Mitchum was having some dispute with the producer. As he's driving up and getting toward this, he said, "...and that goddamn producer." He timed it so that his foul-mouthed complaint would be shot perfectly not to spoil the take. Spader also told me that his ambition was to be a character actor. He said he'd love to be like Charles Laughton. He said, "I'd love to take on meaty roles." Those were nice moments where I didn't anticipate enjoying an experience.

Segaloff: Breaking the code is important, which is what you essentially did there. Were there times when you just said the hell with it and walked out because the guy was such an asshole?

Maltin: The one I should have walked out on was Richard Dreyfuss, which came as a real surprise because I'd met him casually a couple of times. I'd seen him, and I knew he had the gift of gab. What was the problem? Well, the problem was that this was a booking that got fouled up. *E. T.* always was the first on the junket list, as we were first on the line at line at events so we would be the first one to interview them before they were talked out. This time we were the last, Sunday afternoon; they've been interviewed since Friday at the Four Seasons.* This was for the film *Twice Around*. As we were setting up, Dreyfuss popped his head in to say hello. He liked our camera guy, and they exchanged a few words, and he says, "See you soon. Okay." Director Lasse Hallström had a plane to catch, and so did Holly Hunter, and so did Danny Aiello. They're all scattering to the four winds. Dreyfuss was the last, like an hour and a half into the process. His publicist was a jerk and didn't do anything to stop or to prevent this situation, which anyone could see was festering. Dreyfuss stalked into the room, fuming, almost literally fuming, smoke coming out of his ears, pissed off. He sat down and said to me, "All right, ask me something I haven't answered a hundred times already this weekend." Thinking he was teasing me—and I really did think he was teasing me—I said, "How much of you is Harry? How much of Harry is you?" He said, "Ohhhh." He was serious. He was not going to answer any stock question about this movie. I barreled ahead, dense and not getting the message. When I realized what was happening, I felt, if I just keep plugging away, eventually, he likes the sound of his own voice enough that he's going to give me what I need. What I needed was just two or three sound bites.

This was a Sunday, and this piece was going to air on Monday, and I could see it in my head. I could picture, because it was going to incorporate bites from all the principles, except probably Lasse Hallström because *E. T.* didn't care about directors. (It's a long parenthetical sidebar about my producer who always said, "My mother in Flint, Michigan, wouldn't care." He made me stop mentioning director's names. One day

---

* Studios would hold weekend press junkets which involved gathering press and filmmakers into a hotel and running round-robin print and television interviews. Everyone asks the same questions, and it's maddening for the stars, not unlike doing one hundred takes of the same scene.

I did mention Stanley Kubrick. I said, "Stanley Kubrick made *Dr. Strangelove.*" He said, "Maltin, I warned you…" I said, "I've been a good boy, and I haven't dropped any director's name, but Stanley Kubrick is arguably pretty well-known. Even people who don't know who directed most films would know who's Stanley Kubrick." I don't think I won that one.) Anyway, Richard and I do the interview, and I heard a sound bite fly by, then I heard another one fly by, and I said, "All right." The minute we were done, he poses for a picture. He exorcised his anger. I'm bad at confrontation. I'm very bad at confrontation.

Segaloff: He's bipolar, so that accounts for a lot of his behavior. We've been bumping into each other for years. Never for an interview. Always socially or business. He's one of the most brilliant people around.

Maltin: I'd like to think that if that happened today I would stop the camera to say, "Look, Richard, I know you're upset, and I know you're anxious to get out of here. We all are, but if you just play ball for a couple questions, we can all go home."

Segaloff: So you've never walked out on an interview.

Maltin: Oh, no. How could I do that?

Segaloff: Sometimes you realize you'll never get anything good out of the person.

Maltin: I remember flying to New York. This was a memorable one. Whenever *E.T.* sent me to New York, it was usually an overnight trip, and you lose all that time flying East. I considered it a success if I could either have dinner with a friend, and/or go to hear somebody at one of the jazz clubs that night, and maybe have lunch with another friend, or visit my agent, or visit my publisher before taking an afternoon ride out to JFK or Newark the next day to come home. I did pretty well over the years. I would have the cab—in those days it was taxis—I would have the cab take me directly to John's Pizza on Bleecker Street to the point where the owner, Pete Jr.—who I hope is still alive, he retired to Fort Myers, Florida, I believe—would take my suitcase and put it in his office for safekeeping, and he wouldn't let me pay. When that happened, I called out, "If this occurred at Lutece or the Four Seasons,*

---

* John's is (or at least was) the best pizza place in New York City. Ask anyone whose family doesn't have a competing pizza place in New York City.

I could not be prouder than to have the run of the house at John's Pizza." It's one of two places that I had a signed picture on the wall for a while. Long gone now. The other one being the Carnegie Deli.

Segaloff: Of blessed memory.

Maltin: Of blessed memory, yes, where a guy named Sanford Levine gave me a great trivia question, which I've used ever since. Can you name all *12 Angry Men*?

Segaloff: The actors? Because otherwise it's one, two, three, four, five, six, seven, eight, nine — *

Maltin: Yes, the actors. The one that stumps most people is Joseph Sweeney. I had so many really good experiences. Then, of course, last time I went to a reunion of *E.T.*, first-year veterans, I stayed too long. I stayed too long and I started remembering the not-happy things. The fact that they wanted to fire me. The fact that they just kept haranguing me about making my reviews more definitive: "Love it or hate it."

Segaloff: We should talk about how you structure a review, and how you would explain it. You're essentially writing an argumentative theme where you state a premise, support it, and then restate it.

Maltin: Well, you need a good lede. You have to start off with something that's an attention getter or states a premise. Did I tell you my most memorable review, the one that people still talk to me about from time to time?

Segaloff: No.

Maltin: It was a film called *Transylvania 6-5000*. Our director was not always the sharpest tack, but he went along with this; he got what I was trying to do. He did a needle drop on the Glenn Miller record "Pennsylvania 6-5000." I just swayed back and forth, not saying anything, and then said, "*Transylvania 6-5000* — stinks. I'm Leonard Maltin, *Entertainment Tonight*." For years and years and years, people would actually stop me in hotel lobbies and airports and tell

---

* The author got seven right off the bat and then Leonard and I struggled with the other five: Henry Fonda, Lee J. Cobb, Jack Klugman, Edward Binns, Martin Balsam, Robert Webber, John Fiedler, E. G. Marshall, George Voskovec, Jack Warden, Joseph Sweeney, and Ed Begley.

me how much they loved that review. It was not an inappropriate review. It expressed everything I needed to say about that movie. It worked.

Segaloff: How far into the plot of a film did you feel comfortable going?

Maltin: Oh, I never did spoilers. I still don't. What I was doing, and what I did in my *Movie Guide* as well, were not serious in-depth critical essays for which you would have to give away plot points to complete a thorough argument or discussion. These were impressions of the movie. That was never an issue. I remember reviewing a mediocre film with Dudley Moore called *Romantic Comedy*. I said the title is insultingly generic. It's like saying "toilet tissue." They didn't have enough conviction in making this film to give it a name. Sometimes I find a hook like that and that made it easier to write the review. Again, most films that come down the pike don't have anything special about them or don't have anything notable or unique. Of all the things I taught Jessie about language, the one that always stuck with her was that you cannot modify the word *unique*. She still invokes that lesson.

Segaloff: Between you telling her about *unique* and Harlan Ellison telling her not to over-use the word *awesome*—*

Maltin: That's right!

Segaloff: How long did your reviews have to be for *E.T.*?

Maltin: It was one typed page, double-spaced, allowing for a fifteen to twenty-two second sound-up, then a voiceover, and then a finale or summing up. They insisted at *E.T.* that I do a one to ten rating scale which was also being used by Gary Franklin at the time on KABC here, and he was a putz. I disliked being grouped with him in any way. I almost wouldn't know how to write a long review. That would be challenging for me, not impossible but challenging. I'm so used to compressing my ideas and not doing a lengthy synopsis, which most reviews that you read include. If you look at the word count, a lot of that word count is exposition

---

* The Maltins and the author were friends of Harlan Ellison, the speculative fiction writer. Harlan and his wife Susan did not have their own children, but they enjoyed helping to raise other people's, and Jessie was one such beneficiary of "Unca Harlan"'s attention. The author wrote Ellison's biography, *A I it Fuse* (Newton, Massachusetts: NESFA Press, 2017)

describing what happens in the film. I was also asked on the street, "Hey, aren't you Siskel and Ebert?"

Segaloff: That happened to me, too, when I used to do television. People attach whatever name they know to someone they have seen.

Maltin: It's hilarious that Siskel and Ebert became a compound noun, "Siskelnebert." It's two guys. At first, I would say to myself, "Which one do they think I resemble? I don't look like either one. I'm overweight like Roger, but not as big, and I'm certainly not as skinny or as bald as Gene." That's what people would say, but then I'd say to myself, "Wait a minute, there's no entrance exam to watch television. If people see me and associate me with the act of reviewing movies and if I'm reviewing movies, I must be Siskel or Ebert, or maybe Siskelnebert, then it's really a compliment. They know who I am in some vague non-specific way."

Segaloff: Because you're on television, dummy.

Maltin: Because I'm on television, dummy. Right. Yes, exactly.

Segaloff: This is interesting, because it means that people are getting *impressions* from television, but not *information*.

Maltin: Images trump words, always. I found this out early on. I was preparing a review of Clint Eastwood's *Firefox*, one of his lesser films. My words were saying that it goes on too long, it even gets slow and boring, but the images were these cool shots of the fighter jets flying through the air. They contradicted what I was saying.

Segaloff: B-roll is the death of copy.*

Maltin: Well put.

Segaloff: Which is why a lot of producers will cover up talking heads with scenes from their movies. It's a distraction, it's waving your hands in front of a baby.

Maltin: You reminded me of another truism I was taught: "Talent exists to cover jump cuts."† Now, of course, jump

---

* B-roll is what television people call footage that covers a person who is speaking, which is called a "talking head."

† Jump cuts are mis-matched shots where footage has obviously been removed or where spatial relationships get confusing when one

cuts are permissible. *E.T.* kept moving the goalposts, I guess you'd call it. Changing the rules. At one point, their sound guys would carry white, black, and flesh-colored lapel microphones. We wanted to make it look as good and as natural as possible and not remind everybody that we're making a television show, that this is a videotaped interview. Then it became, "It doesn't matter. We don't care." Then they decided for the junkets that we would build a set. We would take a suite at the Four Seasons and construct a backdrop of our own so that we wouldn't look like *Good Morning San Antonio* or *How Are You Denver?* with the same potted palm and the one-sheet poster on an easel. They got elaborate and built pretty impressive sets. But then they wanted to reveal the sets and give away the artifice. I said, "Well then, what's the point of—?" Next, they wanted the actor to respond to the set. I was doing the junket for *City Slickers II*, and they wanted me and the director to go out in the hall and say to Billy Crystal. "We built a set here, and they'd love to get your spontaneous reaction to it when you come in the room." He, not surprisingly, once you get to know him, wouldn't play ball, "Oh, they're going to expect me to say something funny?" "Well, yes. You're promoting your new comedy film, Billy. Yes. I suppose they will expect something funny."

Segaloff: Did he do it?

Maltin: No.

Segaloff: He should have done Bette Davis and said, "What a dump," and they would've torn the whole thing down. When you said talent exists to cover jump cuts, I thought you meant that if you're watching someone as compelling as Cary Grant or Clark Gable, you don't notice that shots don't match.

Maltin: Oh, no. It's not that. This is the wisdom of television at a certain point in time, that if you're playing an interview with a somewhat lengthy soundbite from Robert Stack or whoever, and you want to eliminate a phrase and marry this part of the sentence to that part of the sentence, the way you can hide the edit is by using a cutaway of the interviewer. That was always the toughest part of my job: faking "re-asks," as we called them, which was not an issue when they sent two

---

shot cuts to another. The French new wave in the 1950s used jump cuts as narrative shorthand but it soon yielded to traditional editing, then resurfaced when everybody with an iPhone had a video camera. "Talent," as used here, is not an adjective but a noun for the person seen on camera.

cameras. They often didn't send two cameras, they'd only send one camera, and then we'd have to ask the interviewee if they would have the patience and kindness to let us shoot over-the-shoulder shots of me trying to imitate myself or replicate the cadence and the way I phrased a question twenty minutes earlier, which is hard to do. They made fun of it one night on *Saturday Night Live*, with Martin Short, where he was imitating Robin Leach, and the gag was that every one of Robin Leach's cutaway re-asks was in a different location from the actual interview. I thought, "Well, that's going to explode this ruse," but it didn't explode it at all.

Segaloff: This leads us into the Elizabeth Taylor experience, which you have written about in your memoir, that she gave you more or less stock answers when you asked her questions, but when she was kind enough to stay there for the re-asks, she was the hot ticket and she wasn't being recorded.

Maltin: They had un-miked her.

Segaloff: Has that ever happened with other people? Where the before and after, when you're getting to know them, they're terrific, and as soon as they sit down, they're a lump of clay?

Maltin: It happened to me in a different context entirely. I got a call from the Sundance Film Festival asking if I would be willing to moderate a discussion on stage between Robert Redford and George Lucas. Of course! Where-do-I-go-what-time-do-you-want-me? I'd interviewed both of them before and they were comfortable with me. We did it at the Egyptian Theater in Park City, Utah. They have a top floor, which the public doesn't know about, where they can have a reception. Jessie and I had the best time hanging out with Redford and his, I think it was his wife, maybe one of his kids, and George and his wife Melody Hobson, who was on the Sundance board. She was awfully nice, and they were getting on great, and we were all joking. Everyone was in very high spirits. I had every reason to believe this was going to be a wonderful event. Just before we left the green room, George's wife looked at him, took him by the shoulders and said, essentially, "Now don't pontificate, or don't go off on a tear." When we got on stage, they went dead. They didn't talk to each other at all. There was never a feeling of a conversation. Each one spoke his piece, and then I'd throw another question into the mix, and George pontificated. I don't know if it was evident to the audience. It was live-streamed in the early days of that technology. I don't know if anyone else sensed that or felt that, but I sure did, and Jessie did, too. We were so disappointed, because if you had been in that room for the hour or so that we were up there, you would have been having a great time.

Segaloff: They left it in the green room.

Maltin: Yes, they left it in the green room. That was startling. I've never had an experience as unexpectedly disappointing as that. I got another phone call in 2019 when *The Irishman* was out: would you like to come to the Egyptian Theater a week from Saturday and interview Marty [Scorsese] and Bob De Niro together for forty-five minutes? How much broken glass do I have to climb over to get there?

I didn't want to use notes. I hate using notes, and I was determined to discuss all nine films they'd made together. Marty was not my concern. I love hearing him talk about movies. He's so passionate, and he's so eloquent. He's the best ambassador for the medium anywhere on the planet. Robert De Niro, the first time I interviewed him was like pulling teeth. Many people have had that experience with him, but I've had better experiences with him. He can clam up. He was with Marty, and I knew that, if anything would save the day, that would be it. They arrived two minutes before the event was to begin. I got De Niro aside for one minute and tried to soften him up a little bit, talking about New York. I was just trying to put him at ease as best I could. They were great. They were great. They talked as if they'd never discussed this stuff before. They talked about being aware of each other before they met each other. They were some blocks from each other in New York's Little Italy when growing up, and had apparently some acquaintances or friends in common. When that was over, they vanished as quickly as they appeared. I was on a high. I've never done drugs, but that's as close as I think I'll ever come to feeling exuberant.

The first time I interviewed De Niro was on the press junket for *Awakenings* (1990), a film I liked very much. Because he was in New York and everybody else was here, we all flew to New York. It was a joke, including Robin Williams and Penny Marshall, and others, and the publicists, we were all trekking 3,000 miles. It was the first time I interviewed Robin Williams as well. De Niro acted like he was in pain trying to come up with a sentence or a complete thought. I thought to myself and said to anyone who would listen to me, "Why wouldn't, the day before this event, a producer sit down with him and say, 'Okay, Bob, think about the first time you shot a scene with Robin and come up with anecdotes' and let him memorize a handful of stories and have these answers ready-made. He's an actor. Let him rehearse and prepare to be asked, as he's going to be, such questions as, "Was Robin funny on the set? Did he make you laugh? What was the toughest scene to do? How do you prepare to play a catatonic character?" He struggled so mightily, as opposed to Robin Williams. We had 20-minute loads on our cassettes in those days and from the moment he walked into the room where we were shooting interviews, he was "on" and was funny and endearing and engaging—and then serious when it was called for to discuss the serious movie without seeming false or pretentious in any way. Then he went back to being funny and as we said, "Well, that's it." they kept it running as we said goodbye. I said to my boss, "You could just run this tape. Twenty minutes, start to finish. It's all worth watching and listening to."

Segaloff: This goes to the way the studios used to prepare their people to do these things. Not only were they dealing with extraordinary talents, but they were also teaching them how to manage the press, what to say and what not to say. It was a part of your training. Now they send them out unprepared. When I was a publicist, I used to train new people. I'd have to say to never sign autographs the way you sign your checks. If you shake hands with someone, jam your hand in there because if either of you is wearing rings, they'll crush your fingers. And nowadays if you pose for a picture next to someone, keep your hands visible.

Maltin: Tell me about the autographs.

Segaloff: In a crowd, if somebody hands you something, you never know what you're signing. It could be a blank piece of paper, and they'll add, "I will make a movie for you" on top of it.

Maltin: Oh my, I've never been that paranoid.

Segaloff: Now, they don't send them out at all, which is probably better, they just let them show up on TMZ and hope for the best because they're all expendable.

Maltin: I'm remembering an interview for *Born on the Fourth of July* that was much anticipated by the show. I was going to talk to Tom Cruise and Ron Kovic, the man he was portraying, and Oliver Stone. We had just seen the movie. They had a private screening for me and a few other people who were involved. I think it was an *E.T.* exclusive, actually, or a first. They were getting the cameras and lights set, and Tom said something about my book. Ron Kovic said, "Oh, what book is that?" "Well," I said, "it's a paperback movie guide with little capsule film reviews." Oliver said, "Yes, look up *The Hand* sometime."*

Segaloff: Bringing up Tom Cruise brings up superstar publicist Pat Kingsley who was known to ask journalists to sign releases restricting their use of the interview?

Maltin: I think an *E. T.* producer may have signed such a thing. I don't believe I signed such an agreement.

Segaloff: How do you feel about a publicist who wants to limit what their client will do?

Maltin: It depends on how badly you want the interview.

Segaloff: That's the answer.

Maltin: The screening of *Born on the Fourth of July* was at the tiny Sunset screening room and the publicist on it was the unlamented Andrea Jaffe, one of the nastier publicists I ever encountered. Alice and I parked the car and went up to the screening room, and Andrea gives her the once-over and says, "The screening was supposed to be only for you." I said, "I wasn't told that," which was the truth. She said, "Well, as long as you're here, might as well go in."

Segaloff: What a great way to represent a client.

Maltin: Yes. She preceded Pat Kingsley. It's like, if you're going to let her come in anyway, why bother to be nasty? What is gained by that?

Segaloff: You're a person that's highly recognizable. You're not an asshole. You're a very nice person. How do you deal with all this business of fame and what people expect you to do and people who even talk about you without knowing you?

Maltin: My fame is not the Brad Pitt-brand of fame where people are clutching at my clothing or wanting to.

---

* *The Hand* (1981) was an inauspicious directorial debut for the subsequently multi-honored Stone.

Segaloff: They're not throwing their underpants on the stage.

Maltin: Exactly. Well put. My level of fame is very agreeable and comfortable, because mostly people will say something like, "Seen any good movies lately?" or "What'd you think of _____?" I've seen _____. It's usually positive and pleasant.

Segaloff: Have you ever had second thoughts about a review you had written, and what did you do about it?

Maltin: Of course I've had second thoughts. The only place I was able to do something about it was in the *Movie Guide* because we kept revising it. I didn't want to ever seem like I was flip-flopping. I didn't want to do a cavalier rewrite or re-rating of a movie just because I saw it last night and enjoyed it more than I did the last time I saw it. There were some where I did do exactly that. The one that I always cite is *Alien*. I was on a book promotion tour, and I was in Boston of all places.

Segaloff: Yes, we sat next to each other.

Maltin: Yes, we did. Alice wasn't there. Had she been there, I would have been grasping her elbow repeatedly. I didn't feel the same liberty with you, so I ate my jacket. I kept chewing on my jacket. I'm just the worst patsy for jump scares. While I respected the movie, I did not have a good time watching it. My review reflected that. I didn't want to give it a bomb review. It's not a bomb. It's a well-made movie. Just not my cup of tea. I gave it a middling review. Twenty years later, they reissued it theatrically, and Ridley Scott made some tweaks to it. I saw it again. In that twenty-year stretch of time, I guess my threshold for violence and jump scares evolved. Plus, I'd seen so many rip-offs, so many inferior copies of what that film was able to achieve. I re-reviewed it and gave it 3.5 stars. That's the most dramatic turnaround.

Segaloff: There's a category of films that I call living room movies, which, of course, doesn't exist because nobody has a TV in the living room anymore. Movies like *Casablanca, The Godfather, The American President, Goodfellas*. Are there any films that you love to watch endlessly or if they're on and you're walking through the living room, you'll sit and stay?

Segaloff: Lately, since the pandemic, I must say that the TV rarely veers away from TCM (Turner Classic Movies). I find myself re-watching stuff that I didn't think I would. I've revisited a lot of Hitchcocks that I wouldn't have gone out of my way to see again. I'm really glad that I have done so. I have a whole new appreciation for *Stage Fright*, a better film that I've ever given it credit for. How interesting that it was his return to England and he took the opportunity to cast so many wonderful British actors in parts large and small. I watched *The Man Who Knew Too Much* again, the 1956. Still not one of my favorites, but I came away with a great trivia question. Everyone knows that Doris Day sings *Que Sera Sera* in that movie, but she sings a second song when she's seated at the piano at the foreign embassy. When she sings, she's playing the piano with great emphasis to be heard by her son. On that second song, that's relegated to a sort of background, there's never a shot of her on camera singing that song.

Segaloff: This is going to drive me crazy because I just rewatched it a week ago.

Maltin: The song is called *We'll Love Again*. It was written by Jay Livingston and Ray Evans, and no one had ever heard of it. One night we were tired, we had an early dinner with Daisy and came upstairs. They had just started running *North by Northwest*. We just couldn't stop watching it. There are a lot of films like that in my life.

Segaloff: Let's get back to writing. Which of your books was the hardest to write?

Maltin: I have no fondness whatsoever for *Leonard Maltin's Movie Encyclopedia* because of circumstances. I had an editor at what was now Penguin. I stayed put, but the publisher kept changing ownership. It was called New American Library when I went to work for them when I did the first edition of the *Movie Guide*. Then it was purchased by the Times Mirror Company, which meant the *LA Times*. Then, in an interesting turn of fate, I discovered that they were plagiarizing my book for the Sunday *Times* pullout TV section.

I had a couple of junctures. After getting married and now paying rent, there were a couple of moments along the road where I accepted an occasional gig just for the money. The one that I held out the longest on was the *Encyclopedia*, which my editor, Arnold Dolin, was eager to have me do. He was convinced that because of the success of the movie guide, having a companion volume that was like *Halliwell's Film Guide* or something like it would be a good match. All I envisaged was work, and lots of it. My literary agent, who was always ready to make a deal on my behalf, kept saying, "You can hire people to do this. You don't have to do it. Just have your name on it." I said, "I can't put my name on something that I haven't at least closely supervised." The publisher wouldn't take no for an answer; he kept upping the offer, the advance. I remember clearly, I have a flashback in my head right now of Alice and me in Maui, where we used to vacation on an annual basis, sitting on the veranda of a lovely restaurant in Lahaina. (Poor Lahaina, it was reduced to rubble in those recent fires, and we loved it so much. I hope someday to go back, but I don't want to go back too soon.) I can remember having dinner with Alice and discussing the pros and cons of taking on this *Encyclopedia* assignment. We were thinking about who could shoulder the burden of doing all the heavy lifting. We came up with a person, and I ended up hiring that person who, to make a long story short, screwed it up in ways large and small. One of the guys that he hired used the David Quinlan* book, and being a British book, all of the release dates did not correspond to the years of the original U.S. release. A young man named Spencer Green came to my rescue. He worked for me for decades doing all sorts of things, including transcribing. He was a great transcriber; he checks the names as he transcribes them; no one does that, but he does. He also has a sharp eye, is a good proofreader, and he's smart and he knows his films.

I had a separate building in our backyard in Toluca Lake which was my office. Spencer was out there at 7:00 or 7:30 every morning for months fixing the *Encyclopedia*. My original lofty goal of making it personal and quirky instead of just a recitation of facts sank under the weight of the sheer volume of information we had to convey. I remember writing a cute entry for Frank Albertson, the actor who plays Jimmy Stewart's brother in *It's a Wonderful Life*, who started out as a singing juvenile in the earliest talkies. Then he's the guy at the car rental place that Janet Leigh gets her car from in *Psycho*. A long, long career. I wrote a colorful paragraph or two about him. But I couldn't repeat that feat hundreds of times. As I say, I succumbed to the need to just get it done, and with Spencer's help, it got done. Turned it in, cashed the checks. It was a hardcover, a big, thick, impressive-looking book. The year that it came out, which was 1994, three people came seemingly out of nowhere to gain world prominence: Jim Carrey, Quentin Tarantino, and John Woo. They were planning a paperback edition for that fall but I knew they didn't want to reset type and recalibrate the pages, but I thought if we take a couple of lines out of this review and a couple of lines out of that entry

---

* David Quinlin has published numerous authoritative compendiums of films, character actors, and other subjects.

and out of that entry, we can make room for Jim Carrey and Quentin Tarantino and John Woo, and we did. I was able to at least fix those glaring omissions, but I still don't ever refer to the book.

Segaloff: Let's do the opposite side now. Which of your books has been the easiest to write? I mean the most fun, too.

Maltin: The most interesting experience I had, to answer a question you haven't asked, was the book on cinematographers.* Having gotten my foot in the door at NAL, later to become part of Penguin (which, by the way, was a great leap in the right direction, because Penguin had international distribution, and suddenly my book was on sale in Hong Kong, places it had never been before), my editor, Patrick O'Connor, moved from the company to Curtis Books. His replacement was a nice woman named Nancy Hardin. She came out here and went Hollywood, went into the movie or television business. I was going into my sophomore year at NYU and I had no summer project. I concocted a couple of projects while Patrick was still there. I pitched him three ideas, two of which I thought were commercial, and one that was fun for me. That was *Movie Comedy Teams*, and that's the one that I thought they wouldn't buy. It didn't sound commercial, and that's the one that they took. That was my second book. Great fun to work on.

Segaloff: There's a lot of backstory to *Movie Comedy Teams* that's really about your awakening as a published film historian.

Maltin: Now that the *Movie Guide* put my foot in the door at New American Library and a mentor in Patrick O'Connor, I submitted a proposal with a list of three books that I would like to do. The one I thought was the most commercial was *Sherlock Holmes on Screen*. By now, everything's been done forty times over since that day some fifty years ago, but at the time there was no such book. The films with Basil Rathbone were very popular on television and very present, very visible. I forget what the second idea was. The third idea was *Movie Comedy Teams*, which was sort of the fun idea that I knew they wouldn't buy. But that's the one that they went for, so that was very exciting.

---

* *Behind the Camera* (New York: Signet, 1971), later republished as *The Art of the Cinematographer* (New York: Dover, 1978).

Then Patrick said to me, "But you have to get an agent." I said, "Why? We're talking here, this is so simple, straightforward." He said, "Yes," he said, "but you shouldn't be negotiating for yourself because it's just not a good idea." I said, "Can you recommend somebody?" He said, "All right, I have a couple of people in mind. I think this fellow might be good for you. Meet him, see how you feel."

His name was James McCormack, and he worked out of his apartment on the chic east side of Manhattan. I went to meet him. He was a nice enough guy, so we shook hands and poof! You're my agent. While that was happening, NAL was already writing a contract for *Movie Comedy Teams*. I said to my father, who was the closest thing I had to a business advisor, "Should I be running this through my new agent? The deal's already made." We debated this back and forth quite a bit and decided that if I'm going to have a long-term relationship with this fellow, maybe it would get us off on a good foot to have him complete the terms of the contract, and so that's what I did. In fact, it was a terrible decision because, A, the contract was now written to him representing me, so all communication had to go through him such as royalty statements and money, if any. Two years later, no more than that, he left the agenting business. Extricating my deal and my professional relationship regarding this book with NAL was a giant pain, but everybody eventually signed off. What's more, I had dreamt of getting a hardcover book, and I asked him if he would submit it to Neil McCaffrey at Arlington House. Neil McCaffrey, it turns out, was a rabid right-winger with whom I normally would have had no reason to have any contact. But his hobby was vintage movies and vintage music, and Arlington House was an imprint that he created to publish several Jim Parish books—*The Fox Beauties*, *The Paramount Lovelies*, all that stuff. I later ran into Neil, and he'd never seen the book; my agent did not do my bidding. He took the lazy way out because the deal was there with NAL.

On the other hand, when that book came out, it was before the mall-ing, with a hyphen, the mall-ing of America, and the arrival of B. Dalton, and then Borders and Waldenbooks and all the rest. At the time, most books—paperback and hardcover, but principally paperback books—were sold in Woolworths and drugstores and card and gift shops on racks and only cost $1.50. They were seen and purchased by lots and lots and lots of teenage budding movie buffs and fans. At one time I reckoned that I had met every single person who owned a copy of *Movie Comedy Teams* because so many people said to me in the decades gone by, "The first movie book I ever owned" or "the first movie book I ever read" was

Movie Comedy Teams. It wouldn't have had the same impact as a high-priced hardcover book. Scott Alexander* always tells me that it's his favorite book, so go-know.

Doing research for that book was an education, too. I had a friend in the New York film buff community named Chris Steinbrunner who cut a wide swath. He worked at WOR-TV for years and years and years. WOR-TV was an RKO General station then, and so he had access to 16mm prints of RKO movies and was kind and generous enough to get me all the Wheeler & Woolsey movies which we screened at Joe's Place, aka the Cooperative Film Society, on West 40th Street between 9th and 10th Avenue. Joe's Place was a co-op where people brought prints and passed the hat for $1 or $2 to get to see rare old films together. It was almost literally a hole in the wall. He requested prints of all those films, without which I never could have accomplished anything for that chapter.

Then I got a freelance gig. I'd started doing copywriting for then-called "vee-a-com" (Viacom). That nice man there recommended me to a colleague of his named Harvey Chertok at Warner Bros.-Seven Arts, I think is what it was, in their television division. I met Harvey and he hired me that day to do a catalog of syndicated film packages that they were going to distribute. At the end of this, I quoted him, I think, $2,500, and he said, "Well, this feels more like $3,500 to me." That's the kind of guy he was. I said, "I'm going to ask you a favor, and if I'm overstepping, just slap me down, but there are films that you distribute that I need to see for this book I'm writing." It happened, at that time, that by whatever machinations were going on, they had part of the Universal-International library and part of the 20th Century Fox Library, as well as Warner's films. On a pad on his desk, I wrote down the titles of the Ritz Brothers movies I needed to see and some Abbott and Costello movies I needed to see. Those are the two that stay in my mind. He said, "Hold on a minute." He picked up his phone and he called someone and said, "I'm sending a guy over this afternoon with a list of prints he needs to borrow. Every time he takes one and returns it, you can give him another one." It was Bonded Film Services.

To them, they could have been storing Hydrox cookies. They didn't care what was inside the box they gave me: two 1,600-foot reels of what was inside these boxes. But I got to see all those films. How fantastic is that? The hardest team to research, ironically, was the newest, Dean Martin and Jerry Lewis, who made films for Paramount. Paramount was the

---

* Scott Alexander is, with Larry Karaszewski, the screenwriter of *Ed Wood*, *The People vs. Larry Flynt*, and other biographical films.

last major studio to sell feature films to television. By the time they finally decided that that might be a good idea, there was no market anymore for 1951 films with Mona Freeman and Billy DeWolfe.

Black and white was taboo. You could sell *The Country Girl*, you could sell *Sabrina*, but a lot of that other stuff, no. I had to ferret out prints. Jon Davison called one day and said, "They're showing *Sailor Beware* on a double bill with *Uptight* at the St. Marks Theater for a week." I'd never been to that theater, or that neighborhood, for that matter, and it was an all-Black audience watching Jules Dassin's *Uptight*, and me waiting for it to finish so I could watch *Sailor Beware*. This audience, confronted with the young Jerry Lewis, screamed. They loved it. It played great. It's a very funny film.

Then I said, "Well, I'm just going to have to spend a little money." Films Incorporated was the licensed non-theatrical distributor for Paramount, and the minimum rental for a film like *Artists and Models* was $35. A lot of money to me then. I called Films Inc., tried to book it. They said, "Oh, on Paramount titles, you have to get approval from Paramount directly." "Why? You have it in your catalog." "That's how it works." This was 1969.

I tried calling Paramount to see if I could borrow prints the way I had just done with Bonded Film Services, courtesy of my friend at Warner Bros. I got this guy on the phone and he said, "Do you know how much trouble it is to bring in a print to screen for you? First, we have to go to Kansas City for the salt mines, extract a print, and then someone has to check the condition," and blah blah blah. He went through this whole rigmarole that made it sound like researching the Dead Sea Scrolls, and the conclusion was No. Now, I was willing to pay $35 to the company that rented these films on a regular basis, and he still said No.

This field just seems to attract screwballs. Like Charlie Mogull. Mogull's Film Library. I never went there in person. He had an incredibly rare four-reel comedy produced by Fox in 1929 with Bobby Clark and Paul McCullough called *Waltzing Around*. It was in his catalog, had been for decades, for like $15, so I called myself. I tried to rent it. I didn't try to ask favors. Calling as a customer, I want to rent this film. "What purpose?" Purpose of watching the movie. "What date?" "As soon as possible." "No, I need show dates." "All right, January 14th." He was another obstructionist. He was determined not to rent this film. Charlie Mogull eventually met his maker and the prints were sold and I got to see *Waltzing Around* long, long after, I mean twenty or thirty years after.

Segaloff: They were weird people. Like Roger Hurlock who got the Allied Artists library and I think worked it out of his garage in Connecticut. There was Tim Swank, Kit Parker—

Maltin: Kit is an old friend of mine.

Segaloff: These people were venerated because they were the ones who were providing the only existing 16mm prints.

Maltin: Oh, Kit made it easy. Kit was the opposite of all that. He was the one who would open doors. He just released a two-disc set of rare Charley Chase silents. I was watching them this morning. It's a hobby for him now. So that was *Movie Comedy Teams*, but it finally got done and it came out.

That's when also Patrick explained to me the peculiar mathematics of paperback distribution. He said, "Every month we put out a fixed number of books, and we send them out to the distributors." Newsstands, too, were a big part of the circulation. "We expect to get fifty percent of them back. If a book doesn't get sent back or the scales tip the other way, that's a successful book if you only get forty percent back, or thirty-five percent back, or thirty percent back." I later learned the term *sell- through*. Fifty percent return was considered okay. It was like routine.

Segaloff: Did it have a deadline that you must sell by this day?

Maltin: No deadline. He told me, "You could go into your storeroom and find a musty box that had been shoved aside four years ago and tear off the half covers to prove you hadn't sold it and get credit returns."

Segaloff: Now that you had a relationship with NAL, what followed?

Maltin: Summer was coming along, I guess for my junior year, and I had nothing on the fire. That's when I went to Nancy Hardin and I put together a couple of proposals. One would be a book of interviews with film directors. She said, "We're not interested in that, but we are looking for a book about cameramen." Why were they looking for a book about cameramen? I have no idea. They're a mainstream publisher. It was not exactly a mainstream idea. I said, "Well, I'm not knowledgeable enough to do that." Then a couple of weeks went by and I said, "Who am I to turn down an offer?" I talked to Bill Everson. He said, "Well, you just go to Los Angeles, go to the ASC*, their clubhouse. The old-timers sit around, love telling stories, you'll have no trouble." I made a call to the ASC and spoke to its then-president, Arthur C. Miller, three-time Oscar winner. That book is still highly regarded by some pretty significant cinematographers like Matthew Libatique, who shot *Black Swan*, among others. Ernest Dickerson tells me this every time I see him; it had a big influence. I think that's because the book reflects my experience learning all of this stuff. I'm the avatar for the reader.

Segaloff: Didn't this book come out first as *The Art of the Cinematographer* and then *Behind the Camera*? They're both on my shelf.

Maltin: It came out in mass-market paperback form as *Behind the Camera*. Then, after an unspectacular sale, I regained the rights and sold it to Dover Press. That was an experience because Dover Press was run by Hayward Cirker and his wife Blanche. They were the ultimate mom-and-pop publishing company. They were in downtown Manhattan. All that was missing was a green visor. I don't remember if he had garters holding up his sleeves, but it was very Dickensian. They didn't pay royalties, they paid a flat fee, but they bought non-exclusive rights, so that if I could make a deal elsewhere with the material, I was free to do so. I expanded on the content by adding a lot of photos. It's still in print, because Dover books, for ages, never went out of print. It's a book I'm very proud of.† Quite by chance, the five men that I got to interview span the history of motion pictures, Arthur Miller having shot *Perils of Pauline* in 1914 and Conrad Hall was still in the midst of a stellar career in 1971 when we talked.

Segaloff: You were also involved in packaging books for others to write. What did that involve?

Maltin: Patrick O'Connor, The man who gave me my first job in publishing, a job that lasted for forty-five years, which neither he nor I could have foreseen, moved over to a substantially smaller paperback house called Curtis Books, which was a division of Popular Library, which at that time was owned by CBS. I was still going to NYU and he called me and made a date for a meeting. He said, "I want you to edit a series of film books for me but I can't pay you." I said, "How's that?" He

---

* The American Society of Cinematographers.

† Blanche Cirker died in 2022 at age 104. Dover Publications became part of the Lakeside book Company in 2000.

said, "You're going to become a book packager. You are going to hire the people to write the books, and I don't need to know any details about what you're paying them or how you're paying them, or how you're hiring them but you'll follow through, sort out good ideas from the bad. We'll have a book series." I wasn't eager to do it that way but I became a book packager and I midwifed a dozen or more pretty good books. Some of them were really good. The *Preston Sturges* book was the first book on Sturges. *Hollywood Director* was a book on Mitchell Leisen—go figure. I could get that published. It was by an old friend of mine, David Chierichetti. I learned a lot. I learned that not everybody keeps their word. Some people never turned in a book but did keep the money.

And I learned a publishing or an editorial truism: you never judge a person's writing from the published work. You've got to see the manuscript before it got edited. There's one fellow that I hired to do what we thought was an important book. I judged him by some articles he'd had published in decent magazines. Then I saw the sprawl of badly written, in some cases badly researched, material. That was a painful education.

Segaloff: Did you have to go to Patrick and get final approval or did you have final cut?

Maltin: Oh, no, I had final nothing. He was the one who had to buy them. What drove me crazy was that I brought him *Superman*[*] and he didn't want it. I say, "I finally bring you a commercial book." I had to really fight hard to get that published, and I'm glad I did. Then I gave the rights back to several of those guys because David Chierichetti had greatly expanded his Mitchell Leisen book. Joe Adamson got *Tex Avery* republished. And from the Curtis Books series, I was very proud of this, a guy named Don Miller wrote a book on B-movies all from memory, and his memory was superb. It's one of the few real authoritative handbooks on Chesterfield Pictures from 1934. He also did a great book on B-Westerns, and that got reprinted later on.

Segaloff: Was this before or after the *Leonard Maltin Movie Encyclopedia* experience?

Maltin: These were all before. Patrick also told me that I would never see another nickel, that their sales statements were all fictional.

---

[*] Gary H. Grossman's *Superman: Serial to Cereal*, q.v.

Segaloff: This is right before he left the company or what?

Maltin: No. I accepted it except when I got my statement for one of them; they all came in batches. It said it sold 5,000 books. I said, "If you're going to lie, say it sold 5,023 books." At least I didn't have any illusions.

Segaloff: How did you decide what to accept?

Maltin: I was there to hear some pitches. A guy named Henry G. Saperstein*, Hank Saperstein, came to visit Patrick because Abrams had just published *The Art of Walt Disney* which was a big success as a coffee table book. He owned UPA; he owned Mr. Magoo. He was pitching a coffee table book on Mr. Magoo, which was not a slam dunk of an idea, but not necessarily a bad idea. I said, "Do you have the artwork?" The magic of that Abrams book was that Disney saved everything. "Oh, we got it, we got all that stuff." He was very cavalier about what artwork he had. I was not well informed enough. He was oily, and that came to nothing. On the other hand, I have one of the greatest moments of my life because I happened to be sitting in his office when Richard Feiner† called. We had done a book called *The Laurel and Hardy Book*. Richard Feiner claimed to own the rights to Laurel and Hardy. He bamboozled *The New York Times*. He bamboozled the *Hollywood Reporter.* He bamboozled Hallmark cards. He had what appeared on the surface evidence of ownership but in fact was not. He coined the term "stills rights," which doesn't exist. No one separately copyrights stills for a movie. Ever. He was not a nice man. He was a Raymond Rohauer‡ wannabe.

---

* United Productions of America, the innovative animation studio that was staffed with onetime Disney artists who forged a new, graphic visual style. Among the leading lights was John Hubley, Pete Burness, Jules Engel, and later, Ernie Pintoff. Henry Gahagan Saperstein (1918-1998) bought UPA studios from its founder Stephen Bosustow in 1960 after UPA's *Mr. Magoo* feature tanked. He became a successful rights aggregator, producer, and distributor.

† Richard Feiner (1926-2013) sued several entities claiming he held rights to various Laurel and Hardy intellectual properties which, in fact, belonged to Hal Roach and those to whom Roach had licensed or transferred them. He did own certain rights to Laurel and Hardy silent shorts but boasted of more. His threats of litigation were often sufficient to bluff a financial settlement.

‡ Raymond Rohauer (1984-1987) was a film collector, historian, and distributor who resurrected the work of Buster Keaton, among other silent filmmakers, but who also engaged in duplicitous, intimidating, and nasty actions to assure his primacy.

I was in the office when Richard Feiner called to threaten to sue and all sorts of other stuff. I motioned to Patrick to put him on hold. I said, "He's a fraud. He has nothing. Trust me on this. I know." I got to hear him brush off Richard Feiner, who never followed through.

In fact, he was tied up with my appearance on *The Dick Cavett Show*. I don't remember how that came about, but it was intended to plug *Movie Comedy Teams*. At the time, a fellow I was friendly with a fellow who worked for Walter Reade-Sterling, which had just obtained the TV rights to the Laurel and Hardy package. I spliced a couple of sequences out of my 16mm Blackhawk prints,* and that's what I brought to the Cavett show and which they used. Dick was a real fan. (This is a separate story. The show aired on a Friday night, and I was the first guest. My friend Robert Bader now licenses the Cavett Library for Daphne Productions. He found the episode and burned a DVD for me. When I showed it to Alice and Jessie, they shrieked because neither of them had ever seen me without a beard. I was twenty years old. In that green room I met his other two guests, Veronica Lake, who had just published an autobiography; she was very sweet, she signed my book, and William Saroyan. I got to ask William Saroyan about this short that I'd seen on a Steenbeck [editing table] at the Library of Congress called "The Good Job." It's a one-reeler. I said, "How'd that come about?" He said, "That was part of a big lie that Louis B. Mayer told me that if I did a decent job with this short, he'd let me direct *The Human Comedy* and he never had any intention of letting me direct *The Human Comedy*."† I got that from his lips.)

Cavett, when we went to commercial, said to me, "Veronica Lake is spiffed." He says, "I'm always uncomfortable with that." He says, "So if you want to jump in and ask something, please do. Feel free to do that." I said, "Okay." But he was too fast. He left no room to jump in.

Segaloff: Did he talk about you at all that night or did he only talk about himself?

---

* Blackhawk Films of Davenport, Iowa had licensed the nontheatrical rights to the Hal Roach Laurel and Hardy films and sold first-quality 16mm and 8mm copies to the public for home use.

† *The Human Comedy* (1943) was an original screenplay written by Saroyan for MGM with the studio's promise of being able to produce and direct it himself. When MGM decided to have house director Clarence Brown direct the film, Saroyan turned his script into a novel. It is the story of a telegraph boy, Homer McCauley, and his experiences in a small town during World War II.

Maltin: No, we talked about Laurel and Hardy.

Segaloff: That's a good change for him.

Maltin: I stopped watching him when he talked more about himself, or when he was telling Laurence Olivier anecdotes to Ralph Richardson and John Gielgud. Anyway, I was on *The Dick Cavett Show* when it was a big deal on ABC at 11:30 at night. The next morning my phone rings and it's Richard Feiner saying, "It was nice seeing you on TV last night. Who gave you permission for the clips?" I said, "Walter Reade-Sterling" "Well, they don't have excerpt permission. I'll have to look into that." Then he proceeded to get me blackballed off *The Dick Cavett Show.* They had said they wanted to have me back to do other comedy teams. I don't know if they paid him off. He rattled the cage.

Segaloff: How did you find out that you weren't going to get any more bookings on the Cavett show again?

Maltin: I didn't get any more bookings on the Cavett show.

Segaloff: You never hear anything in this business. It always just happens and then you look back and you realize.

Maltin: I was still going to NYU and, earlier that week, I'd gotten a call from WNET. They were doing an arts roundup show on Friday nights, and wanted to have me on, and it dovetailed with the Cavett taping, but Cavett was using a theater on West 58th Street, I think and WNET was on 10th Avenue in the '50s. Geographically, it was doable. I managed to juggle the two. On the WNET show, they had a great lineup that night. I can't remember everybody who was on, but I was going to be discussing some film event or release with Penelope Gilliatt. In one of their teases coming up later in the show, they referred to her as a film critic. She said, "I don't like to be called a critic, I am an essayist." Whatever. They said "critic" again and she said, "That's it," and walked out. Wasn't rude to me. She was very pleasant to me. She walked out leaving me to do the segment by myself and apparently, I was "on" that night because they were full of thanks and praise which led to nothing. As I came out of the Cavett taping, my best friends at the time, Dennis Fine and his fiancé Rosalie Palladino were there cheering me on, but I didn't have a girlfriend, and I felt really rooked. That was the kind of thing you wanted to do to show off for a girlfriend.

Segaloff: Oh, Leonard.

Maltin: I've made up for it since.

Segaloff: You said your long-time dream was to write a newspaper column.

Maltin: Yes. Growing up in Teaneck, we got the Bergen *Record*, which was a very good newspaper that subscribed to the AP and UPI. It's where I read Bob Thomas on a regular basis when he was doing a daily column for the AP, which was forever. It was a good paper. My parents got *The New York Times* delivered every morning. I was never a news reader, I confess. Never much on current events or anything like that, but I read the entertainment pages. My dream was to write a column. I wanted to write a column, and I didn't know what exactly it would look or read like. I was doing enough in my junior publishing days that I liked the idea of having a voice, plugging things that I cared about and all that. I'm trying to put a date on this. Then the opportunity arrived. Patrick O'Connor, the man who gave me my first job, was friendly with Andrews-McMeel, which syndicated Gary Larson's *Far Side*. They were hot. They were the new kid on the block in terms of syndication. I wrote some sample columns for them, trying to get into the mushrooming home video market. This way I could write about different films and filmmakers. This would be the springboard for two columns a week or whatever it was going to be. They liked the columns well enough to make an offer, which I assigned to my lawyer, Les Abell. He's more like an uncle who looks out for us. The first thing is that they wanted a ten-year commitment. Les said, "I thought Abraham Lincoln signed a proclamation of some sort. Ten years?" They said, "It takes time to build a column into a success. We're experienced. We know it takes time. We don't want to invest that time only to have you say you don't want to do it anymore." There was absolutely no financial guarantee of any kind. If I started writing these columns and they yielded only $75 a week, I was stuck. I would have been stuck.

Segaloff: For ten years earning $75 a week?

Maltin: That's right. If it became popular, the revenue would go up according to how many papers signed on. The size of the paper, the size of the market, the upside was that there was no limit to what it could earn. But I didn't want to make that commitment. The irony is that I walked away.

Segaloff: You were so young that you had your future in front of you. Why should you be anchored to a column?

Maltin: Yes. It was a real disappointment. I said, "I'll sign a restrictive covenant that if I decide it's not worth doing, I won't go to a rival syndicator or rival newspaper. I'm happy to sign that." No, all in or not at all.

Segaloff: How close did you come in your *Entertainment Tonight* commentaries and features to approaching what you would have done in a column?

Maltin: It was a different thing, different medium. I find I write differently in every different medium, and for a particular audience. People over the years wanted to do things with the content of the *Movie Guide*. You don't understand. Those little capsule reviews work in the context of that book. As soon as you take them out of that context, you say, "Why isn't he more descriptive" or "Why doesn't he mention the writer" or "Why doesn't he single out the cinematographer?" All that does is magnify the shortcomings of that form.

Then I had a second opportunity, because an old friend in New York had charge of the North American Newspaper Alliance, one of the first syndicators.* It may have been the first real national newspaper syndicate. It was the same deal, essentially. Not time-wise, but revenue-wise. It was essentially writing on spec. By the time that loomed as a possibility, I was so busy that the idea of writing on spec, possibly for a year or two, because it would take time to build a successful column from a standing start, didn't appeal to me.

Segaloff: You did write, though, for something that I've never heard of called *Greater Amusements*.

Maltin: In the garage, I have copies I can show you. I forget how this connection was made, but somebody got me an introduction to a man named Ray Gallo, a lovely man who was the editor-publisher of an ongoing trade magazine called *Greater Amusements*, which had swallowed up another small magazine at some point. He was very kind to me. I was in my teens. He threw things my way, little freelance things. He was supported by the industry, which still took trade ads in his—the word I want to use is *woebegone*—his woebegone publication.

_____

* Founded in 1922 by fifty major U.S. papers, including the *Los Angeles Times*, it lasted until 1980.

Segaloff: It was a national magazine?

Maltin: Yes.

Segaloff: Boy, I escaped that one.

Maltin: He had a friendship with the very talented and renowned Hong Kong watercolorist Dong Kingman, who did the cover art for their anniversary issue. Their office was around Times Square. They had columns with regional reports: Midwest, Northeast, Southwest, whatever. They subscribed to a very famous clipping service called Burrelles.* My actor friend Jimmy Karen said he used to have a Burrelles subscription so that if he got mentioned in the *Denver Post* or the *New Orleans Times-Picayune*, they'd find that clipping and send him a copy. *Greater Amusements* would send me these mounds of Burrelles clippings. From that, I did a dot column† from the Southwest region about whatever was going on with theater owners, releases, innovative marketing ideas, and things like that. But the news was too old by the time it filtered through me and got back to them. They had a guy on the staff named Spencer Hare. The name of his column was, "Hare's What They Do." One week Spencer Hare was going on vacation, and he said, "Can you fill in and go to all the trade screenings this week and file reviews?" Sure. I became acquainted with the six, seven, eight people who were on that beat for other publications, *Variety* and *New York Daily News*, I think.

Segaloff: This was your first immersion into the movie beat in New York?

Maltin: Yes. Screenings at 10:30 AM and 2:00 PM. Columbia was at 711 Fifth Avenue. UA was at 729 Seventh Avenue, Universal was at 445 Park Avenue, like that.

Segaloff: What did you learn, Dorothy?

Maltin: The most interesting thing about it was we wouldn't talk much to each other. They were not unfriendly, but we saw mostly mediocre stuff that week. On Thursday, we

---

* In June 2024, Burrell's announced that, after 180 years, it was leaving the "media monitoring business."
† A "dot column" was a series of short notices connected with dots, called "leaders" in journalism. *Variety*'s Army Archerd was a master at it: "John Smith has a new movie out ... Jane Doe moving from LA to Gotham... Vincent Van inked a three-pic deal at Metro..." etc.

saw something that was pretty good. While waiting for the elevator, the talk was, "Hey, that was pretty good." Because everything else had been so blah, this one stood out and got a stronger positive reaction than it would have in any other circumstance. That was my takeaway from that week: that it's not a great movie, but compared to the other crap we sat through, it's a masterpiece. No one went that far, but it was very interesting that, when you do that day after day, week after week, you look for one unpolished gem, something that isn't a drag to sit through.

Segaloff: We used to have a ritual at our critics' screenings in Boston, which were not competitive, except for one person. If anyone had to leave to go to the bathroom in the course of a screening, when they'd come back, they would always ask, "What did I miss?" As a chorus, we would all call out, "You missed the car chase." This was especially funny watching a Bergman film.

MALTIN AND THE MOUSE

Segaloff: For years and years you were the spokesperson for Walt Disney Home Entertainment. You were producing. You were hosting. You were the leading authority, which I think is wonderful. Can you tell me how your association with Disney came about and how the dynamics worked? They can be tough to deal with.

Maltin: I can tell you very specifically. That's a saga in itself. I became aware as I was attending screenings of new Disney films in the late 1990s that the man who was running the company was a very nice man named Dick Cook.* I approached him one day at a party behind the El Capitan Theatre† after some new movie. I said, "I have an idea I'd like to run by you." He said, "Well, let's have breakfast." He liked having breakfast meetings at the former Mo's on Riverside Drive in Toluca Lake. I met him there at 8:00 AM one morning and brought with me a one-page typed proposal, but it was really a verbal pitch. The pitch was, "You've been releasing your cartoons helter-skelter, like the *Best of Pluto, Micky and Friends* and things like that, and there's no rhyme or reason. I think you're missing out on a substantial audience of Disney buffs and serious Disney collectors. You wouldn't be cutting off your general family audience, you'd just be adding to it. He said, "Okay, let's do it." That's what he said. He said, "Okay, let's do it." Of course, it took months after that to get a contract hammered out with the business affairs people. Essentially, it was the shortest meeting in Hollywood history.‡

Segaloff: Who chose which subjects to do and which you did?

Maltin: Me. All me. There were a couple of executives at Walt Disney Home Entertainment who were riding herd over this project, and they gave me a producer to work with. The first producer was Jeff Kurtti, and we worked well together§

---

* Richard W. Cook held ascending executive positions at the Walt Disney Company from 1996 to 2009 capping a long earlier career with several phases of the Disney organization.
† Disney held high-profile premieres and VIP screening at their El Capitan Theatre on Hollywood Boulevard. Behind the venerable showplace was an alleyway that the Disney artisans decorated in the style of the film being premiered and guests gathered there to party following the screening.
‡ The Disney Treasures series consisted of thirty-seven two-disc DVD sets in prestige cases of classic Disney films and television shows curated by Maltin. The series was issued in several waves between 2000 and 2009 when Cook left Disney.
§ Jeff Kurtti is a prolific producer, author, and consultant who has produced innumerable special features for home video and other productions, often with his business partner Michael Pellerin.

Segaloff: For things like *Davy Crockett* and *Behind the Scenes at the Walt Disney Studios* and all of these wonderful compendiums, you were the man.

Maltin: Yes. Subject to approval, of course. They liked everything that I proposed. When things went south with Kurtti-Pellerin, I went to work with Sparkhill Entertainment. That was Eric Young, another experienced video producer, and we also made a good team. Now, everybody in the home video department knew that I had pitched this to Dick Cook, their boss, so there was no deception going on. I learned early on not to bother him with trivia. He was not a micromanager. That was not his M.O. as a boss, but when I needed him, I could call on him. I decided on year-one to start with Mickey Mouse in color and not Mickey in black and white because I thought that would be the wiser way to go both for sales value and entertainment value, and frankly, to dodge censorship issues that would inevitably arise from the earlier black and whites. That was my call. I made another judgment call that I regretted, which is that we showed "Three Little Pigs" on the *Silly Symphonies* disc and didn't show the original version with the wolf as a Jewish peddler (which later we did). The first four were very well received. The idea was they were going to number each of them and have Roy E. Disney sign a facsimile signature on what they called the belly band that surrounded the tin.

I learned pretty early on that, despite the enthusiasm of the boss, most of the people at the home video division didn't care about this series. They bought a three or four page insert in *People* magazine keyed to gift-giving for Christmas and didn't mention the four new releases that we were doing. That's how little they thought of them. By year five—I forget which year it was that we did *Silly Symphonies Volume 2*— they were getting sloppy and/or lazy in choosing which video master to use. They would pull video master D off the shelf when in fact video master A had the best resolution and color. I started getting heated emails and petitions because I was the face of the series. They hung me out to dry. This is still in the early days of internet communications. Even then, they were able to show that in an earlier release on a *Best of Donald* set sold at Walmart the color was better than the version we were selling on our collector's deluxe edition. Disney actually went back and reprinted the discs and made them available to angry customers who wanted satisfaction.

A year two later, I get a cryptic phone call from somebody who was passing along information in just a *pro forma* manner that, "We can't use the following eleven Mickey Mouse cartoons because there's offensive material in it." I said, "No, the whole idea of this series is that we're going to show them and explain them and put them in historical context. Also, we will separate them on the disc so that kids would have to make an effort to see them and wouldn't stumble onto them unawares." That's when I called Dick and said, "I thought the whole idea was—." He said, "Of course, that's the whole idea. I'll take care of it." He did. That subject never came up again.

I learned through our annual breakfasts with Dick that he was a Zorro fan. We had one of our periodic meetings with the Home Video people and Bob Chapek (when he was in charge of consumer products) about what to do next. I said, "I want to do the complete *Zorro*." And Bob said, "Oh, no. We haven't had any luck with television on the DVD. *The Golden Girls* was a big disappointment." I said, "This is not *The Golden Girls*. This is Walt Disney's *Zorro*." "No, the TV stuff doesn't sell." I called Dick and Dick said, "Oh, I think I can do something about that." Stan Deneroff, a very nice guy in the division, called me. He said, "What did you say to Dick Cook?" I said, "Why?" He said, "He says we're to do complete restoration of both seasons and all six of the hour-long shows." I said, "I just told him I want to do *Zorro*." That was all there was to it. The year that we did *Dr. Syn, Alias the Scarecrow*, that was them responding to a groundswell of interest from customers. It sold out in three weeks. I called the head of marketing and I said, "Are you going to reprint it? You can't buy it on Amazon now, except at speculator prices." He says, "No, we said it was a limited edition. That's fine." I said, "There are people making big money reselling copies. Shouldn't *you* be making the money?" He said, "No." Their indifference knew no bounds.

Segaloff: Did the series end when Dick Cook's employment did?

Maltin: Yes. We had the last hurrah. The day that Bob Iger fired Dick Cook was the day the series came to a close. Everybody associated with Dick Cook had a black mark on their backs.

Segaloff: Disney is what everybody grew up with. They have a near-paranoid philosophy about protecting their brand name and making sure that everything is the Disney way. As the years went on, since you are really as much of a Disney historian as Howard Green or Dave Smith,* has Disney changed?

---

* Howard Green is the beloved press contact for any reporter seeking

Maltin: In some ways, yes. They've spent serious money on restorations. They've backed projects like "Once Upon a Studio," a wonderful short. In other ways, they're not so very different from other studios, where it's all about the egos of the current regime. "How does this help me? How does this reflect well on me?" As long as Howard Green is still breathing, and their wonderful archivist Becky Cline, there is still hope. We had thirty-seven volumes of the *Walt Disney Treasures,* for crying out loud. I can't complain. I was well compensated and grateful for the opportunity and worked with great collaborators, too. My only regret is that they never made them available on iTunes. They never reissued them on Blu-Ray. They're still living in purgatory.

Segaloff: You must have had the chance to go through some original drawings, materials, sketches, Walt's stuff. It sounds so romantic, almost as if you were able to touch a piece of the true cross. What things were you able to get access to and what does that feel like?

Maltin: Mostly, it was the people that I got to. It was getting the people on camera because even though it's not that many years ago, a great many of them have died, not the least being Roy Edward Disney [son of Roy O. Disney, Walt's brother]. To have him reminisce about being a kid riding his bike on the studio lot when the military moved in in early 1942, that's precious. John Hench, who worked with Salvador Dalí on the unfinished *Destino* project. The longtime voices of Mickey and Minnie, Wayne Allwine and Russi Taylor, who, by a fantastic turn of events, were husband and wife. Wayne learned his craft from Jimmy MacDonald, who worked directly for Walt. Joe Grant, who had his finger in so many different pies over the years. Tommy Kirk, who died much too young, and who was so talented. Fess Parker, who gave us an unforgettable day up at his winery, could not have been more gracious. Those are memories that will never fade for me. I don't mean to sound Pollyanna-ish, but those were gifts to me.

Segaloff: You were literally meeting your childhood heroes.

Maltin: Yes, absolutely. At age four, I sang a stanza of "The Ballad of Davy Crockett" in nursery school, wearing my coonskin cap. Then there I am sitting with Fess Parker.

---

interviews or contacts. Dave Smith (1940-2019) established the Walt Disney Archives at the studio in 1970 and wrote numerous books and papers about the studio.

Segaloff: How many of the nine old men did you get to meet?[*]

Maltin: I got to know Frank Thomas and Ollie Johnston reasonably well, and also Ward Kimball. I heard Milt Kahl speak at the School of Visual Arts, but never really met him. Sorry to say, never met Eric Larson, John Lounsbery or Les Clark, but I came close. Then I was befriended by Diane Disney Miller, which was an incredible privilege. She opened up with me in ways I could not have predicted. She remembered weekends when the animators would come over to her family home and swim in the pool. That was before the strike and before all the bad blood came bubbling to the surface.[†] That's rather extraordinary. When I was very young, I had a book of *Grimm's Fairy Tales*. One of them ended with only a third of the page covered in print. There was a blank space at the end of that story. I took a crayon, and I drew a box, and I wrote in the box, "A Walt Disney production." I guess you could say I was brainwashed by then. It turns out that that book was illustrated by Gustaf Tenggren, a great European artist who went to work for Walt doing concept art.

Segaloff: At my newspaper, nobody wanted to do cartoons, so they made me review all the animated features, which was asking Br'er Rabbit if he'd like to visit the Briar Patch. Fortunately, dear Howard Green set me up either meeting or on the phone with not only Frank and Ollie. going out to the house, but with Eyvind Earle, Woolie Reitherman, Art Stevens, the same people you knew, these extraordinarily gifted artists.

Maltin: Here's the saga of the book. *The Disney Films*.[‡] When Walt Disney died on December 15, 1966, I was home sick from school. I heard the news on the radio. You remember radio? Though I was living in New Jersey, we had a copy of the Manhattan phone directory, white pages, which was a great resource. I looked up Walt Disney Productions, as the company was then called, on Madison Avenue. I made a cold call and was connected to Arlene Ludwig[§] who was then a

---

[*] Disney's primary animators were called "the nine old men" in reference to the U.S. Supreme Court of Franklin D. Roosevelt who were called the same.

[†] A bitter 1941 strike and lockout between many of Disney's animators and Disney over wages, credit, and rumors of Communist infiltration. It divided the studio and continued to infect relationships for the rest of the participants' lives.

[‡] Originally published by Crown Books (New York) in 1973, it covers every feature film released by the Disney studios. There have been several updated editions.

[§] Arlene Ludwig, daughter of Irving Ludwig who created the Buena

junior publicist. I didn't know any of this then. I said, "Hi, my name is Leonard Maltin. I publish a magazine called *Film Fan Monthly*. I want to devote an entire issue to the work of Walt Disney." She said, "What do you need? How can I help you?" I said, "Well, I have the research already done pretty well, but I could use some stills." She said, "Tell me what you need." I prepared a list. She sent them to me in a matter of days. Then when the issue was complete, I sent her four or five copies. She called me and she said, "We don't have anything like this. We don't have a chronological list of our films. This is amazing. How can I get more copies?" I said, "How many do you need?" I sent her whatever she requested. That was in 1967. A couple of years later, I made my first trip to Los Angeles for Cinecon. I had stayed in touch with Arlene, I got on her press list. I went to screenings of Disney features. She said, "Let me set you up with Tom Jones," who was the head of publicity on the West Coast. He gave me an unforgettable day at Disney Studio in 1969. I got the nickel tour, and then he took me into the office of Ward Kimball. I had a tape recorder. I talked to him about his favorite sequences that he worked on in *Dumbo, Three Caballeros*, and all that. I got on a stage where they were shooting some Kurt Russell film. Norman Tokar was directing a bit player in a scene against a blue screen backdrop. Then they led me into a screening room, which I now know is on the third floor of the animation building, and they ran from me a nitrate Technicolor print of *The Reluctant Dragon*, which was otherwise unavailable. You couldn't see it anywhere for love or money. At the end of the day, I wound up back in Tom Jones' office. He said, "This issue you did is so great. Are you going to turn it into a book?" I said I hadn't thought about it. He said, "Well, I'm encouraging you to think about it. It seems like a natural."

A family friend knew somebody who knew somebody who knew an editor at Crown Publishers in New York before they were acquired by Random House. In fact, the man who, I think, founded the company, Nat Wartels, still signed the checks in a little scrawl. He always waited till the fourth or fifth of the month to squeeze every last drop of interest out of those royalties. We made a two-book deal for *The Great Movie Shorts* and *The Disney Films*. My first two hardcover books.

Vista Distribution Company that handled Disney films after Walt left RKO and UA, rose to run West Coast publicity for the studio. In 2011 she tripped and suffered a fall at the D'Cache restaurant and snapped her spinal cord. Mostly paralyzed and requiring around-the-clock care, in 2014 she was awarded damages in a contentious lawsuit against the restaurant.

When it came time to work on *The Disney Films*, I called Arlene. She said, "I'm going to set you up with a guy who runs our non-theatrical distribution outlet in Paramus, New Jersey." That was right next to Teaneck on a busy highway, Route 17. It was a stealth office; there was no signage anywhere. They didn't want anybody poking their heads in to see what Disney was doing in Paramus. It was mostly women sitting at rewinds inspecting the prints and doing stuff like that. The guy who ran the operation was very sweet. Every Friday, they called him in the afternoon to make sure he was still there and hadn't snuck home early.

Segaloff: That is so Disney.

Maltin: It's very Disney. Arlene said, "I'm going to set it up so that every Friday, you can go and borrow one print and return it on Monday, and then next Friday you can take another film home." I said, great. I was given access to the VIP library. They had a set of 16mm prints of films that were not available non-theatrically. Not *Fantasia*, notably, not *Snow White*, but almost everything else. For the next year, I watched every Walt Disney feature film in chronological order. When I was showing *Dumbo*, or I was showing *Three Caballeros* or *Ichabod and Mr. Toad*. I had a full house in my basement. By the time I got to *White Wilderness* and *Ten Who Dared*, it was just me.

Segaloff: You had your own 16mm projector at that point?

Maltin: Yes. The basement had a good throw. I had to borrow a CinemaScope lens from a collector friend to watch *Westward Ho the Wagons!* I don't remember if I had *Lady and the Tramp* or not, but there were a couple of 'Scope movies that I managed to show on a good white sheet. When I finished, after well over a year of screening—I realized the ladies at the rewinds found this very amusing—I realized that the credits that I could find in print form didn't match the credits on screen. They didn't put everybody's name in the printed official credits such as music editor Evelyn O. Kennedy. She's done dozens and dozens of films. I used a projector lens like a loupe and wrote down the credits. When that job was done, I checked in with Arlene and by that time they had hired Dave Smith. Roy O. Disney had hired Dave Smith to come on board because he had done a bibliography on Walt Disney as a grad student at UCLA in library science. I was told I had to talk to a man named Vince Jeffords at the studio in California. In the interim, between the time Tom Jones encouraged me to do this book and the doing of the book, they had made a deal with Harry Abrams, the art book publisher, to do the first-ever Disney coffee table book, which became *The Art of Walt Disney.*[*]

Mr. Jeffords was not happy about this kid from Teaneck, New Jersey doing something that he saw as competitive. I had an answer for him. I said, "Harry Abrams' book is going to be lavish and in color, right?" He said, "Yes." I said, "Well, my book is not for the same audience. My book is for film buffs. It's going to be in black and white. There will be no color illustrations. The illustrations are just there to support the text. I think they can coexist quite naturally." To his great credit, he heard me out. He never hung up on me. He never said, "That's it, conversation over." I had most of these conversations while my family was having dinner. I was on the phone. We had a kitchen phone that extended into the dining room. I'd be swaying back and forth, shifting my weight back and forth, foot to foot, trying to salvage my book here. I kept saying—I forget how we finally got around to this—that I wasn't asking for their *permission.* I was asking for their *blessing* to do the book. I did say to Mr. Jeffords at one point, "I don't need your permission to write whatever I want to write. It's been granted by the First Amendment." I never was a wise guy with him. I was always respectful. He appreciated that, but he was a businessman.

I also had done my homework to determine that movie stills were not separately copyrighted from the movies, that though Disney had a slug stock caption on every still they issued in the '30s saying "copyright Walt Disney Productions, blah, blah, blah." they never actually registered anything. That was my ammunition: in case of fire break glass. What we finally agreed to was that I would submit any biographical material I wrote about Walt Disney to Dave Smith for him to vet. In return, they granted me permission. I think that's how they saw it all along. That was our compromise. They never saw a nickel from that book. Nor did I have to alter what I was doing. Oh, that's right; I left one ingredient out. I was refused access to the archives.

Segaloff: How odd.

Maltin: I had to do it on my own which, as it turns out, was not an impossible feat. All of Walt's films were well documented, even then. Not as well documented as they are today, fifty years later, with so much more deep research

[*] *The Art of Walt Disney* by Christopher Finch is a landmark volume published in 1973 by Harry N. Abrams. There have been several subsequent editions.

having been done. Because I was working for the Directors Guild magazine, I got their annual membership directory and wrote to people like Ken Annakin and Byron Haskin and all the freelancers who did the live-action stuff for Walt and got wonderful responses. Just great responses. That gave me wonderful resource material in a couple of the live-action films. The book turned out pretty well.

When it came out, it came out almost the same time as the Abrams book. *Time Magazine* did a four-page spread on the Abrams book saying it's the only book of its kind except for Richard Schickel's *The Disney Version*. I had several friends of mine with impressive letterheads write to *Time Magazine* saying, yes, but you're leaving out this other book that just came out. They said, "Well, we meant the only major book." Then two weeks later, they did it again. They plugged the Abrams book and ignored mine. In spite of that, my book sold pretty well and stayed in print for a long time. Then I got to do three revised editions. Irony of irony, the last edition, which I think was the fourth, was published by Disney. It was when Michael Eisner was running the company. I heard this third-hand. He said, "Don't worry about it. Let him write whatever he wants." I was able to even be critical of some post-Walt work. More recently, when the Taschen book called *The Walt Disney Archives* came out, I was assigned to write the chapter on *Song of the South* and *So Dear to My Heart*. Again, I think I passed muster because of my previous work.

Segaloff: *Song of the South* is considered Disney's land mine.

Maltin: I grew up loving the film and loving the score. I've never changed my mind about that film. They had me host a screening at the studio fifteen years ago when they were pondering doing some more merchandise with Br'er Fox and Br'er Rabbit. Uncle Remus is the hero of that movie and that story. He's the smartest guy, the smartest grown-up, in the film. The white adults, the Caucasian adults, are all dunderheads. When Bobby Driscoll is in the grip of a fever, only Uncle Remus can save him. There's a close-up of his hand in Uncle Remus' hand. A black and white hand clasping together in 1946! Unheard of. Unprecedented. I think the film gets a bum rap.

Segaloff: Agreed.

Alice and Leonard strike a pose in movie-rich Monument Valley, Arizona in 1983 but the Western garb didn't fool anybody.

Alice and Leonard with Patrick O'Connor, the New American Library editor who changed Leonard's life by offering him a job creating a movie guide. Decades later Patrick and his life partner moved to Southern California and a friendship was rekindled.

At Leonard's high school's twentieth anniversary reunion, he and Alice posed with his close friend Louis Black and the gifted singer-songwriter Phoebe Snow, whom they knew as Phoebe Laub when they were growing up together.

When Leonard and Alice moved to Toluca Lake in the San Fernando Valley, they told friends back home that they were "Bob Hope adjacent." Bob and Delores were the village's most prominent residents and rode in the town's 75th anniversary parade in 1999.

Jessie was five years old when she first saw the MGM musical *Good News*, which she thoroughly enjoyed, so when there was a chance to introduce her to its star, June Allyson, Leonard jumped at the chance. Says Leonard, "I love this picture."

Two of Leonard's heroes: film historians Kevin Brownlow and William K. Everson at the Telluride Film Festival in 1981.

Leonard with director-writer Sam Fuller at Telluride.

Leonard with directors Joe Dante and Allan Arkush
at the Telluride festival.

Another golden moment at Telluride with
director Don Siegel and festival co-director William K. Everson.

Leonard with Clayton "Lone Ranger" Moore,
whom he interviewed in 1989 on *Entertainment Tonight*.

This shot was taken on the patio behind Clint Eastwood's
Malpaso Productions offices on the Warner Bros. lot.
They were both a lot younger then.

George Lucas looks cool and relaxed. Leonard is putting on his
game face to experience the Indiana Jones ride with him at
Disneyland—he, who cringes at the very thought of a
"thrill ride."

Leonard engineered the first-ever reunion of Robby the Robot, from the classic science fiction film *Forbidden Planet*, and the man who provided his thunderous voice, Marvin Miller, in 1983.

Leonard says, "I got a lot of reaction from viewers who couldn't believe I was interviewing the actress who played Esmeralda opposite Lon Chaney in *The Hunchback of Notre Dame*. It was 1988 and the film was shot on this particular outdoor set on the Universal back lot in 1923."

Leonard says, "When I was four years old, I simply loved Pinky Lee. Decades later he reminded me why."

What's the point of being able to interview Martin Scorsese if one can't get him to autograph his latest book while he was promoting *Kundun*?

Leonard says: "I never dreamed I would take a picture with two comedy giants like Sid Caesar and Carl Reiner" This was on New Year's Eve 1999 at the Playboy mansion.

When shown this picture, Sophia Loren said they looked like newlyweds. "Who is to argue?" asked Leonard.

Leonard never got to host *Entertainment Tonight*, although he came close one morning when Mary and John Tesh and even their subs were ill. Mary posed with him to prove that he could have done it, sort-of.

Eleanor Keaton, Buster's widow, irons his iconic porkpie hat.

NEW YORK TIMES BESTSELLER

LEONARD MALTIN'S

2015

MOVIE GUIDE

THE MODERN ERA

NEARLY 16,000 ENTRIES,
INCLUDING 300+ NEW ENTRIES
AND MORE THAN 13,000
DVD LISTINGS

Leonard Maltin's 2015 *Movie Guide: The Modern Era* was the swan song of the *Movie Guide* that he began publishing in 1969. Updating it nearly every year was a major endeavor.

"Another rare instance of having my camera handy at just the right moment," says Leonard." James Earl Jones, Sidney Poitier, and director Robert Wise at a function he attended in 1998.

Behind the scenes on the interviews that George Lucas and Leonard did for the home video release of his *Star Wars* trilogy. Says Leonard: "I am still getting recognized for this by fans who collected them."

June Haver and Leonard standing in front of an advert
she did for Royal Crown Cola.

"It's easy to pretend you're a celebrity photographer when
you're in a room with celebrities," says Leonard. Lauren Bacall
and Roddy McDowall, two of the great stars from Hollywood's
greatest era, in 1989.

Trying to help the irrepressible Charles "Buddy" Rogers in an impromptu bit of entertainment for the folks attending the Cinecon in 1990.

Leonard relaxing with Jerry Lewis—if anybody could zver relax with Jerry Lewis.

Alice and Leonard with Chuck and Betty Fanning McCann at a 1999 New Year's Eve party at the Playboy mansion.

Leonard with actress Gloria Stuart, who had begun her career in Universal horror films of the 1930s and capped it off by coming out of retirement to play "old Rose" in James Cameron's *Titanic* in 1997.

Leonard with Milton Berle at TV station KCET. Uncle Miltie, known as "Mr. Television," in the 1950s, was always "on."

Relaxing with bandleader, voice actor, and personality Phil Harris at Disneyland while the *Entertainment Tonight* crew was setting up for their interview.

Leonard with actors Richard Crenna and Janet Waldo at the
Museum of Television and Radio (now the Paley Center)
in Beverly Hills.

Louis Black, Kurt Russell, and Leonard.
Kurt was looking a little stiff that day.

Leonard with the incomparable Katharine Hepburn in 1988.

One of Leonard's better snapshots: Roddy McDowall and
Maureen O'Hara on the *Only the Lonely* press junket (1991).

Leonard says: "I scored again by having my camera ready at a reception preceding the Golden Boot Awards in 1998." That's Roy Rogers and his wife Dale Evans, if I have to explain."

Leonard's first venture into publishing was *Profile* magazine, long before he became involved with *Film Fan Weekly*.

Leonard finally got to meet one of his comedy heroes, Albert Brooks, when he appeared on *Hot Ticket*.

Here is the great filmmaker and film scholar Bertrand Tavernier presenting Leonard with his Telluride Silver Medallion onstage at the Telluride Opera House in 2007. Says Leonard, "I couldn't have asked for a more meaningful individual to hand me that prize."

Every now and then the phone rings with an offer Leonard can't refuse, like interviewing Budd Schulberg on stage in Los Angeles.

"The lunch of a lifetime," says Leonard, "courtesy of my pal Howard Green": Buddy Hackett, George Segal, Richard Benjamin, Jan Murray, and Louis Nye dining on fried chicken at Dinah's in Glendale, California.

Leonard participated in the popular *Los Angeles Times* Festival of Books for many years and happily accepted such assignments as interviewing Ellen Burstyn, who had just published her autobiography.

ReelzChannel started booking guests for interview segments on *Secret's Out.* Leonard especially enjoyed talking to character actors like J. K. Simmons some years before he won his Oscar.

In 2007 Leonard was given a luncheon tribute by the Pacific Pioneer Broadcasters, which meant he had achieved seniority in Hollywood. "I was touched that people I so admired came to speak on my behalf," he says. Pictured: June Foray, Margaret O'Brien, Norman Corwin, Bea Wain, A.C. Lyles, Art Gilmore, Darryl Hickman, Stan Freberg, and local radio personality Chuck Southcott.

Says Leonard: "My friend Jeanine Basinger (R) doesn't visit L.A. often, so Alice and I arranged for us to have lunch with one of her longtime favorites, June Haver. I wish I had a tape recording of the conversation that day."

One year the Publicists Guild invited a handful of MGM contract stars to its annual luncheon, and Leonard got to spend time chatting with Gloria DeHaven, Howard Keel, and Kathryn Grayson. "What a treat."

"When I was growing up, staying up late to watch Steve Allen's show whenever I could and committing Stan Freberg's record albums to memory, I never could have envisioned I would be with them both one day." The occasion was June Foray getting a star on the Hollywood Walk of Fame in 2000.

Leonard's interviews with Bob Hope inevitably took place in the back yard of Hope's Toluca Lake home.

Says Leonard: "This was the first time I met Walt Disney's daughter Diane. She kindly signed me the paperback she supposedly wrote about her father that was actually ghosted by celebrity journalist Pete Martin—as she readily confessed."

Leonard didn't attend the 2006 Oscar ceremony, but he got to greet people as they left the Shrine Auditorium, like celebrated writer-producer Ernest Lehman. Could he look any happier?

"I came home from school every day when I was little and faithfully tuned in *The Mickey Mouse Club*. What were the odds that I would meet a handful of them years later on Stage One at the Disney studio, where they hung the curtain that was their backdrop? As icing on the cake, they made me an honorary Mouseketeer." Pictured L-R: Cubby O'Brien, Sharon Baird, Lonnie Burr, Leonard, Doreen Tracy, Karen Pendleton, and Bobby Burgess.

When Leonard found an original 78rpm album of Norman Corwin's masterful World War II broadcast, "On a Note of Triumph," he says, "I asked him to pose for this picture. He was one of a kind, and I'm grateful to have earned his friendship."

Peter O'Toole won everyone over during his trip to the Telluride Film Festival in 2002. He also astonished all of us by trying out Bill Pence's bicycle. Explains Leonard, "In those pre-cell phone days, I was the only one who had a camera ready to take this snapshot to prove it happened."

Holocaust survivor Renee Firestone was happy to meet Leonard's USC students, and they were eager to have contact with her, when she came to class with James Moll's heart-rending documentary *The Last Days*.

Says Leonard, "Jessie has grown up at Telluride, and Alice and I have decades of wonderful memories to sustain us. Here we are posing for a family photo in the heart of town."

Two animation titans, Chuck Jones and Ward Kimball, catch the spotlight at the Telluride Film Festival's Opera House in 2004.

THE PUBLICITY CIRCUIT

Maltin is a holdover from the days when book publishers sent authors on publicity tour to draw attention and generate sales. Having started writing so young, there was a curiosity factor as well as his achievements that made him a prime talk show guest.

Maltin: In 1971, I got booked on the *Mike Douglas Show,** which was a great booking, of course. It was a national show, very popular. I have a picture of me. I was on it twice within a year or so. One time I was on, the guest host that week was James Coco. The guests that day included Otto Preminger and Moms Mabley.† I sat in the dressing room, a big green room, and got to see Moms Mabley take her teeth *out* in order to go on stage. I was plugging *The Great Movie Shorts* and she said, "I always did like a man in shorts." The other time I was on it was with singer Johnny Paycheck, and Ben Vereen was the co-host. I have a picture of me and Ben Vereen, who is still above ground. I discovered that people I met, by and large, were more impressed that I was on the *Mike Douglas Show* than with the fact that I'd written a book that got me on the *Mike Douglas Show*. This is fifty years ago.

Segaloff: He was huge. You had to go to Philadelphia for the taping.

Maltin: Oh, yes. Took the Metroliner out of Penn Station in New York.

Segaloff: Was he a nice guy or was he painted as a nice guy by a strong staff?

Maltin: No, no, no, he really was a nice guy. Totally off-topic: I later ended up working more or less with his two producers. The two lead producers were Vince Calandra and Erni Di Massa.‡ Erni is still plugging away.

Segaloff: Unlike movie stars, who had publicists accompany them, authors were usually sent on the road on their own. What kind of adventures did you have?

---

* A weekday syndicated talk show starring the uncontroversial Mike Douglas (not actor Michael Douglas) who, each week had a celebrity co-host. Produced by Group W (Westinghouse) for their own TV stations and syndicated nationally.

† Loretta Mary Aiken's stage name was Jackie "Moms" Mabley (1897-1975), a beloved, raspy voiced actress-comedienne who told naughty jokes.

‡ E. V. DiMassa, producer-writer.

Maltin: I was promoting *Movie Comedy Teams*. There was going to be no promotion for *Movie Comedy Teams*. It was a paperback original and they had no plans to do anything. I had to explain to people that I lived in New York City and the expense would've been a subway token and another token for the return trip. Then three weeks before its pub date, it got a really strong review in *Publishers Weekly*. Suddenly, the publisher got interested. It required an outside source that they respected to give it that review, and then suddenly they got busy and, among other things, got me the *Mike Douglas Show*. Well, I realized I had to prepare a clip reel and that, if I didn't do that, doors would be closed to me that would otherwise open. I had my first experience, I don't remember who I called on for this favor, but I found a friend who was able to transfer some 16mm public domain footage onto a three-quarter inch video cassette. It had Ted Healy and the Three Stooges from *Hollywood on Parade*, a public domain short. Abbott and Costello doing, "Who's on First" from *Command Performance*.* Mike ran a bunch of those clips but somebody screwed up and didn't take the volume directly from the cassette. Somehow they thought we were going to get it from the audience mics.

Segaloff: To get their reaction laughing.

Maltin: Yes, but the main mic was off. It was funny because people were ready to laugh at Abbott and Costello doing that routine, and they could faintly understand what was being said, but not really. It sounded distorted. It taught me a lot about television that day. They said, "Can you send the clips?" I said, "No, I'd really rather bring them." They said, "If you want to bring them, you have to come earlier." They had me show up at KYW at noon. I took a 10:15 train from Penn Station and got to TV station at noon. I sat there for four hours, having brought a book to read because even at this early date, I'd learned Einstein was right: time is relative. Finally, somebody came in and asked me for the clips, and we did the show.

When Alice and I moved out here, CNN, Ted Turner's Cable News Network, was fairly new then, early '80s, '82. I started commuting here in the summer of '82. CNN had just hired Mike Douglas to host a nightly one-hour showbiz show, which they used the backdrop that the L.A. nighttime studio backdrop. What were Mike Douglas' chief assets? Affable,

---

* Filmed programming produced expressly to be sent overseas to America's fighting forces.

likable guy. Worked well with an audience of his target demo, middle-aged women. And had a pleasant singing voice. Now they took away the audience. They took away the ability to sing, and they had him interviewing people, and this was not his strong suit. It was dreadful show.

Segaloff: When you brought your three-quarter inch U-matic cassette into KYW, did you encounter any union situations?

Maltin: No, but in 1983 we visited Joe Dante on the set of *The Twilight Zone*, on the Warner lot, and, oh it was funny. Anyway, we went to visit Joe and it was afternoon, and we told whoever we got to talk to on the perimeter of the set that we were here to just say a quick hi to Joe. He came over ten minutes later and apologized for keeping us waiting, and he said, "If I was back at Corman, I'd have half the movie done already, and today I'm on my second shot." At one point he told me he'd picked up a vase and right away somebody pounced on him: he couldn't touch a prop on the set.

Segaloff: Do you consider yourself to be in show business?

Maltin: I've always had an odd relationship with show business. As I said, my father subscribed to *Variety*. They gave me one of my first plugs when I was publishing my first fanzine, *Profile*. I used to go to New York for a day and have an agenda. When I look back at this now, it boggles my mind that I had the chutzpah that I apparently had. I would stop at *Variety*, and I got to know the managing editor, who was named Robert Landry, and one of his editors, Bob Frederick. I got into one of the dot-dot-dot columns. "Young 13-year-old Leonard Maltin, publishing fanzine… could use a good proofreader." It got a lot of attention for me, which was cool, but they made an error in writing it up. On my first ever piece of stationery, which had cost $4.95 mail order, X number of envelopes, X number of letters, and they were five by five and a half, I wrote politely back to him saying, "I so appreciate the plug, thank you very, very much, but you misspelled the name of so-and-so, so even experienced professionals can make mistakes." He sent it back to me, and he wrote on the bottom, "Nice riposte."

IT TAKES A VILLAGE
TO RESEARCH FILM

Maltin: *The Great Movie Shorts*, my first hardcover book for Crown, became a permanent remainder book. This was a gimmick. I haunted bookstores, I loved books, and there used to be a big business in remainder books, which is to say unsold books. Then, some bright person posited the theory that, "Well, if these books are selling now," because we've lowered the price, sometimes drastically lowered the price, what if we republished them or reprinted them on slightly cheaper paper, and kept them alive for a period of time? That's what happened to me on the two books I did for Crown. *The Great Movie Shorts*, which had a retail price of $9.95, which was pricey then, because it wasn't really a coffee table book. It sold a respectable number of copies. At the time, Crown owned an imprint called Bonanza Books, which was in the business of doing these lower-priced, so-called remainders, and that kept that book alive for a long time. Also, *The Disney Films*. When I interviewed the director Elliott Nugent in New York, where he lived, for *Film Fan Monthly*, I had purchased his autobiography called *Events Leading Up to the Comedy* at Marlboro Books, which was a New York-centric chain that specialized in remainder books. Remainder books also was where I had a lot of humor books, cartoon books, books by *New Yorker* cartoonists and the like. Anyway, I realized, to my great embarrassment, that he was either unaware, or too polite to say anything, that when he opened the hardcover book to sign it to me, in pencil it said 59¢.

I used to do all my research at the Lincoln Center branch of the New York Public Library, which is one of the great show business reference libraries in the world. The equivalent out here in Los Angeles is the Margaret Herrick Library of the Motion Picture Academy. I'd spend the day doing research, taking notes. If only I'd had a digital camera. Such things didn't exist, and they certainly wouldn't have allowed me to use it if I had it then. I'd get home to Teaneck, New Jersey, and think, "Oh, shoot, I forgot to look up ____." I'd be so frustrated that I determined then that I really wanted to have a comprehensive reference library of my own. There's nothing worse for a collector than having justification. That's it. You're sunk. "This isn't a good book, but it might be useful for blah, blah, blah." Same thing with films.

I bought runs of magazines. At one point while doing the *Guide*, I learned of the existence of a publication I had not known about, the British Film Institute's *Monthly Film Bulletin*, which solved an ongoing problem I had of getting accurate running times. They figured their running times from the footage count. Now I can look at the DVD or Blu-ray and there could be no question, but for a long time, before video, you could look up a brand new movie that just opened on a

Friday, and go to five sources, and get five different running times. I came to trust *Daily Variety* because I learned that Todd McCarthy, their chief reviewer for thirty years, used a stopwatch. The publicity department at Paramount may have been saying the movie was 96 minutes. He timed it at 94 minutes. I took his running time. Eventually, *Monthly Film Bulletin* became a great resource for older films. I bought a complete 1951 to whatever run. I subsequently donated them, because I didn't really need them anymore.

I found that, at every studio or distributor, there was one person who was nerd enough to soak up those details. They became my contacts, my sources. I called United Artists. I got through to a guy. I said, "What do you rely on for running times? Do you do footage counts? Does the projectionist tell you?" He said, "Gee, we use your book." It was a lovely compliment. Not useful, but lovely.

Joe Dante was the one who told me about a Philadelphia-based trade paper, *Independent Film Bulletin.* They printed on colored paper stock, almost newsprint-like stock of a back-of-the-book section of their magazine, which was just film reviews. They prided themselves that they reviewed everything, the synopsis, paragraph of opinion, and maybe sales pitch or whatever, and release date and running time. That included cartoons and shorts, and no one else pretended to do that. Others reviewed shorts, but not diligently. I had a chance to buy a run, and they're in loose leaf binders, because they came with three-hole punches. That was how they expected you to maintain them.

Somebody sent me a letter saying I had the wrong running time for *Wells Fargo* with Joel McCrea from 1937, and it was off by twenty minutes. What? Well, a one- or two-minute discrepancy. Didn't make sense. A twenty-minute, and my first go-to was the *Film Daily Yearbook,* a run of which I studiously, and diligently accumulated over many years' time, only because New York Public Library sold off some duplicates they had, and the Academy sold off some duplicates that they had. I have Sol Lesser's volume of 1936 or something embossed on the cover. That was the industry. Everybody turned to that book. It's an annual compendium of facts and figures, so I look it up in 1937, and its 110 minutes. Then I look it up in a TV directory, and it's eighty minutes. What happened to that twenty minutes? It's not a classic film. It's not a film by a director who the people care about, and then the light bulb went on. Paramount sold its backlog to MCA in 1958.* This is really deep in the weeds.

---

* MCA (Music Corporation of America) took over Universal Pictures

Segaloff: I know what you're saying. Go ahead.

Maltin: In 1957, Paramount tried to wring every last drop they could out of their library, and they reissued a number of films, theatrically, and trimmed them, so that they could do double bills, so I went to the *Independent Film Bulletin*, and got confirmation that in 1957, they put it back in theaters at eighty minutes.

Segaloff: What does that say about the existing versions that the audience could see?

Maltin: That they're missing twenty minutes. I love solving riddles like that, and very few other people do, or would, but I love doing it when there's an answer. I don't mind the hunt if there's a resolution. It's when you can't resolve it, that it gets —

Segaloff: You know what comes to my mind, is we're talking about running times, and that is somewhere in the bowels of the Motion Picture Association, must be paperwork on every single film, every trailer, every short.

Maltin: When my first hardcover book came out, which was *The Great Movie Shorts*, I really craved a review in *Variety*. They didn't review many books. It was not part of their beat, but I brought a copy and I left it with Robert Landry. I couldn't have crafted a worse review if I'd tried. Something to the effect of, "Well, I guess all it takes is a trip to Cinema-bilia* downtown" —which was a film bookstore—"to come up with something that passes as a film book these days." It was a harsh review. It's one of the lessons I learned early: be careful of what you wish for. The same thing happened with *People* magazine when my *Great Movie Comedians* book came out some years after that. I had a string I could pull, and at least got it to somebody there who would consider a review. In that review, they accused me of being an egghead. They accused me of being so scholarly that I drained the humor out of the subject. It's like the old saying, "By princes you're no prince, by eggheads you're no egghead." I'm about as middle-brow as you can get in terms of my taste, in terms of my style of writing. Be careful what you wish for.

---

in 1962. To bolster its library of intellectual properties, in 1958 it bought the pre-1950 Paramount library.
* A movie-intensive bookstore at 10 West 13th Street in Manhattan, next to the Waverly Theatre in Greenwich Village, New York. Opened in 1965 by Ernest D. Burns, it was an oasis for collectors, scholars, and fans. It closed in 2018.

Segaloff: If it mollifies you any, in the years since, the trades still don't review film books. That astonishes me because that's the place where they could be reviewed by the most knowledgeable people. But let's talk about getting bad reviews.

Maltin: Walter Kerr* told this story to my friend Herb Graff. He went to a dinner party, and one of the other guests was Laurence Olivier. When they were introduced, Olivier proceeded to quote from Kerr's unkind review of his performance twelve years earlier in some play. He had it committed to memory.

Segaloff: This doesn't surprise me. Joe Mankiewicz reportedly carried in his wallet the one negative review that *All About Eve* had received. It sounds to me like the story they use at the end of *Patton*, somebody whispering in your ear that all glory is fleeting.

Maltin: For instance, doing book tours, and being on all those morning shows and afternoon shows, and occasionally even a nighttime show, I once took a late afternoon train down to Baltimore so that I would be there overnight and ready to be on the 7.30am *Good Morning Baltimore*. I knew ahead of time that I was going to meet the other guests, Vincent Price and Gina Lollobrigida. I brought a nice portrait of Vincent Price from one of his Fox films from the '40s, which I knew he would appreciate, instead of an AIP photo of him as *Dr. Goldfoot*. He did appreciate it and wrote me a lovely inscription. I didn't have anything for Gina Lollobrigida that day, unfortunately. I had the experience of being on the air but not being in control of what was happening on the air. It gave me a heady taste of show business, at one level of show business.

Segaloff: That was your first on-air appearance?

Maltin: No, an early one. The first one was on *AM New York*, which preceded the creation of *Good Morning America*. The host was a really nice guy named John Bartholomew Tucker. This was for *Movie Comedy Teams* (1970). I'd given them cues of what clips to use in the WABC-TV library. I had to get there at 6:45 in the morning. Then and now, I'm not a morning person, but I did as told. I forget who the first guest was, but the big guest that day was going to be Bill Moyers. I met him

---

* Walter Kerr (1913-1996) Lead drama critic for the *New York Herald-Tribune*, and then *The New York Times*, who could close a show with a bad review. He also wrote film books such as *The Silent Clowns* (1975).

when he was shown as the green room. We chatted a little bit. It was a live show, and I could tell that John Bartholomew Tucker was lackadaisical that day, there was no urgency in him. I intuited what was going to happen. He was going to run long with the first part of the show. He knew he had Bill Moyers for the last segment of the show. Where do you squeeze? The middle. I was introduced, and he said, "Let's look at these film clips you brought." We cued up Abbott and Costello, we cued up the Marx Brothers, we cued up the Three Stooges. Then he said, "Gee Leonard, we're out of time, but it's so nice to get to talk about these wonderful comedians." I said, "If people want to learn more, they could read my book." He picked up on it instantly, held up the book, and said, "Right, Leonard's new book is called *Movie Comedy Teams.*" I got my plug, but only because I spoke up, I was assertive.

There was a host in Detroit who screwed me twice, two years running. I found that other people who went on with nonfiction books got to talk about the subject of their book. But when I went on certain shows like this one, they would come up with a movie-themed quiz or gimmicky segment as if I was just in the neighborhood and happened to drop by and wanted to participate in their little fun movie segment. They would never discuss that I was there to promote a book. I came to learn these things.

Segaloff: That's the quid pro quo of doing a booking.

Maltin: Well, yes. Fair is fair, after all, I'll give you my ten minutes of chatter about movie-going in general, or what next big Christmas movie is going to be, and you in return will mention that I have a new book on sale, and it's called whatever. They got me twice, and on the second time they did it as they were fading out. After that, when I would be in the wings or backstage at a show, and I had my book hermetically sealed and attached to my hand, they would say, "Oh, we have one out on the stage." I would say, "Ah, I just like having it with me." "Well, we took a slide already." "I just like having it with me."

Segaloff: You have to. You're out there naked, and they have the control. Have you ever caught grief from someone you wrote about?

Maltin: Writing *Of Mice and Magic.* Getting a book published, especially by an established publisher, is no small feat. Keeping it in print is something else again. But because *Of Mice and Magic: A History of American Animation* is adopted by teachers of animation history it sells just enough copies that Penguin maintains a stockpile, and I still get a modest royalty check every six months.

I knew I wanted to pen a history of animated cartoons early in my career but I was stopped in my tracks when I learned that Mike Barrier, the publisher of the erudite fanzine *Funny World*, had embarked on the same project. As much as I learned from Barrier's groundbreaking interviews with major figures like Bob Clampett, I also knew that Mike was not exactly a speed demon. After waiting several years I decided to take the bull by the horns and write my own book; if and when Mike published his was none of my business.

An imposing number of men (mostly men) were still alive, and in some cases active, in the world of animation. I spoke to pioneers like Walter Lantz. I met Al Eugster, whose first job was filling in the black ink on the body of Felix the Cat. I corresponded with Dick Huemer, who worked with Max and Dave Fleischer on their *Out of the Inkwell* cartoons. Some of these veterans lived in New York, but many of them had long since decamped for California. My long-distance phone bills mounted up, but I couldn't pass up the opportunity to talk to people like Chuck Jones, Friz Freleng, and less-celebrated artists like Harry Love.

When I worked for Viacom writing copy for their new Showtime venture I came upon a storeroom with file cabinets full of paperwork relating to Terrytoons, the New York-based studio that CBS had bought outright from Paul Terry in 1955. What's more, the studio's longtime executive William Weiss still worked in an office just around the corner from the files. I started talking to him and gained a great deal of knowledge, especially about the company's attempts to stay afloat and remain relevant in later years. I think he was pleased that anyone was interested in talking to him about his career.

The story of the business of animation is dotted with personality clashes, occasional lawsuits, and conflicting memories of what actually took place. I was determined to dodge those pitfalls and did, for the most part. But there were a few notable exceptions.

When I attended the World Animation festival in Zagreb, Yugoslavia in 1974, just before I started dating Alice, I met many interesting people, from John Hubley to Terry Gilliam. At a mid-week picnic some fellow Americans told me that as nice as it was to be sitting on a hillside in the outskirts of the city, eating pork from an open spit, the picnic in Annecy was even better. I said, "What and where is Annecy?" Animator Lee Mishkin said, "Have you seen *Claire's Knee*?" referring to a recent film by the great French auteur Eric Rohmer. I said,

"Are you kidding? I've seen it *twice*." "Well, it was filmed in Annecy." That's all I needed to hear to convince me that I had to attend the festival the following year.

In the interim, I met and married Alice, and she agreed that it would be fun to make the Annecy trip part of our honeymoon, following a week in London. Little did we know that our Annecy experience would be nightmarish in many ways, but one positive takeaway was meeting Jules Engel. He was Charming and elegant, and we were happy to have dinner with him when he passed through New York on his way home to California, where he taught a new generation of animators at Cal Arts, the Disney-funded university.

Jules told me how he created "The Dance of the Sugar Plum Fairies" for Walt Disney's *Fantasia* and I took him at his word. He described his fellow animators as plebians who had never even seen a ballet.

Then one day my phone rang and at the other end of the call was Art Babbitt. The Art Babbitt who helped revolutionize character animation at Disney's in the 1930s, who later had a major falling-out with Walt, and whose first wife was Marjorie Belcher, the dancer who would become famous as Marge Champion. Art Babbitt was renowned for his explosive temper and I'm sure if he could have wrung my neck via long distance, he would have done just that.

All I could do was to tell him the truth and apologize for my gaffe. It wasn't difficult to determine that he was correct in refuting Jules' version of history. Fortunately, the paperback edition of my book was due in a few months and I would be able to replace the offending paragraph. Whew!

Almost as bad was the fury that surged through the phone lines when I received a call from Bill Weiss, who was aghast at my harsh critique of Terrytoons. As someone who avoids confrontations whenever possible, I paced back and forth as I held the phone and tried to calm him down. I told him that it was my job to recount the history as it was, even if it wasn't always upbeat. Terrytoons were at the bottom of the barrel for most of the company's existence and there was no getting around it. He seemed less apoplectic at the end of our lengthy call.

Izzy Klein, who signed his work I. Klein, had given me many anecdotes and observations from his decades of work at the New York studios and his relatively brief sojourn to the Disney company in California. He was insulted that, while I quoted him extensively, I never said anything, positive or otherwise, about *his* work. I had to admit it was true, but I couldn't tell him it was because no one else ever mentioned him.

There were land mines in the history of Warner Bros. animation but I seemed to make it through intact. Friz Freleng's only complaint was that I compared one of his Bugs Bunny cartoons to a similar one directed by Tex Avery and he thought that was unfair. He was probably right.

In 1980, while I was doing some traveling for *Of Mice and Magic,* Elliot Wilhelm at the Detroit Institute of the Arts booked me for an evening. I had a program that I did. I brought seven or eight prints of milestone animation shorts. He called me a couple of weeks before and said, "I hate to do this, but there's a really popular noontime radio show here hosted by a guy named J. P. McCarthy, and he's on WJR, which has a 50,000-watt signal, and everybody listens to him. But you'd have to come in the night before to do this. It's going to drive people to your show Friday night at the institute." I said, "All right, I trust you. Fine." I fly to Detroit and Elliot's a great guy. People in Detroit used to kiss his feet thanking him because there were no art theaters in the city. He booked all the new Miramax products for his film series because otherwise, they would get no exposure, and the people of that area wouldn't get a chance to see a lot of great movies, foreign films, and American-made films.

Elliot and I go to the Fisher Building. It's an Art Deco masterpiece, an incredible-looking place. I take an elevator to a very high floor, and there's WJR. We go into a studio that obviously was built for an earlier form of radio with a live orchestra and an announcer. It's a very spacious studio, not a little closet like you have at most radio stations. They told Elliot and me where to sit. He had a number of guests booked that day for his ninety-minute show, and a big clock on the wall.

Just before noon, an announcer—they still had an announcer, an older guy—said, "Stay tuned now for JP McCarthy," blah, blah, blah. Well, JP comes in thirty seconds before air with his arm around Ron Powers,[*] a fiction writer of some success. He even worked for *E.T.* for a while doing editorials when they briefly thought that was a good idea. It was not. We other guests, we peons, were already seated, but he came in with someone he felt was on his level intellectually, socially, whatever it was. He gave us a passing wave. Ron Powers is a good guest, a pro at doing this thing, very interesting, and he ate up the first half hour.

Then he had a doctor, and as McCarthy is reading his written introduction, I see in his face that he realizes this guy

---

[*] Author and Chicago *Sun-Times* columnist, the first newspaper television writer to win a Pulitzer Prize.

really *is* interesting. This may be an obligatory interview he's about to do, but this guy's worth hearing out, so he gives him a good chunk of time. There were some other guests and then there was me. By the time he got to me, it was seven minutes to go on the show. He's a pro, and he says, "Tell me about this book, why should people be interested in the history of animated cartoons?" "Well, JP," I said, "blah, blah, blah." He adds a wrap-up statement and says, "That's what kids are still watching today, right, *Morton*?" Now I have a choice to make. I see the second hand going around and we have a minute and a half to go. I have to decide whether to take the time to correct him and say, "No, my name is Leonard" or to answer his question. I like to think that's the moment I became a professional because I didn't correct him. Then the minute the clock hit, he was gone with no need to say goodbye to the "unwashed" guests.

Segaloff: You were a pro, because if you say nothing you win and make him look silly, but if you correct him, then you look silly because it's his show. There's hardly any way to defeat a host on his own show, or a king in his own country. I'm sure it's a lesson that has stuck with you.

Maltin: Oh, yes. In another experience I had, I was represented by New Line Lecture Bureau. New Line Cinema was a scrappy little company that made its mark by distributing John Waters' *Pink Flamingos*.*

Segaloff: Back when Robert Shaye was still called Bob Shaye.

Maltin: Robert Shaye, indeed. Somehow or other, they realized that they had developed a network of connections and contacts at colleges all over the U.S. and that these colleges would eagerly book John Waters to come in person with *Pink Flamingos* because it had this notorious reputation. Audiences would walk out. People would be insulted. People would be horrified, but they'd already paid their admission. They started a lecture bureau to take advantage of this network of people who would book speakers. I became one of those speakers. I remember my initial fee, asking price, was $750 out of which I kept, I think, $450. I'm pretty sure I'm right on that. Alice and I were about to get married. We were about to get married when I got my first booking in Bloomfield, Indiana, speaking at Indiana University. It was a good gig.

---

* The 1972 breakthrough film from iconoclastic filmmaker John Waters, *Pink Flamingos*, starring Divine, is about the filthiest people in the world and ends with what can only be called a climactic movement.

This meant—and they apologized to me—there's only one connecting flight per day from Chicago to Bloomfield. You have to get on a really early flight at Newark, like at six in the morning. You have several hours to kill when you get there. It's worth it. It's a good booking. Okay, great. I'm thinking to myself, gee, if they only book me twice a month, that'll cover our rent. As a freelance writer, you're always thinking that way. Okay, so the day comes, and I carry my films with me. I go to Newark, and I get on the plane, which is going to fly to Chicago, where I have to switch to a puddle jumper. The distance from where I land in Chicago and the puddle jumper is at the farthest extremity of that airport. I was walking twenty-five minutes, and I walked fast in those days. I got to the plane just in time and it's a nice day, easy ride. After forty minutes or something, we land in Bloomfield. I get out. The airport is small; you can see from one end to the other. There's nobody there.

I go to the pay telephone, which tells you how old this story is, and I put in a quarter or whatever, and I dial. I have the letterhead of the confirmation of the booking, and I get a *boop* sound, "That number is not in service," or "You've dialed a number that doesn't exist." On the third try, I dialed a zero. In those days, you could get a human operator. I said, "Operator, I know I'm dialing the right number because I'm reading it right off their stationary." She said, "Who are you trying to call?" I said, "Indiana University's Student Affairs Office." She said, "Indiana? You're in Illinois." I was in Bloomfield, *Illinois*. I had done nothing wrong. It was an incorrect booking. Apparently, this was not the first time this had happened to a passenger. The nice people who ran the airport—who had little to do, by the way, because there weren't that many flights coming and going—showed me on a map that if I rented a car and I drove like crazy, it was a straight line to Indianapolis, and then due south, I would get to Bloomfield by the end of the afternoon. It meant driving for five and a half hours.

The only flight going back, reversing what I had done, would come in too late for me to do the gig that night. With a heavy sigh, I went to Hertz and I rented a car, and I drove it eighty-five, ninety miles an hour. I was driving mostly through cornfields or wheatfields or whatever they were, and there didn't seem to be any cops anywhere. Someone later said to me, "They use helicopters for tracking." I'm glad I didn't know that because I've never driven so fast before or since. The only thing that sort of buoyed my spirits was seeing a sign go by that said, Indianapolis, 110 miles, ding. Indianapolis, ninety-two miles, ding. I got there. I pulled in at 5.20 in the afternoon, and my gig was at 7.30 that night. I went on, it was well-received, and I got home safely. Then, Alice and I got married right around that moment in time because she had to coach me on how to convince New Line that I shouldn't have to pay for the rental car because they wanted me to pay half.

Segaloff: Had it been New Line's bad booking?

Maltin: Yes. A travel agent, whoever, somebody was responsible, and it wasn't me. They never did get to two bookings a month. It was nine months before I had another booking. I played Bluefield, West Virginia. I played Ames, Iowa. When the kids would pick me up from the airport, I'd say, "How did you happen to book me? I'm just curious." This was before my television fame. They'd say something like, "We had $1,000 left in the budget."

Segaloff: The places you were naming, did they check and see if you had horns?

Maltin: Oh, Kearney, Nebraska.

Segaloff: Yes, same question.

Maltin: No. Kearney, Nebraska, however, they were a little apologetic because they didn't realize when they did my booking that it was also the first night of the school production of *Kismet*. We had a very small turnout, and you could faintly hear the strains of *Kismet* down the hall. I had seven 400-foot reels, and they had a projectionist, so I did this impassioned introduction to maybe Disney's "The Band Concert," it was one of my standbys. The wrong film came on. They realized it and stopped. I'm sitting there in that auditorium, and I said to myself, I swear this is true, I said to myself, "Look, this is not your fault. You are doing what you're supposed to do. You're going to continue the show and see it through to the end and then get a good night's sleep, and you'll be on your way home tomorrow morning and get paid." That was the moment I became a professional in that arena. It was humbling, all of those experiences, those speaking gigs, really humbling. Ames, Iowa, which is Iowa University, they did a very professional film festival there and brought in people like Robert Altman and other A-listers. They decided to do an offshoot in the spring. I think the other one was in the fall. I was speaking in what was normally a ballroom that seated like a thousand and I had eleven people there. They said I had the best turnout all week. It was an animation festival. They brought in Ralph Bakshi. They brought in Frank (Thomas) and Ollie (Johnston). These are humbling experiences to keep you from getting too full of yourself. Would I have wanted these experiences? No.

Segaloff: Do you do your own bookings now? Your website has a click-through for bookings.

Maltin: I'm represented by American Program Bureau.

Segaloff: They're still around?

Maltin: Well, they haven't booked me in two years, so I don't know.

Segaloff: They started off in Boston. They handled everybody for a while.

Maltin: Oh, yes. I don't remember how I came to be with them.

Segaloff: Guy named Bob Manofsky used to run it I think and somebody else. This was before your time.

Maltin: Alice talked to somebody who talked to somebody who talked to somebody. I got some good bookings from them. There's a woman who does all their booking of air and hotel. She's worked for Delta Airlines. She's an old pro. I love working with people like that, who really know what they're doing. I value that more than ever.

WHERE THE MONEY IS

Segaloff: You seem to have done well, but it sounds more like it's from lecturing and from *Entertainment Tonight* than it is from book sales.

Maltin: Yes, for sure.

Segaloff: TV is still *The Glass Teat.**

Maltin: I learned that, but before I learned that I learned something else. A guy I knew who worked at Walter Reade-Sterling went to work for what we then called "Vee-a-com" (Viacom) in New York. He called me and said, "There's a guy I work with named Bill Aden, a really nice guy. He's got a freelance job that you might be good for," so I went to meet him. They were doing something to reissue or re-syndicate *Perry Mason*, and he wanted a background piece on Raymond Burr that they could print as a brochure. He offered me a nice fee. At that time, I worked a year and a half to two years on some of those books. I used to say I could have done better working at Arby's, and it wasn't an exaggeration. My advances were like $1,500, $2,000—pennies, given the time and effort. Some of them paid off. Some of them went on to considerable success and some did not. Ultimately, The *Movie Guide* became a profitable book. The *Our Gang* book, which Crown had no faith in, especially after Book Club turned it down and the Nostalgia Book Club turned it down. They just had to keep going back to press, and back to press, and back to press, and back to press, and wound up selling over 100,000 copies.

Segaloff: That's wonderful.

Maltin: All of that paled in comparison to what I could make dashing off copy for Viacom. I became one of their regular guys that they called on when they were doing a new package for syndication of films that they'd acquired. I would write the pitches or the descriptions. It was anonymous for me, and I could use clichés like "torn from today's headlines."

Segaloff: You wouldn't be held responsible for banality?

Maltin: No. In fact, they liked it. As some people do crossword puzzles, I wrote copy. I became a well-paid copywriter. It was the inverse of what I made as an author. That's what paid the rent.

---

* Alluding to the two books of essential TV criticism written by Harlan Ellison, *The Glass Teat* (1970) and *The Other Glass Teat* (1975).

Segaloff: Industrial work is not usually spoken of, but that's where the real money is.

Maltin: Oh, yes.

Segaloff: Especially if you don't want your name attached to it for various reasons.

Maltin: Yes. One day, Bill Aden says, "They're starting up a new service here called Showtime and a guy named Jeffrey Reiss is going to run it. I recommended you to him. Drop by his desk and make an appointment," so I did. I sat down with Jeff, and he described what Showtime was going to be. As I learned to say for the next four years, "It's like HBO" because that's what it was. I became the fifth employee of Showtime writing the viewer guide. This was in 1976. When he got done describing what he needed me to do, I said, "Here's my situation. I'm a freelancer, and I don't want to give up my other freelance jobs, but I can do this work for you, and it won't be a full-time job for me." He said, "Well, I don't know if that's going to—." I said, "Look, I will vouch to you that I will be available for a meeting anytime you call me, and I will come in on a regular basis if you want me to, but I'm not going to be here full-time." He said, "Let's give it six months, and at the end of six months—" or maybe I said that. One of us suggested that we do it on a trial basis. This is just before computers; word processing was starting to be a thing, but I was still using an IBM Selectric as most people were, and somebody said to me, "Don't ever show them anything with crossed-out lines. Only show them a clean copy. If they see lines crossed out or Xs, they think that gives them the freedom to make more corrections." It was sound advice. I worked for them for the next four years, and it was fun. It was fun writing that copy. I enjoyed writing the way some people relax by doing crossword puzzles or crostix or sudoku.

Segaloff: You still kept on that same freelance basis?

Maltin: Oh, yes.

Segaloff: For four years.

Maltin: I showed up one week a month. They gave me an office space which I shared with someone else, and I would show up for one week and seem to be working. I wasn't, but I seemed to be working. I went to see Sammy Cahn at the 92nd Street Y and he said that when he and Saul Chaplin were hired as the house songwriters at Vitaphone in Brooklyn, they would do all the songs for the new short subject on Monday morning and then go to the track. Sam Sacks was their boss, and they'd show Sam what they had done, and he'd say, "You guys have just tossed this off. No, this is not good work. This needs polishing. This needs revisions on it." They learned not to show anyone their work till Thursday. I functioned in much the same way and had fun and was in on the startup. We went to the ad agency that he hired to produce the viewer guide, and he was not happy with the photos that Fox had sent for *Young Frankenstein* or whatever film it was. He marched around the office of this ad agency looking for a secretary to dial the number so he could talk to someone at Fox in California.

Segaloff: His own finger wasn't good enough?

Maltin: No. By the way, they had to hire his wife as one of their graphic artists. So many things to learn. Anyway. His cousin Randy Reiss was the vice president of Paramount Television whom I wound up working for.

Segaloff: Nepotism never goes away.

Maltin: That was interesting being at the beginning of Showtime and seeing how that worked, how that functioned. One of the perils of being a freelance writer is you have to set your fee, and you never know what to ask. Is this too much? Is this too little? My mother had that all the time for club dates, so she never knew what to ask. Alice solved that ultimately for me. At the end of 1979, Sumner Redstone* said Showtime had grown faster than they anticipated. They were trying to keep up with whether we hire more people to handle this additional business or do we wait to see if the business is going to stay and work our people harder? He said, "Get rid of all part-timers and freelancers," so they very unceremoniously said goodbye to me at the end of 1979.

Five months later, the phone rings, and it's Jeffrey Reiss as if we had just finished talking a day before saying, "Leonard, we're about to go to the NAB [National Association of Broadcasters] convention and several of the studios

---

* Sumner Redstone (1923-2020) had a storied career. A theatre owner in New England, he leveraged his cash flow into becoming a major stockholder in Paramount, then got aboard Viacom and bought the studio. He kept adding to it and, by the time he died at age 97, was a huge force in all areas of media. His daughter, Shari Redstone [Korff], continues to manage her father's empire.

have joined forces, and they're going to start a rival pay cable network. I need you to write a treatise on why it's never a good idea to be in business with studios because they always screw their partners. Can you do this?" "Yes." "I need it pretty fast." "Okay." "What will it cost me?" and I said, "$5,000." "$5,000? Jeez, Leonard, you got me over a barrel here. I need to have this, but, geez, $5,000? Is that per week or is it for the piece, the finished piece?" I said, "Per week." I had left there very insulted. My ego was bruised that after four years of loyal service, no one really said goodbye or anything like that. He put the idea in my head when he said, "Per week?" I said, "Well, yes." It turned out they needed it Tuesday night, so it went into a second week legitimately, but then John Sie, who later became the head of Starz/Encore, called me after I turned in the piece and he said, "I need you to come in and do some stuff." He gave me busy work. Writing letters to the affiliates, things like that just to get things to work out my week's salary.

Segaloff: They're so petty.

Maltin: I have a flashback in my head right now. The first time I saw a fax machine was at Showtime, and it was like a wire-photo machine. It was so strange, and it smelled of sulfur.

Segaloff: That's because it was the devil's tool. We can go back and get nostalgic. I remember being in a newspaper, a real newspaper. It was a tabloid with the wirephotos coming in in a separate room and tearing off sandwiches of white and yellow rolled carbon paper from the AP and UPI machines. Every afternoon you'd feel the whole building shake when the presses started printing the 3 PM predate first edition. That's when I fell in love with newspapers. Now, of course, all you have is a computer showing you a little flag that you've got mail.

Maltin: When I went to work at *E,T.*, they still had teletype machines. Then you get a ding, ding, ding when there was some priority item coming in. Alice has a solution, by the way, about collecting the freelance fee. She says, "What's in your budget?" They say, "Well, we don't really have a budget, we don't know. Give us an idea of what you're going to charge." Alice: "$50,000." Them: "*$50,000!*" Alice: "Well, then you *do* have a budget. You have a price in mind. What is it?" That sometimes shakes the trees.

THE MOVIE-GOING EXPERIENCE

Segaloff: I want to talk in general about the moviegoing experience. Not just Leonard Maltin's, but going all the way back to Koster & Bial's Music Hall in 1896. It's a huge topic, but I know you lecture on this. What is the hypnotic nature of movies and what is the appeal? We're talking about everything from a train coming into the station to the Death Star blowing up.

Maltin: If I had to define it in a word, I think, ultimately, movies are about escape, and that's what movies offer people. That can be *Francis the Talking Mule,* or it can be *Goodfellas* or it can be *The Godfather* or it can be *Rules of the Game* or *Seven Samurai.* There are different kinds of escape, but I think, pretty much, it's taking you out of yourself and out of your preoccupation with your day-to-day activities and taking you on a journey of some sort.

Segaloff: Was it always like that? At the beginning there was Thomas Edison's "Cripple Creek Barroom" scene.

Maltin: I think so, yes. There was a novelty to it in the early days.

Segaloff: That's where I wanted to go, starting with the novelty.

Maltin: In the very early days, there was the sheer novelty of watching pictures move, but it didn't take long for that novelty to start to wear off and require the early producers and distributors to give people more than simply random movement or exotic sights. Thus, storytelling became part of the evolution of motion pictures and storytelling involves escape.

Segaloff: We need a Noam Chomsky of cinema to divine how the vocabulary of cinema developed. How did a "cut" work to change a shot or a scene without the audience having to see the curtain come down first?

Maltin: A friend of mine, Tracey Goessel, is working on something called The Biograph Project where she's restoring, from paper prints, new fully realized copies of the earliest D.W. Griffith films. You can track these things. She's shown us samples. You find that in 1908 they're doing things a certain way and by 1910 that's changed. When you see the use of cross-cutting in *Intolerance,* you understand that Griffith fully expected his audience to be engaged and to be attentive and to comprehend what he was doing.

Segaloff: It's fascinating when you see the language of a new medium developing in front of you. Whoever invented this or that is immaterial to the fact that audiences could adapt as it advanced. One tries to relate to a general audience of 1896 cringing when a train pulled into a station or 1896 or ducking under their seats in 1903 when a bandit shot his gun into the camera.*

Maltin: At the same time, when the Japanese video company NHK did their home video version of the Chaplin Library, some of the bonus features were quite good. One of them was done, I think, by the Dardenne Brothers who brought Chaplin to a tribe in Africa. They got it and they loved him. As who wouldn't? That's his rare understanding of human nature. If we all had that, we'd be sitting on top of the world. He had a keen appreciation for and a discerning eye for the human animal.

Segaloff: Since you're a historian as well as a fan, I wanted to point out something that struck me. In the 1940s, before the Consent Decree,† there were 15,000 *theaters* in America. By the 2008 recession, there were 23,000 *screens* in America. The difference, semantically as well as commercially, between having 15,000 theaters and 23,000 screens pretty much describes what's happened to movies over the last sixty years. Theatres are now "chair factories" and showmanship is out the door. I'd like to start talking about showmanship and about what you remember as a kid and how things have changed.

Maltin: I never saw much first-hand evidence of showmanship in my early years as a moviegoer in North Jersey. The Linwood Theater in Fort Lee still showed serials and a series of shorts—I've yet to learn the name of this series, but it was a series of comedy races made in 1930s with old-time silent movie comics, second-tier people like Billy Bevan, Snub Pollard, people like that. They each have a big number on their outfit, whatever outfit they're wearing in that week's film. As you come into the movie theater, you're given a ticket with corresponding numbers. If your guy wins, you get a prize. It turns out that these films were made by Andrew Stone at some point in the 1930s. The same fellow who did *The Last*

---

* "The Arrival of a Train at La Ciotat" (Lumiere, January 25, 1896) and "The Great Train Robbery" (Porter, December 7, 1903).

† *US v. Paramount et al, 1948* was a court agreement that forced the vertically integrated studios to divest their theater chains and exist solely by producing and distributing films. It opened the industry to independent companies but broke apart the major studio monopolies.

Voyage and *The Song of Norway*. My friend Herb Graff had a print of several of them spliced together, but I don't think they had a main title.

Segaloff: I remember race*horse* films, 8mm reels that you could buy for home use. They were un-labeled so you never knew when you threaded them up which horse would win. You'd take bets and send your party guests home broke.

Maltin: I remember seeing them in a catalog.

Segaloff: Of course, the person people think of in our generation as being a showman was William Castle.*

Maltin: Well, okay, now you have it. I saw *13 Ghosts* (1960) twice. I was so taken with it. I still have my original Ghost Viewer/Ghost Remover.† I used to do a pretty fair imitation of William Castle's spiel at the beginning of the movie: "If a friend comes in after the movie has started, show them how to use it." I didn't see it again for decades, then they showed it at the Nuart one night with Terry Castle (William Castle's daughter) there. What a clunker of a movie. It's indefensible, it's so bad. At age 12 or 13, I thought that was just the coolest thing in the world.

Segaloff: It's like the prize in the popcorn in the Cracker Jack box. Kids want to come, whether it's *The Tingler* or *Mr. Sardonicus*, which was also a fraud.

Maltin: I saw *The Tingler*‡ in the theater without the gimmick. *Lack* of showmanship!

---

* Producer-director Willian Castle sold his films with gimmicks that attracted young viewers: "a nurse will be standing by," insurance policies in case you died of fright, etc. For *House on Haunted Hill*, he devised Emergo (a skeleton that flew across the theatre); for *The Tingler*, there were vibrating seats. For *Mr., Sardonicus*, Castle stepped onto the screen near the end for a show of hands to let the audience decide the villain's fate, and the projectionist would switch to the appropriate reel (but never did). Castle eventually acquired the rights to *Rosemary's Baby* (1968) but Paramount refused to let him direct it, preferring Roman Polanski.

† It was a cardboard viewer with blue and red cellophane windows. Colored ghost sequences were spliced into the black and white prints. To see the ghosts, which were white on blue-tinted film, you'd look through the red cellophane that turned the blue into purple and made the white stand out. To not see the ghosts, you'd look through the blue cellophane that turned everything blue and rendered the ghosts invisible. No kid worth his salted popcorn ever used the blue, except to test if it worked.

‡ *The Tingler* (1959) was a centipede-like parasite that fed on fear

Segaloff: I've never spoken to anybody who was actually in a showing that had the vibrating seats.

Maltin: Or Emergo.

Segaloff: Emergo!

Maltin: *House on Haunted Hill.* I never got to do that. I never saw 3D during its brief heyday in 1953; I was too young. I never saw Cinerama; again, I wasn't old enough. In the '90s, a guy who has become a friend, Larry Smith, and his wife Jenny (both of them have just retired from the Library of Congress motion picture unit in Culpeper, Virginia,)* ran the new Neon Theater in Dayton, Ohio, and decided he was going to bring back Cinerama. There was a fellow who lived in Dayton named John Harvey who outfitted his house, his home, to show Cinerama films.† He broke a wall to do it. He was no longer married; go figure. He put a volunteer corps together to construct a special screen. I didn't realize that the Cinerama screen is like a Venetian blind.

Segaloff: They're lenticular, yes.

Maltin: With tiny holes. The new Neon was an intimate theater, 225 seats, a little jewel box of a theater. Joe Dante emailed me and said, "I just went to Dayton. You've got to go. Don't miss this." I said, "Okay, I won't." I went a week or two later, and they arranged the weekend that I went they showed prints of the four Cinerama films they had. They invited, from *Cinerama Holiday* (1955), the American couple and the European couple who were experiencing new things

---

and attached itself to the victim's spine. It could only be dislodged by screaming. Some (very few) theaters spaced vibrating seats throughout the auditorium to jolt random audience members into screaming at the right moment. The rumor was that these devices gave electric shocks. (This was satirized in Joe Dante's 1993 movie *Matinee*.)

* Fearful that a nuclear war would destroy America's cultural heritage, in 1969 philanthropist David Packard funded a preservation and restoration facility for the Library of Congress in Culpeper, Virginia. It has ninety miles of shelves and thirty-five climate-controlled rooms.

† Developed by Fred Waller, Lowell Thomas, Merian C. Cooper, Hazard "Buzz" Reeves, and Mike Todd, Cinerama involved three projectors and a separate seven-channel sound system synchronized to throw a 146-degree image onto a curved screen. Premiering in 1952, it was an all-encompassing but cumbersome process that eventually gave way to easier (but less impressive) 70mm systems.

in each other's homelands. It was a good print, but just a faint pink.* I think that's the one that has the toboggan ride.

Segaloff: It is. I saw it in Cinerama at the Warner Theater in Washington, D.C. I'm just a little older than you are. It was amazing.

Maltin: The toboggan ride is amazing. It was the sound as much as the image. The sound was so incredibly real; it blew me away. Then the overture to *How the West Was Won* (1962) by Alfred Newman—I thought the orchestra was sitting in front of me playing because it was a very small space.

Segaloff: The Cinerama sound system was the best there was.

Maltin: It was magnetic.

Segaloff: Absolutely. On a separate roll.

Maltin: Right. Normally, Larry explained, you need eight to ten people to properly present and project a Cinerama feature. They did it with two people: Larry and this guy, John Harvey. They did a great job.

Segaloff: Did you ever have anything to do with Dave Strohmaier?

Maltin: I know Dave.

Segaloff: Oh, he's the God of Cinerama now. That was show-manship.

Maltin: Chapin Cutler. Do you know Chapin?

Segaloff: Yes, all the way back to Boston Light and Sound.

Maltin: We interviewed him on our podcast this past week. He and I did several shows together at Telluride. One of them was a Cinerama show. They built—they jury-rigged—one of the auditoriums to actually be able to show Cinerama. The highlight of the show was the breakdown reel with Lowell Thomas. There's a fifteen-minute reel in black and white. It said, "In case of emergency, click this 'on' switch and I will come." It features the famous newsman and world traveler

---

* Eastman Kodak uses a dye-coupling photochemical process that fades over time until the prints look pink by the absence of the blue layer of dye.

Lowell Thomas, who was a Cinerama investor, saying, "Mr. Projectionist tells me that you're having little trouble right now. I'll just talk for a bit and fill up the time. I hope you'll excuse me if I wander around several topics. Cinerama has been in development for fifteen years now, and it was originally used for military purposes," blah, blah, blah. Then after a while, he'd say, "How's it looking up there? Can we go back to our feature?" He'd pause for a bit. "Not yet? All right." He'd talk again for five minutes and then say, "Mr. Projectionist, are we ready to go back to our feature film?" What a great fallback film to be able to show—but most people never saw it.

Segaloff: Cinerama was a great process but thoroughly unwieldy for intimate storytelling.

Maltin: I also remember standing under the marquee outside of the theater. I used to examine the stills and lobby cards on my way in and again on my way out. That's how I came to understand that sometimes there were scenes that were cut from the movie but still appeared in some of the promo materials. I remember going to see *How the West Was Won* at the Teaneck Theater in its "flat"* version and I was hypnotized by those join lines which now digitally they're able to remove in SmileVision.†

Segaloff: Showmanship costs money, but it yielded something. I don't think anybody really ever developed a formula. No one knows what good publicity does, except you spend money and you hope you get it back at the other end. Showmanship took initiative and it took extra people, and that, I think, may have had something to do with its downfall. Do you remember ballyhoo?‡

Maltin: Not firsthand. I remember reading about ballyhoo. I remember those punch cards for the Western serial. That was close. I don't remember anything more elaborate.

---

* After the first-run engagements ended of the three-strip Cinerama films *How the West Was Won* and *The Wonderful World of the Brothers Grimm* (1962), they were optically printed onto a single anamorphic image and run in standard theatres, but the blurry joining lines and wide-angle lens distortion were still visible.

† New Blu-ray and DVD transfers use computers to almost completely remove the blurry joints and introduce a "SmileBox" aspect ratio that suggests the effect of watching Cinerama in a theater. The restorations are remarkable.

‡ Ballyhoo is a circus term for outlandish stunts that draw public and press attention.

Segaloff: You wouldn't have been around for Dish Night or anything like that?*

Maltin: No, no. I've gotten friendly with a woman named Kathy Fuller Seeley. Do you know her? She's at University of Texas, Austin. She's also a published Jack Benny aficionado. She's working on the films of Francis Ford now. Very interesting woman. She did a lecture on Dish Night and contacted the company that manufactured some of those dishes. It was fascinating.

Segaloff: It's a great idea. Just like going to the gas station and if you filled your tank, you got a set of glassware.†

Maltin: When Alice and Randy Haberkamp‡ and I hosted the Cinecon in 1990, Warner Brothers had a deal with Texaco where they made up special Bugs Bunny 50th anniversary glassware. Since we were having a banquet at the Hollywood Roosevelt that Sunday night, Alice said, "Wouldn't it be great to have one of those glasses at every place setting?" I forgot how she finagled it, but she did it. That was neat.

---

* In the 1930s, theaters would give patrons one dish each time they came on a traditionally slow night such as Monday or Tuesday, the purpose being to assemble place settings with continued patronage. See a reenactment in the 1994 comedy *My Summer Story,* aka *It Runs in My Family.*

† In the 1950s and '60s filling stations used to give away glassware. Banks would give away toasters with each new account.

‡ Former program director for the Academy of Motion Picture Arts and Sciences.

TEACHING AND STUDENTS

Segaloff: How long have you been teaching at the University of Southern California (USC)? How did that start, and what are your subjects?

Maltin: I was taken to lunch by Rick Jewell in 1998. A very nice man who held the Hugh Hefner chair at USC School of Cinematic Arts, SCA for short, and just a good guy. He was then Associate Dean of the school. He took me to lunch and essentially wooed me to take over this class, which was a famous class known by its course number rather than its name: 466. It has a terrible name, "Theatrical Film Symposium," but no one has ever come up with a better one, so we've let it stand. It was started by Arthur Knight in the early '60s. Apparently, he went to the school and said, "You're missing a bet here. You're in Hollywood's back yard and you're not taking advantage of it. Why don't we invite filmmakers to bring their newest movies here?" He started doing it. Alfred Hitchcock came, but so did young talents like John Cassavetes. He taught it for a number of years. When he retired, Charles Champlin took it over. Charles was not only the senior film critic for the *Los Angeles Times*, he was a cultural ambassador of our town. George Lucas took the class with him, and Ron Howard took the class with him. Hitchcock came back. There's a picture of Chuck Champlin and Hitchcock in the Coffee Bean café that they have on campus. Fred MacMurray's daughter, Laurie, was his teaching assistant.

Rick said to me, "Can I tempt you into doing this?" I said, "It's a famous class. I'm very flattered. I just don't know if I have the time." He said, "You don't have to grade papers. The TAs do that. You don't have to attend faculty meetings. You don't have to book the films or book the guests. We have someone on staff and that's their job. We just need you there every Thursday." What had happened was in the fall semester they'd hired a guy who worked for the *Hollywood Reporter* who was having a drinking problem, which they did not know about. They needed a replacement, and they needed him or her right away for the new semester, beginning in January. I said, "I'll give it a try."

There was a woman at the time who was doing the booking. I said, "What have we got lined up?" She said, "*Jackie Brown.*" I said, "Great," because we were friendly with Robert Forster, the nicest man in show business. I didn't know if he was going to be in London for the London premiere with Quentin. I said, "Who's not going to be in London for the premiere?" She said, "The sound mixer." I said, "The *sound mixer?* We have Quentin Tarantino's first film in five years and we're going to have the sound mixer?" I was very condescending about this turn of events, but that night came, and I did my opening night spiel. I watched it again, and this time I really listened to the movie. *Listening* stimulated all sorts of questions in my mind. Somebody gets whacked in a panel truck. How do you simulate that hollow sound with the ricochet? They filmed at the Del Amo Mall. How do you get live sound in a public place like that, etcetera, etcetera?

It turned out that my guest, Michael Minkler, was a *third-generation* sound man in Hollywood. Now he has three Oscars; then, he had two. He's still very active and working at a very high level of achievement. I learned several lessons that night, but the most important one is that he's not a technician. That was my knee-jerk reaction: "Oh, he's a sound mixer. A technician turning knobs." Wrong! If he doesn't understand the dramatic context of a scene or the importance of what's going on in the scene, he's not going to help the movie. He may even hurt the movie. He's a creative contributor. Everybody is a creative contributor, essentially. That was a lesson I learned and keep relearning.

I took a show of hands with 350 students that first semester, and I said, "We're going to be showing the new version of *Great Expectations* by Alfonso Cuaron. Just out of curiosity, how many of you have seen the classic 1946 version by David Lean?" Five hands went up out of 350. I said, "Oh, I've got to do something about that." I wasn't able to do it that semester, but the next semester I got a good 35mm print of the David Lean film, and Ronald Neame came.* He didn't want to see the film again. He came an hour in. I was walking him down the aisle. He looked up at the screen and said, "The timing is a little light." That was a small triumph, but I said to myself "I've got to find a way to get my licks in for Hollywood history." On the last night of that first semester, I knew exactly who I wanted as my guest, and she was more than willing: Gloria Stuart, who they all had just seen in *Titanic*. I called Universal and said, "Do you have a 35mm print of John Ford's *Air Mail*? They said, "Yes, we just restored it. How'd you know?" I said, "I didn't know. Would you be willing to loan it to USC?" "Sure." Then I did a song-and-dance introduction where I explained this was not a classic movie or a great piece of cinema. This is a bread-and-butter movie but executed by professionals with a clear understanding of how to tell a good story. The film played well, and then there was Gloria. Gloria talked about the famous stunt pilot Paul Mantz taking her up in the air, showing off.† My students didn't

---

* Neame was a director of photography before he became a director.
† Paul Mantz (1903-1965) was Hollywood's greatest stunt pilot. He

know what to ask her. Finally, one girl raises her hand and says, "What do you think of your performance?" She said, "Oh, honey, I was terrible. I'd been studying at the Pasadena Playhouse, getting ready to be a theater actress. I didn't understand working with the camera or any of that stuff." She said, "Let's face it, they just signed me because I was pretty." Now where are you going to hear that in 1998 from someone who made a movie in 1932 that you've just watched?

The next semester, I had Robert Stack with *To Be or Not to Be*. Probably the only time it didn't get its opening laugh. The first laugh in that movie is Jack Benny coming out in tights to perform the Hamlet speech. Well, they didn't recognize him or know anything about Jack Benny, but then they got into it. They liked it. At the end of that evening, the last night of the semester, a guy came up to me and said, "Normally, I wouldn't watch a film like that, but I really enjoyed it. I'm going to try to see some more." I wanted to hug him. I wanted to say, "You're the reason I'm here. You are the reason I'm doing this."

Segaloff: I gave up teaching at a certain point when this sort of thing happened. The antipathy toward black and white films, the hatred of subtitles, the fear to try anything new. At a time when almost every movie ever made was available on home video, there was no interest. Have the students changed that same way at USC since 1998, for you?

Maltin: Well, I taught two or three semesters on Zoom, which was no fun at all because I couldn't hear if they were laughing at my jokes. They didn't get cheated. They got the full ride because when they asked a question of the filmmaker, and the filmmaker responded on that full screen. They're sitting in their kitchen or their dorm room or whatever, having a one-on-one with a director or a writer or producer. They still got the benefits of taking the class but for me, it was a drag. Since then, my observation is that the classes sit there like a lump. They don't seem to have a sense of humor when I'm showing them shorts and stuff, but individually, they're great. They participate in the discussion period at the beginning of the class, and they ask good questions. The filmmakers are always impressed with the caliber of their questions, which is a good measure. But I think they aren't yet over the isolation that the Covic pandemic imposed on everyone.

---

died doing "one more shot for safekeeping" on *The Flight of the Phoenix* (1965).

Segaloff: These are all declared cinema majors?

Maltin: No. On the contrary, the majority are not.

Segaloff: What they bring is curiosity but not experience?

Maltin: Exactly. Early on, I used to have the whole football squad, and they would sit in the back of the hall, as far from me as possible so as to not engage.

Segaloff: Too cool.

Maltin: One winter break, the person who was booking the class said, "We have an opportunity to show *City of God.* It's a Brazilian film set in Rio de Janeiro made by Fernando Meirelles. It's a devastating movie. It takes place in the favela neighborhoods of Rio. Many middle-class and wealthy people in Rio don't even know they exist. It's like another world.

Segaloff: Like *Metropolis.*

Maltin: Yes. Meirelles had won Clio Awards. He was a very proficient filmmaker, but this book just spoke to him, and he went to the author and personally pleaded his case to get an option on the book. The author gave it to him, but he then decided he needed to make a smaller movie first, to have the experience of directing a feature-length film under his belt. While that was happening, he hired an acting coach to work with kids, to get them ready, get them up to speed. Have you ever heard of anybody doing this?

Segaloff: No.

Maltin: This guy was a prosperous, successful, commercial filmmaker. Then he made this incredible movie. Incredible movie. He explained when he came to the screening that the first section is all on tripods and it's at eye level. The second section, some handheld and different points of view. The third is chaos. Even the football players got hooked on this movie. They read the subtitles. I've had several successes like that. Not always, but several successes like that where we've overcome what would seem to be obstacles to what is really a general audience of twenty-somethings.

Segaloff: Would this be considered an easy course?

Maltin: No. There's a midterm and a final. If you haven't paid attention and you fail, it's going to bring down your GPA.

Segaloff: Are there term papers?

Maltin: It depends on my head TA every semester.

Segaloff: Correcting 350 papers is not my idea of anything you want to do.

Maltin: It's all online now, open-book, take-home. It's the history of technology; when I started teaching, everybody had spiral loose-leaf notebooks and pens. Now, nobody does that. It's all being recorded or typed up, whatever. We used to show 35mm prints. Now, mostly digital. About four years ago, I realized that they may never have actually seen film. What does film look like? I showed a 16mm short that night and handed it to our projectionist but I also brought another one so I could unreel it a bit and show them what that looked like, that there's a relationship from one frame to the next. I also brought a reel of a colored 35mm leader that I had rescued from a dumpster at Paramount years ago. I brought a pair of scissors, and I said, "If you want to come and snip off a piece of film, use it as a bookmark, amuse your friends, be the first on your block," whatever. I've done this every semester since and it's like I'm Santa Claus. They are so thrilled. They are thrilled to have some tactile relationship with motion picture film.

Segaloff: It may be called photochemical, but there is something emotional about it, too. You speak to editors who are holding film and moving their hands left or right "feeling" where to cut, and you know *this* is a bad edit, but *that* is a good edit. I can't tell you why, but that's the case. What have you been able to learn in your engagement with the students over these years of their changing attitude towards film in society, film as a medium, the potential of film? Does it hold the same magic quality as it did when you were their age?

Maltin: You're asking me at an interesting juncture because I just showed *The Wild Robot* last week. I think it's a beautiful film. It played stupendously well. We discussed it last Thursday. A lot of them said, "This reminds me of my childhood, I haven't felt this emotional watching a movie in a long time. This is the kind of thing I used to see when I was growing up." It was though they'd missed that experience. They were really happy to have that level of engagement with a movie.

Segaloff: Presumably, these are kids who go to the movies anyway. Why is this different?

Maltin: Well, first of all, they *don't* go to the movies very much. It's hard to make generalizations. It's 300-some kids. I say "kids," they're mostly kids but they're not necessarily movie-savvy. They don't all follow what's coming. I gather it's not important in their lives. It's not a big presence in their lives.

Segaloff: That's a change from our youth, certainly.

Maltin: Yes. Bob Zemeckis is coming with this new film this semester.* He's very loyal to the school. They have a digital film center that he built. He said, "When I was going here, just before home video in the '70s, we used to borrow 35mm prints from the studios every weekend. We watched seven Westerns in a row. But now I walk around the campus, I don't get a feeling of that kind of commitment. We used to eat, drink, sleep, film." Which is interesting.

Segaloff: Particularly because this is one of the two or three most significant film schools in America.

Maltin: The best answer to a possibly trite question was when I had Scott Alexander and Larry Karaszewski come with *Dolemite Is My Name*. After the formal Q&A one young man said to Scott, "What advice do you have for a young filmmaker who wants to make movies?" He said, "Make the kind of movie you would want to see. Don't try to second guess, 'what are they looking for?' Make the kind of movie you would pay money to go and see." I thought, "Well, that is a perfect answer."

Segaloff: If more people would do that, we'd have more movies that you want to see instead of what focus groups want to see, and safe sequels.

Maltin: I haven't asked them if they were watching miniseries. Do they watch *The Bear*? Do they watch the new Nicole Kidman show? I'm given to believe they don't watch conventional television at all. I don't know. It's a different group of students every semester.

---

* *Here* (2025) starring Tom Hanks and Robin Wright, based on a graphic novel and short story, about what happens on a specific plot of ground from Creation to present time.

Segaloff: That's interesting. Thinking about what Frank Capra wrote in *The Name Above the Title*, that flips it around. He says the audience knows everything at once and they know it faster, and yet—well, maybe that's a factor of social media. People relate alone to a tiny screen, not together to a big screen.

Maltin: I showed *State of the Union* when Angela Lansbury came to class; she's so good in that. The film gets a bad rap, I think. It was heavily rewritten from the play, but I think it's very relevant. It's about the first television-era election campaign. Spencer Tracy is a successful self-made man, an industrialist who discovers early on that he has to make compromises. If he wants to have that union's vote, he's got to do some quid pro quo. The last set-piece of the film is Tracy and Hepburn at an election night party and there's a TV crew there, and friends and associates of theirs are coming. Tracy gives a bartending job to an old crony of his played by Irving Bacon. Things happen, a lot of incidents and embarrassments and faux pas. Capra keeps cutting away to Irving Bacon doing bits of business, schtick. I swear, every laugh he built into that reel, landed with my twenty-somethings decades later, and that, to me, is fascinating.

Segaloff: Are there prerequisites to the students coming to the class having had to see a certain wealth of films?

Maltin: No. I wish there were otherwise, but no. I have a repertoire of shorts that I show. Opening night is always a Max Fleischer Betty Boop cartoon, and that always goes over well, never fails. I show Robert Benchley's "The Sex Life of the Polyp," and this is a little dicier. Some of them get it, and some of them don't. Some of them are chuckling fairly early on, some of them are triggered by one or another of his foolish statements. I love it. I never get tired of watching it. I show them Cecil B. DeMille's "Hollywood Extra Girl." I never get tired of watching that or watching him. Then I show vintage cartoons.

Segaloff: It sounds like you're creating a baseline so you can gauge their reactions and know how far one way or the other you can go.

Maltin: Well, I used to show the Fox Movietone interview with Sir Arthur Conan Doyle (1927), until I came to realize that they didn't care about Sir Arthur Conan Doyle. This was of no interest to them at all. I showed that one night when

Guillermo del Toro came with one of his films. He knows that interview backwards and forwards, of course, but he's interested because of Doyle's explorations of the supernatural, but I took it out of my rotation because it just wasn't playing.

Segaloff: When do the students at USC see *Citizen Kane*?

Maltin: Probably in the Introduction to Film class. When Jessie was in the 11th grade, her school asked if I'd come and talk about *Citizen Kane*. "Sure." "Come at 10:45 on Tuesday." I go into a classroom where the blackout curtains aren't really blackout curtains. Light is leaking in everywhere and they're sitting at a school desk, not in a comfortable chair. How many strikes can you put against a movie? Then they're told this is the greatest movie ever made. "Sit down and watch it now. I dare you. I dare you not to like this movie. It's the greatest movie ever made." I wouldn't do that again.

Segaloff: That is a problem. People come with a chip on their shoulder to see *Citizen Kane*. A lot of movies you have to discover. You have to be up at 2:00 in the morning if something is on and you say, "My parents don't know I'm watching this." It's like eating a stolen watermelon. It always is better if you shouldn't be seeing it.

Maltin: I remember a roughly equivalent story. I remember sifting through my parents' collection of 78 rpm records and discovering Fats Waller. "This guy is great." There is that element.

Segaloff: Are the screenings held in Norris or some other auditorium?

Maltin: It's Norris Theatre and Frank Sinatra Hall. About twenty years ago, Frank's children donated all of his memorabilia to the school. Why? No one really understands. Nancy's (Frank's daughter) son went to USC, but that's as close as we can figure. They renovated the auditorium, paid for an overhaul of the seats and everything. There are window cases in the lobby where there are snapshots on the streets of Hoboken. They have personal letters from FDR. And his three Oscars: the one for "The House I Live In," one for *From Here to Eternity*, and the Jean Hersholt Humanitarian Award, as well as Grammys galore. On one tall wall, the atrium entryway to the theater, we have all his Gold and Platinum albums. It's stupendous. I tell them, "The music you hear when you're filing in every week is Frank Sinatra, and this is why. He was one of just a handful of people who had equally successful music and movie careers: Bing Crosby, Frank Sinatra, Doris Day, and Elvis Presley." Would you add to that list?

Segaloff: What does it take to be able to judge an old movie on its own terms rather than by today's standards? It's something that you can imbue in your students.

Maltin: They have to be willing to meet the older film on its own terms. If they aren't, then it's a lost cause. One year, a long time ago, Ray Harryhausen was in town. A guy I knew was acting as his host here in L.A. I said, "Would he be free to come down to my class at USC next Thursday?" He said, "Yes, I think we could make that happen." I called Grover Crisp at Sony, because I'd heard that they had restored *The 7th Voyage of Sinbad*. Indeed, they had; they had a new 35mm print and he was willing to loan that to us. To get the students in the right frame of mind, I took several segments from a DVD where various current visual effects people had done homages to Ray for his milestone birthday. I gave them a taste of what was to come. I said, "You have to embrace your inner 10-year-old to watch and enjoy this." They couldn't do it. Couldn't or wouldn't. They who grew up on CGI had no appreciation for the hand-crafted antecedent. That was discouraging. I've had many successful forays into this arena, but that was one that didn't work.

Segaloff: Is it a matter of setting the film in historical context or giving them some hints?

Maltin: Yes, as best you can. I've done that a lot. Just two weeks ago I showed my class chapter eight of *Zorro's Fighting Legion*, which I've shown before in its entirety on a week-to-week basis. The first thing that is noticeable is that the guys go for it more than the girls. I'm just reporting what happened. It happened that night as I was leaving to go home, as I was leaving the building, one of my students who lingered said, "I'm really glad you showed that Zorro chapter tonight. I heard about those old serials, but I'd never seen one before. I really enjoyed it." I said, "You just made my day, my whole week." When I interviewed William Witney[*] some time back, he said they were aiming for the 10-to-12-year-old boys.

Segaloff: That says a lot.

---

[*] William Witney (1915-2002) was a prolific director of serials, many for Republic, distinguished by their solid action sequences.

Maltin: That was their ideal demographic. Even today's boys or young men, whatever you want to call them, respond to it because it's good storytelling. Clear, linear storytelling. Many other things, great stunt work and wonderful practical visual effects by the Leyendecker* brothers and all of that. That wonderful voice of Reed Hadley's.† There's one chapter where the last scene is Zorro standing on the second story of an adobe building. He jumps down to his waiting horse, lands perfectly in the saddle, and the horse takes off all in one shot. A student came up to me and said, "How'd they do that?" I was taken aback for a moment. I said, "*How'd they do that*?" He said, "Yes." I said, "That was obviously a stuntman behind the mask and costume of Zorro. They had a movie-trained horse who was used to standing still until a signal was given. The stuntman jumped down onto the horse, made a perfect landing, and the horse took off." I said, "What you saw actually happened in real time." Maybe they had to do a second take, but they didn't often have to at Republic, nor did they want to. It was a marvel to him.

Segaloff: The story reminds me of that moment in *Hearts of the West* where Jeff Bridges says he'll do the stunt for no extra fee, and he jumps on the horse and hurts himself. Later they say, "Didn't anybody tell him to wear a cup?" Have you ever had a film get canceled or #MeToo'd in class because it's politically incorrect?

Maltin: Being aware of the pitfalls, I think I've dodged and weaved pretty well on the whole. I always show an *Our Gang* comedy at some point. The one I've been showing most recently, the last ten years or so, is called "Framing Youth" (1937). That's one of the one-reelers in the latter part of the series' history. It's got Alfalfa, Buckwheat, Darla, Porky, Spanky, and Butch. They're all in it. Porky and Buckwheat are equally unintelligible. Nothing untoward there. Darla is Spanky's secretary. It's an office, and she calls him 'boss.' "Yes, boss." No one's complained about that. There are some shorts I've taken out of the rotation because they don't respond to them. I don't want to beat my head against the wall. No, I haven't had that particular problem, thank goodness. I've had many others, but not that.

---

* Howard "Babe" (1911-1969) and Theodore (1908-1990) Lydecker were visual effects siblings whose work with miniatures included *Lost in Space, Voyage to the Bottom of the Sea*, and scores of modest-budget theatrical features where their economy was essential.
† Reed Hadley (1911-1974) played Zorro in *Zorro's Fighting Legions*. He had a mellifluous speaking voice.

THE GRIM REAPER

Because he knows so many people from the Golden Age, Leonard has also been "on call" over the years to write or comment on their deaths. (See also the Appendix.)

Maltin: One of my specialties—I don't know if that's quite the right word—is obits. For many, many years, I was on speed-dial with CBS Radio News in New York. When we had our landline the phone was on Alice's night table. She'd pick up the phone, and if it rang at an odd hour, and if she was in the right mood, she'd say, "Who died?" The poor person on the other end of the line would say, "Actually, Lauren Bacall." Then Alice would hand the phone to me to ad lib. I did it in my sleep.

Segaloff: Ad-libbing a comment about the person who just died?

Maltin: Yes. This is stuff I know really, really well. They've tracked me down over the years in all sorts of places. We went to the Grand Canyon about fifteen years ago. We weren't going to do any white-water rafting; that's not us. We did the old- people trip on a rubber raft on the quiet part, the other side of Lake Meade or something like that. We got off and look at some petroglyphs and then came back to the restrooms. People were reassembling, maybe fifteen people on this water-craft. Alice's cell phone rang, and it was CBS in New York, asking if I could talk about Art Linkletter, who just died. She said, "Call back in five minutes, and he'll be here." She was trying to explain to the skipper of this raft what I was doing. Could they please be quiet for a few minutes? The connection was as clear as a bell. I don't get Van Nuys that clearly.

One time in Hawaii, on the Island of Maui, they tracked me down, another time in a very noisy pizza parlor next to the Egyptian Theater in Park City during the Sundance Film Festival, in the men's shirts department of Barney's. All sorts of places. One time my agent was annoyed with me because he said, "You should be paid for this." I said, "Yes, but who's going to pay me?" He poked around. No was willing to pay for this service. I'm happy to be associated with having the knowledge to do this.

The most exceptional story I do tell in my book was getting friendly with Roy Rogers and Dale Evans' daughter, Cheryl. Roy was a pack rat. He saved everything. He gave me a tour, a walking tour. He saved the original drafts of the song that he and Bob Nolan wrote for the Sons of the Pioneers. He had everything.

Segaloff: I cannot imagine being given a tour of Roy Rogers Museum by Roy Rogers himself.

Maltin: Amazing.

Segaloff: My friend Arnie Reisman was the entertainment editor of a paper in the Boston area, the *Quincy Patriot Ledger*. When word came over the teletype that Trigger had died and that Roy Rogers had had him stuffed—

Maltin: Mounted! I was always corrected.

Segaloff:—Arnie's headline was "Trigger Mortis."

Maltin: Wonderful. Great. Years later, when Roy was in extremis, Cheryl said, "The Apple Valley newspaper wants to be the ones to break the news. I don't want them to do it. I'd rather you do it." I said I'd be honored. She sent me the obit that she had. I suggested rewrites, faxed it back to her, and she approved it. Then I got the contact numbers for AP, *LA Times, New York Times*, and KTLA because I watched KTLA, and KNX, the all-news station here in Los Angeles. I wore a pager for three or four weeks. (That dates the story.) The pager never went off, but one morning the phone rang at 4:20 in the morning. Alice picked it up and it was Cheryl advising of Roy's death. She told us that the family was all together in his home, singing as he passed away. We said a few words of condolence to her and then we sat there. We're just sitting, Alice and I, in the middle of the night, contemplating this news. Suddenly, I realized I'd better get moving; I am the one to tell the world that this famous celebrity has just died, and he didn't die in a hospital, so nobody knew about it yet.

Segaloff: You were the only one who knew at this point?

Maltin: That's right. They have a very large family. I started making calls. We had an office in the backyard then. I went out there. Then Jessie woke up and she wanted to help. She was twelve. There's a reason I remember that, which I'll tell you in a minute. I was using a fax machine, and when I called AP, I swear I could hear the guy sitting up a little straighter in his seat. I said, "I've been authorized to inform you that Roy Rogers has died." He started firing questions at me about when, cause of death, what time and all that. I said, "Do you see the fax coming through your machine now?" He said, "Yes." "Okay, good. There'll be five pages." There was no going back to sleep after that. We were up and talking to different people and watching TV. We watched CNN, and CNN had some file footage. Not a lot. It just kept recycling the same fifty-second B-roll footage of Roy. CNN put me on a phone line live, even though it was TV, not radio. I said to Jessie, "This is so unusual for me, honey. I don't often deal with breaking news." She said, "No, you deal with *broken* news," which I thought summed it up pretty well.

Segaloff: Have you had to do many obits of people that you have known well?

Maltin: You're going to want examples (see Appendix). I've done a lot on my website especially. I've done a lot of obits of genuine friends. I interviewed Henry Mancini in his home, knowing he was dying, and the next night, there was a big gala for him at the Pauley Pavilion at UCLA. Julie Andrews, Luciano Pavarotti, a whole wealth of people. *E.T.* set it up for me to go and sit down at his house for an interview and then be there at the event, during cocktail hour. It's so strange talking to a man facing mortality like that. He didn't make me feel uncomfortable, but he knew he was dying. I just felt strange.

Segaloff: When I interviewed Louise Fletcher for my *Exorcist* book, we had known each other years ago. I was one of her publicists on *Cuckoo's Nest*. I interviewed her a few times after that when she was acting, but we fell out of touch. We reconnected by telephone, and we have a wonderful chat. I said, "What are you up to?" She says, "I'm going to move to France. I invested in a cottage there. I'm rehabilitating it and I'm going to go over there." I joshed, "Oh, you don't like America anymore?" She said, "I'm going there for dialysis." She was over 80, so I knew she had about six months. In fact, she didn't even have that much.[*]

Maltin: Oh, my.

Segaloff: Did you meet anyone as a star who later befriended you?

Maltin: I was a huge fan of Mel Tormé and I got to know him a little bit. This story is worth telling, but just for the final moment. He was not in a good place. Alice went to a matinee at the Laemmle Royal and Mel was sitting either just behind or just in front of her. He kept buying snack bar food. Crap.

---

[*] Louise Fletcher died September 23, 2022, in Montdurusse, France.

There was a lot of leftover stuff on the floor. He was part of Hef's (Hugh Hefner's) band of merry men. They went on a field trip. Kevin Burns* wanted to show them some rare Fox footage he had dug out. Mel couldn't walk back to the car after the screening. He was having a series of mini strokes and not responding to them, not doing anything about it. He didn't have a personal physician. Then he had a major stroke that put him out of the running. He was in a very bad place. I'm thinking, "What a waste!" At some point in my young life, I learned that Mel Tormé was a film buff and a film collector. He called a friend of mine once and said, "Hi, this is Mel Tormé, but I'm not calling you as a star. I'm calling you as a fellow film collector."

I was booked on *The Dr. Joyce Brothers Show* at 30 Rock (NBC studios in New York) and her co-host for that week was Mel Tormé. I wound up sitting in his dressing room with his drummer Donny Osborne, I think his name was. I had copies of *Film Fan Monthly* with me. He said, "Oh, this is great stuff." He said, "Put me on your comp list." I said, "I don't really have a comp list because it's a labor of love and I can't just give it away." He said, "I'll buy every back issue you have, but I can't keep up subscriptions because I'm traveling all the time, and the subscriptions run out and I can't renew them." I put up a good fight, but I finally said okay. We made a date. He was performing at the St. Regis and staying there. He said, "Come and have breakfast with me Monday in my room. Room service breakfast." Great. I brought a shopping bag full of the sixty or sixty-five back issues that I had and an invoice which was never paid. He said, "I've even got a story I can give you. I wrote it for *True* magazine, and they killed it. It was about the silent-era stunt pilot, Dick Grace. I've got pictures and everything. I'd love to see it published." "I'd love to publish it, Mel." "Great. I'll send it to you when I get back home," blah, blah, blah. He would say, "We were just in—Donny, where were we? Cleveland?" "Yes, Cleveland," like he needed a foil. What's that old saying about being able to hold two contradictory thoughts in your mind at the same time? Anyway, on *The Joyce Brothers Show*, the stage manager came to do a rundown. Segment one, Mel's going to sing with this trio. Segment two, Joyce is going to interview Mel about how he became a movie buff and what turned him on, blah, blah. Segment three, blah, blah, blah. Segment four, Leonard comes out and plugs his Disney book, and segment five, blah, blah, blah. Mel says, "No one cares about how I

---

* Kevin Burns (1955–2020) was a prolific producer of movie history documentaries, based at Twentieth Century Fox.

became a film buff. Spend more time with Leonard." What a generous thing to do. What a selfless, generous thing to do.

Now I have this dilemma: how do I dun Mel Tormé for an unpaid bill? Very awkward. I wrote a note on my stationery and sent it to the address that he had given me and said, "Hey, Mel. I'm sure you're out doing the circuit, but if you have a moment, I would appreciate payment of this invoice. I work on a very small margin and every dollar counts. Also, I'd still love to publish your Dick Grace article." Silence. Nothing. About a year later, Alice and I go to a screening at 711 Fifth Avenue, the Columbia Pictures building. After the screening, I see Mel is there with his bass player. We're all at the elevator bank waiting to go down. He says to me, "I've got an article I wrote for *True* magazine about this silent movie pilot, Dick Grace. Would you be interested in printing it?" "Absolutely, Mel." I just played it straight. Like the earlier conversation never happened. What can you do? C'est la vie.

Segaloff: You're telling the story years later, that's what you can do. There's some stories that you have lunch on.

Maltin: I never lost my enthusiasm for him as a performer. He was great. I got Jessie turned on to him many years ago too.

Segaloff: He's enormously talented—was—but there is a duality in these people. Whether they develop it, or they're born with it, but it enables them to compartmentalize everything.

Maltin: I have a theory. I don't know how good it is. Mel was a child radio actor in Chicago. Sammy Davis Jr., Mickey Rooney, Mel Tormé, these are people who didn't have a lot of formal education but grew up in the world of show business. They're self-conscious about their lack of education, and they try to compensate by using big words, but they're all a little hollow. Talent they've got. That's what got them where they are. It's a gift. They each have an extraordinary gift.

Segaloff: Look at the moguls, the ones who, as I think Joan Crawford said, should be fed out of a trough. They had their fingers so firmly on the public pulse that they survived for decades and decades without even really knowing how to read the contracts that they signed. There was something about them, there's something about people who are autodidacts, who have the knowledge but not the confidence that goes with it.

Maltin: Interesting. One night I was seated next to Mel at the Playboy mansion, and I asked him about how long it took to make a record album back in the heyday.

Because he'd done mostly live albums in later years, which were awfully good, a lot with George Shearing, he was happy to answer me. In a three-hour session, you might get two or three tracks done, and you built an album that way. It was a matter of days, not weeks or months. He said Billy May, one of my heroes, used to pick him up sometimes, and they would drive over to Capitol Records together. At red lights Billy was still filling in the arrangement.

Segaloff: Yes, you hear these stories. Billy Friedkin talked about working with Sonny and Cher on *Good Times*, and he said they'd be in the recording studio and Sonny would be there with his friends writing, and then they'd go right out and do "I Got You Babe." There are some people who need the pressure. We knew Sammy Cahn. He could get a phone call, go to a typewriter, type up a lyric just like it was written in stone from the previous century. He's amazing. Some people can do it. Lorenz Hart. You know the stories.

BECOMING AS AN INSTITUTION (AND OTHER GAMBITS)

Segaloff: You are at the stage of your career and your life when you're starting to get awards and recognitions and such things. How does it feel to suddenly be on the receiving end of these?

Maltin: I got a phone call or a letter saying the Temecula International Film Festival wanted to give me a career achievement award. They would send a car and pick Alice and me up and drive us down to Temecula and put us up at the casino hotel there, and there'd be an award ceremony Saturday night. I have an ego like everybody else. The previous awardees were on a very impressive list. Robert Wise, Eva Marie Saint, solid people. I said, "Yes. I'm not doing anything else that weekend. Let's do it." Then they say, "Who would you like to present the award to you?" Who am I going to saddle with that burden of schlepping to Temecula, which is not around the corner? That's a drive. The nicest man in show business, Robert Forster was the answer; he came with his friend Frank Pesce, a real character with a capital K. We get there and we go into the ballroom for the event, and we're seated at the same table as Jean Firstenberg.* I say, "They hooked you too?" We all treated it as a goof. The woman who was hosting it kept saying, "Are you having a good time?" She kept begging the audience. "Is this fun? Is this great? Isn't this something?"

Segaloff: You're lucky that they didn't hit you up for a list of all your friends to donate money.

Maltin: That's the other thing I learned. We dodged a bullet because they didn't have a program book full of congratulatory ads. Thank goodness. They obviously were not desperate for money or else I would have been asked for—

Segaloff: —everybody you ever met.

Maltin: That's right. It's not like being George Clooney. It's nice. I don't know anybody who spits in the face of someone handing them an award. It's all well and good to be professionally cynical about awards—until you get one. Have you ever heard Doug Benson's podcast? Doug Benson is a very funny stand-up comic who is high most of the time. In fact, he has a video podcast called *Getting Doug with High*. Word reached me through Jessie, I think, that he was doing a popular podcast where they played The Leonard Maltin Game.

Segaloff: The Leonard Maltin Game?

---

* Then the head of the American Film Institute.

Maltin: It was when I was still doing the *Movie Guide*. The object of the game is to name a movie based on the number of cast names you bid, but it's from the bottom up... the stars of the movie come up last.* There are people who are really good at this game. I'm not one of them, but there are people who are really good at this game. Freakily good. One is a young actor named Samm Levine.

Segaloff: No relation to Sam Levene.

Maltin: No relation to the co-star of *Guys and Dolls*. It's double M and Levine. He's an actor.† He was in *Freaks and Geeks*. He makes a decent living going to autograph shows as a cast member of *Freaks and Geeks*. He's also in Quentin's World War II movie, *Inglorious Basterds*. Anyhow, Samm is amazing at this game. I forget how it came about, but I got through to Doug that I would like to be on the show. He invited me on as a guest. Usually, it's other stand-up comics and sometimes actors. It's done live at the Upright Citizens Brigade Theater. Jessie said to me just before I went on stage, "Be a little bit of a dick." It was good director's note, and I had a great time. I've done it many times since then. He's invented other games now because the book is no longer current, but he does a show on Wednesday night of ComicCon week in San Diego at the San Diego Comedy Club. For six years in a row, I've done that Wednesday night show with him and it's always fun.

Segaloff: Did you become a dick when you went on?

Maltin: Yes, I tried.

Segaloff: You can't be a dick. You're Leonard Maltin.

Maltin: I was a little smart-ass a couple of times.

Segaloff: Were you less dicky as the years went on?

Maltin: Yes.

Segaloff: I just had to straighten this out.

---

* *Leonard Maltin's Movie Guide* listed cast members roughly in order of familiarity from highest to lower.
† Levine was also a sidekick on *Kevin Pollack's Chat Show* online.

Maltin: One of the things I enjoy about it is that it gives me a taste of show business with which I've always had a conflicted relationship. I have to write about it as a critic and as a journalist, but I'm also a part of it. Inescapably, I'm part of it. I'm out on the margins. I'm not a movie star. I'm not a television star, but I'm on TV sometimes. At one time, I was on TV a lot. I still have podcasts, and I turn up as a talking head in a hundred different documentaries, so I'm *sort of* in it. There was a period just before the pandemic, which spoiled a lot of things for a lot of people, goodness knows, when I felt like I really was in it because I met people doing Doug's show. I met Jon Hamm, who was a big movie buff, a very nice guy. I met a number of people. Do you know Paul F. Tompkins? He's a comic who does a hilarious Werner Herzog, a sputteringly funny takeoff of Werner Herzog. He can just talk as Werner endlessly. COVID put a damper on a lot of things, including live entertainment. I miss that.

When I was at the early peak of my success on *E.T.*, I called my agent and said, "Do you think *The $10,000 Pyramid* would book me as a celebrity guest?" He said, "We'll ask them." They said yes. They said, "Don't be insulted, but you'll come to their office and play the game with them there." I wasn't insulted. I went over and I met two associate producers who had been with the show a long time. After we played both positions, giver and receiver, she said, "You're really good at this." I said, "I've been watching the show forever. Didn't my agent tell you I'm a big fan?" She said, "That's what they *all* say, and then they get up here and they haven't a clue." That was fun. I helped a woman win a $10,000 vacation. Then I did *Password Plus*, where my fellow celebrity that week was Phyllis Diller.

You have to bring five changes of clothing because they tape five episodes in a single day. I go to CBS Television City, which in itself is freaky. When I got up to the second floor in the elevator, someone comes rushing over and says, "Why didn't you tell us you were here? You shouldn't be carrying your clothes like that. We've got a rack." I said, "I work at *E,T.* No such niceties there." Anyhow, the second time I did *The Pyramid* with Dick Clark, he was doing ten shows that day. The man was a machine, yet he came across as genuine. I wore one of my 1939 New York World's Fair pins. He said, "Oh, are you into the '39 fair?" I said yes. He said, "Me, too. I have a bedroom set in that style." Phyllis Diller said, "What's with the pins?" I said, "I collect lapel pins, cartoon characters, advertising pins, old movie pins." For the next fifteen years, wherever she traveled, she sent me pins with a little note: "Hi. Enjoy."

Segaloff: Oh, what a sweetheart.

Maltin: One morning, I walked into the green room at *Regis and Kathie Lee*. In that green room were Walter Cronkite, Jane Goodall, Nadia Comaneci, and Joanne Woodward. I made a point of introducing myself to each of those people, shaking their hands and making a little small talk just so I could say I met them all. Now, what does that mean in the grand scheme of things? Not much, I guess, but I met those people.

Segaloff: Your wonderment is charming. No, that's condescending. I think it's empowering that someone who is as well-known as you are can still be impressed by other people because you don't take yourself seriously. That's what makes you long-lived in this business.

Maltin: I just remembered this recently and told Alice. When I did *The Pyramid* for the first time at CBS Television City for the CBS Network a guy came up to me during a break and asked if I would do a PSA [Public Service Announcement]. I said, "Sure." So I did a PSA about "don't share needles." I, who have never inhaled a puff of marijuana smoke from my vast experience in the drug world, was telling people, "Don't share needles."

Segaloff: This leads us to whether you have ever done any product endorsements?

Maltin: No, but I came close. Red Lobster, years ago, pitched a campaign where they were going to sell Red Lobster like a new movie. It was not a bad idea, actually: "The curtain has risen, the reviews are in, the critics are raving." When it said, "the critics are raving," I was to be seated at a Red Lobster booth with a meal in front of me. I didn't have to say a word. It was very tempting because that's serious money, but I just felt I couldn't or shouldn't do it.

Segaloff: You have appeared in movies, however. *Gremlins 2*, and, of course, the great Peter Jackson spoof *Forgotten Silver*. How many films have you appeared in?

Maltin: Those two. There was a definite reason for being in *Gremlins 2*. That was to atone for my sins. *Forgotten Silver*, that project was just irresistible. The guy who made it with Peter Jackson, Costa Botes, just called me a month or two ago. He's writing a book about the making of *Forgotten Silver*.

Segaloff: Have you ever had to recuse yourself from doing a review?

Maltin: I've never had the ability to. That was how I got in trouble with Joe Dante and *Gremlins*. There was no alternate film critic on *Entertainment Tonight*, and that was a big, big movie that had to be covered.

Segaloff: You wrote in your book about the experience of interviewing Robert Mitchum for *Ryan's Daughter* and how he was breaking up a brick of marijuana while you were all talking, and the MGM publicist asked you not to use it. Have you ever killed stories?

Maltin: No. I've never killed a story. I've chosen not to write about some films.

Segaloff: Isn't that recusal?

Maltin: If you want to call it that, yes, I've done that often now. I do it all the time when I don't want to. I go into my "Thumper"* mode—"If you can't say something nice, etc." I don't review that many films anymore now on my website. I'm a part-time critic, so to go out of my way and devote the time and energy to trash a film, why would I do that? As often as not, I just won't weigh in on that film and the world continues to spin.

Segaloff: Why did it take so long for you to be asked to join the Motion Picture Academy?†

Maltin: My wife and daughter were bent on that happening. I didn't have a great desire. I felt I was already getting the best of it as a friend of the Academy. The truth is now, as a member, if they give me special treatment of any kind, it's like, "Why is he getting special treatment?" Because I hosted a lot of events there. I appeared in a promotional film they did about the activities of the Academy. I've had nice relations with them for many years. It's an entirely different organization now. It couldn't be more different than it was under Bruce Davis'

---

* The young bunny rabbit in Disney's *Bambi*.

† In 2023, Leonard was formally invited to membership in the Academy of Motion Picture Arts and Sciences. After many years, the Academy began changing its rules to reflect outreach and diversity. Bruce Davis was the last Executive Director under the old rules, having served from 1991 to his retirement in 2011.

leadership. We can leave it at that. It's not better or worse necessarily, but it is different.*

Segaloff: I was having a meeting in the '80s with a production executive. We were describing the old adage, "Nobody ever sets out to make a bad movie." She went through her list of the studio's next season films. She said, "Here's our buddy cop film, here's our Western, here's our youth film." She says, "They're all terrible." I said, "You mean people actually do set out to make bad movies?" She said, "We know what these pictures will cost to make, and we know how much they can possibly gross." I said, "Why can't you spend a little extra money to make them better?" She said, "We could, but it wouldn't show up at the other end, so why bother?" That has stuck with me for nigh on to thirty years.

Maltin: I've never heard anyone say that.

Segaloff: She did. She later quit her job and became a very good screenwriter. We had mutual friends, so she was honest with me—foolishly, perhaps. These are things you can't report, but by God, I used to teach it. So: do people set out to make bad movies, or does shit just happen?

Maltin: First, we have to define what is, in this context, a bad movie. Is a bad movie a failure financially? Does that make it a bad movie? Is it a bad movie because it isn't successful at what it purports to be or wants to be? I remember seeing *Battleship*, based on the board game. What is their excuse for this? Why would a board game be a good springboard for a movie? I don't get it. Given that, I still don't think anybody sets out to make a bad movie. Even if it's overtly a commercial product. You want to be a successful commercial product. Therefore, it has to be good enough to please the target audience. The target audience may be slightly slow-witted tweens, but if you please that audience, they consider it a good movie.

Segaloff: In the studio heyday, each company had to grind out thirty or forty films a year. Not all of them could be *Casablanca*.

Maltin: Even Warner Bros couldn't make lightning strike twice with *Casablanca*. That's my all-time favorite movie.

---

* In 2015 an #OscarsSoWhite campaign criticized the Academy for its lack of diversity, so in 2020 a campaign began to be more "inclusive." This drew widespread criticism (ongoing) of "woke-ness" that stressed diversity over traditionally defined achievement.

I find so many things interesting about it. One of them is that Warners tried to recapture all the ingredients. They tried to essentially make another *Casablanca*, and it never worked. *Passage to Marseille* and *Across the Pacific*. Some combination of Bogart and Peter Lorre or Sydney Greenstreet. Nothing worked. Nothing came close to working the way *Casablanca* did. The stars were in alignment for *Casablanca*.

Segaloff: I remember having a conversation with the late Anthea Sylbert, who at the time had stopped doing schmattes (she was a major costume designer) and was involved at United Artists. She talked about a Columbia project called *The Fortune*, written by Adrien Joyce, who was really Carole Eastman, and directed by Mike Nichols. It starred Warren Beatty, Jack Nicholson, and Stockard Channing. It was a disaster. I said, "How does this happen?" She says, "I don't know. We knew the script wasn't that great, but figured these people are smart, they'll fix it. They didn't."

Maltin: That's right. Every movie is a miracle.

Segaloff: It is. I'm very sympathetic.

Maltin: I love the story that Scott Eyman tells in his Louis B. Mayer book about Mayer being at a dinner party or a cocktail party in New York, talking to a literary type who was very condescending about movies. Mayer said, "You'll admit that every now and then, two, three times a year, we do make a good movie." Guy said, "Oh, yes." Mayer said, "We don't have to."

Segaloff: What is it when Billy Wilder had made three flops in a row? He said, "I don't know, I made *Sunset Boulevard*, *Lost Weekend*, *Fortune Cookie*, *Some Like it Hot*. I didn't suddenly get stupid." But to segue back, you've said that you don't feel comfortable doing commercial endorsements such as for Red Lobster, so what pulled you onto QVC, the sales television network?

Maltin: There's a pre-story that leads into the story. When *Titanic* came out in 1997, the soundtrack album or CD by James Horner sold over one million copies. That was unprecedented; no orchestral music for a movie had never attained that level of success. That sparked an idea in a couple of fellows who I hadn't met before, who were old-school music industry veterans. They had produced several CDs of film music with an orchestra in Slovenia, very capable musicians and a conductor. The idea they had was that I should "front" an album of themes from my favorite recent film scores. They had a company interested in producing such an album on CD. I was well paid. They were good to their word. They really wanted my picks. I think I had two Jerry Goldsmith scores in there. One of them for *First Knight*, I remember. I really liked the score for the Coppola-John Grisham film, *The Rainmaker*. The only thing that didn't turn out right was the cue I liked that used an electric organ, a Hammond B-3 electric organ. They didn't have one in Slovenia, or at least not accessible. They chose another cue. That was a minor quibble on my part, but they did a very good job of getting ahold of the necessary materials. I wrote liner notes for the booklet. I happened to interview Steven Spielberg around that time for something for *E.T.* and I got a great quote from him about John Williams and what John Williams adds to his movies.

I was very pleased. I thought the essay turned out well. Then at the eleventh hour, the company that was going to produce and sell the album backed out. One of their colleagues put the guys together with QVC, which was launching its own record label, Q Records. Their first release was the original cast album of the then brand-new production of *The Music Man* on Broadway with Dick Van Dyke. We were going to be the second release from this new venture, but it required my going to Westchester, Pennsylvania, outside of Philly, and going on the air. I said to them, "I can't be a sales pitchman. That's not what I do and that's not who I am." I equated this with that kind of selling out. They said, "You don't have to do any of the selling. That's what the hosts are there to do. You're going to be talking about why great soundtrack music is great to listen to, why soundtrack music is valid as a form of music to enjoy." Okay. We get there, I was going to do two shots, one at 3:00 in the morning and one at 3:00 in the afternoon. Just a week or two before going, John Tesh, then the host of *Entertainment Tonight*, had just gone on QVC with an album of his new-agey piano music, and he said, "Oh, you'll have a great time. You're going to love it because as soon as you're done with the segment, you go into the green room and you can see this counter, and the numbers start flying by as they're making sales. It happens in real time, and it's great." I hadn't watched QVC. The error I made was that I should have watched the channel for a little while just get a sense of how it worked, and I shouldn't have been so precious about being a pitchman. Because if I believed in the music, there would have been nothing wrong with saying, "I think you'd really enjoy this." The poor hosts who are moving on—five minutes from now, they're going to be selling a lawnmower—so there's a limit to how invested they can be in the product at hand. At 3:20 AM when I finished the first segment, one of the two producers for the album came with me for moral support.

We looked at the counter and it went [tick] 119, [tick] 120, [tick] 121, [tick] 120. Somebody backed out. Somebody cancelled the order! It wasn't flying off the shelves. It was trudging through. Very weak response. Somebody told me they were very excited that I was coming. Why would I believe that? Why on earth would I believe that? Nobody greeted us or waved goodbye either. Q Records died a painless death. It was an experience. Now, if I were doing it today, I'd like to think that I would be more successful because I'd go on and do a real sales pitch and hopefully persuade more than 120 people to give it a try.

Segaloff: It isn't like you came on with a clothespin on your nose.

Maltin: No, not at all. The hosts were very congenial, but I wasn't helping them.

Segaloff: Another useless experience.

Maltin: But nobody saw it.

Segaloff: 3:00 in the morning.

Maltin: Nobody saw either appearance. I got no feedback, ever. Never, in a hotel lobby, in an airport, no one ever told me that they saw me on QVC. I think I dodged a bullet.

Segaloff: Let's get into some memorable interviews, using a broad definition of "memorable." You interviewed Robert De Niro and Al Pacino together; this must have been for *Heat* in 1995. Neither one is known for being terribly garrulous. How did you blast them into speaking?

Maltin: I had nothing to do with the booking. An *E.T.* producer pulled that off, but because they had both spoken to me before for *E.T.*, I passed muster with both of them. Whereas dragging a quote from Mr. De Niro was an effort, at best, Pacino was always talkative and ready to play. That permeated the air. They were so comfortable with each other. I think that was the real key, that they were comfortable with each other. They'd known each other a long time, though they hadn't worked together. They said they almost made *The Pope* *of Greenwich Village* together.* I remember that. It was all of ten minutes because they were on a press junket schedule. It was very exciting. Did I tell you the photo story?

Segaloff: It's going to have to be in the book.

Maltin: When the time was up, no one was going to linger because they had to get back on the schedule. They were seated next to each other in straight-back chairs in this hotel room. This was before the age of camera phones. I had a point-and-shoot camera. I threw it to the *E.T.* intern who was there. I said, "Take a picture." I ran behind the two chairs, and they were willing. He took one picture, and then I said, "Take one more." Just as he was about to press the shutter, De Niro said, "Cheeeeeese." We all cracked up. Not only do I have a photo of me with them, but we're also all laughing. That's a really rare souvenir.

Segaloff: Do you get more out of people if it's a good film?

Maltin: The broad answer to that question is yes, because then they're not lying. They're not putting on a face, a mask, when they really don't like what they're promoting.

Segaloff: Let's go to another impenetrable celebrity, Mr. Warren Beatty. You've had encounters with him.

Maltin: Friendly meetups. I was there when he did his hand-prints and footprints at Grauman's [Chinese Theater, known for its forecourt of celebrity hand and shoe impressions in cement]. He and Annette Bening were there. We had a nice chat. Then I saw them at the Oscar nominees' luncheon. Had a nice chat. Those were just casual interactions. I lose my timeline here. At least fifteen years ago, Alice and I were at our Malibu apartment, which we don't have anymore. Jessie called us from home. She said, "I just took a phone call. He said it was Warren Beatty. He gave me a number to call back. Wanted to talk to you." I returned the call and it was Warren. He was entangled in a legal wrangle with *Chicago Tribune* over the rights to *Dick Tracy*. He maintained that he had the right to make a sequel or a spinoff of his movie. They believed he did not. He wanted to assert his ownership or put a stake in the ground to prove that he did own the right to drama-

---

* Eric Roberts and Mickey Rourke did instead, in 1984, written by Vincent Patrick and directed by Stuart Rosenberg.

tize *Dick Tracy*. His idea was to have Charlie Rose* interview Dick Tracy. Not Warren Beatty, but to interview Dick Tracy, who'll be portrayed by Warren. He told this to one of the execs at Walt Disney Home Video who said, "Oh, you don't need Charlie Rose. We work with Leonard Maltin all the time. He could do that." "Okay, great." He called me and told me what he had in mind. It'll take a day or an hour or whatever to shoot. They were going to use a stage at Disney Imagineering, which had a small stage in Glendale. I didn't know till I got there that it was going to be shot by the great Emmanuel Lubezki, known as Chivo.†

Segaloff: Shot on film, of course.

Maltin: I think.

Segaloff: Warren always shoots on film. 35mm film with top crews.

Maltin: The first thing I got out of this was a wonderful lunch. A wonderful getting-to-know-you lunch where I heard his repertoire of great stories. His first Hollywood party when he met Clifford Odets and gawked at Rita Hayworth. He's a great raconteur. He called and then he sent me the script. He wanted to run lines with me.

Segaloff: A script for an interview?

Maltin: It was not an interview. It was a performance piece.

Segaloff: As Dick Tracy. To establish his proprietorship of the remake rights.

Maltin: Yes. He came to our house when we were in Toluca Lake. He sat in our library room and read through the script. He said to me, "If this was Arthur Miller we're reading, I wouldn't vary a syllable, but I wrote this. We can dance around a little bit." "Fine." At the last minute, he said to me, "I want to talk about Ralph Byrd and Morgan Conway who played Tracy in the serials and the older movies." I had to frantically write something that they could put in the Tele-

---

* Best known for his no-frills PBS television show in which he spoke to people across a round table in a darkened studio. He was unfailingly gracious.

† Lubezki shot, among other titles, *Children of Men* (2006), *Gravity* (2013), and *The Revenant* (2015), and is considered one of the world's most innovative cinematographers.

prompter and all that. I did. Then the day before the shoot, for which I was well paid in addition to getting the benefit of being with Warren Beatty and working with Warren Beatty, one of his PAs called and said, "I wanted to set his call time for tomorrow." I said, "How long this will take, an hour or two hours?" "It'll be an all-day shoot." "Really? All day?" I had a screening I had to go to that night. Alice said, "He's got to be able to come home and take a catnap so he'll be fresh for the screening." "Let's say a 4:30 p.m. out and 8:30 a.m. will be his call time." "Fine." Jessie came with me.

Warren said to me the day before, "Let me tell you, the yellow coat makes a big statement." He wasn't wrong. When he sweeps in wearing that hat, the fedora, and the yellow overcoat, it's imposing. It really is. Got makeup and all that. We agreed on my jacket color, shirt color, whatever. I sat at a round table. They made it look like the Charlie Rose set. Round wooden table and brightly lit subject and interviewee. We did it over. I had read Oliver Platt about working on *Bulworth*, about Warren's tenacity doing something over and over and over and over. That's what we did all day. The same dialogue over and over and over and over again. No direction such as, "Hit this a little harder" or "Slow up." Just do it over and over and over again. At about 3:45, the assistant came, stage-whispered to Warren, "Just so you know, Leonard has a hard-out in about 40 minutes." "Fine." They didn't give me any trouble about that. A week later, I said to myself, "What if he's still on that stage shooting his lines?" Then I heard nothing. I ran into Annette at LAX and she said, "Oh, the show is adorable. You'll be very happy when you see it." It was done for Disney Home Video in collaboration with TCM and aired once on TCM on July 4th. They buried it so deep in their schedule, I'm amazed anybody saw it, but people did see it and didn't know what to make of it.

Segaloff: Did he send you a copy?

Maltin: No. It went into a video purgatory somewhere. I don't think it was on YouTube for long. Then, a year and a half ago, I got a call from Warren Beatty. He wanted to do it again because something happened in the legal case.

Segaloff: The legend is that every time the rights are about to lapse, he makes some cheapjack version of a *Dick Tracy* film and never shows it anywhere, but it's what he needs to do to retain the film rights. These phantom productions are listed on IMDb which makes them look more legitimate.

Maltin: Right. Did it again. Different style, different content, different approach. This time, he did it with TCM. Ben Mankiewicz and I were both hired. A nice fella who works for AFI directed it. We did it in a suite of offices that he leases or rents on top of Beverly Glen Drive. We did it over and over. The throughline, such as it is, was about us trying to convince Dick Tracy to let Warren Beatty play him or something like that. This you can see. I've gotten quizzical responses from people saying, "What was that about?" It was a long day, long day. At the end of the shoot, I'll tell this, he was using Zoom as a device where he could talk to himself. Warren could talk to Dick Tracy or vice versa. First he wanted to get just wild shots of us reacting badly supposedly to some of the old footage, earlier Dick Tracy. It's not easy to do [Leonard mugs reactions] for five minutes. Then at the end, he wanted us to go, "All right," he says, "give it two thumbs up." I said, "No, I can't do that." He said, "Why not?" I said, "That's really the property of Siskel and Ebert, and I'm friendly with Chaz Ebert, and I wouldn't want to upset her." Warren didn't get it. He said, "He doesn't own a thumb." I said, "No, no, it's associated exclusively with him and Siskel, and I can't do that." He tried to talk me into doing it. Meanwhile, it's late in the day, and I will pat myself on the back, because I didn't back down.

Segaloff: You're one of the few people who's ever been immune to Warren's charm.

Maltin: I wasn't immune. He's a charming guy, and he took Alice and me to dinner before we did the shoot, but I was not going to succumb on this one. Then finally he said, "Well, what if you both applaud?" I said, "No problem." We were acting, and I'm not an actor. Ben's not an actor, so it was inherently awkward to begin with, and he didn't understand what the thumb is.

Segaloff: What's this I hear about you writing a script for Troma? Was it like Roger Ebert writing *Beyond the Valley of the Dolls*?

Maltin: This was a fluke, a fluke of circumstance. Alice and I got married on the Ides of March 1975 and moved into a brand new seventeen-story building at the corner of 79th and Amsterdam on the Upper West Side. Our next-to-next-door neighbor, two doors down, was Michael Herz, the cofounder of Troma with his more flamboyant partner Lloyd Kaufman. We were friendly in an apartment-friendly way. We didn't have dinners together. We saw each other in the hallway and in the elevator, and we'd chat. I think he offered me the opportunity to write a screenplay for a film that they had just greenlit for themselves called *Squeeze Play!* about a women's softball team, and this was to be a titillating R-rated movie. Not X-rated, but R-rated. One day, his wife Maris knocked on our door and invited us to go to the screening of their newest film. Michael and Lloyd had gotten their way into the business by doing budget breakdowns on scripts, working with John Avildsen, and that was their entree. They wanted to make their own movies, but they concluded that there was no way to break in except from the extreme margins, one of them being pornography. Maris said, "We'd like you to come see our new movie called *The Divine Obsession.*" Or maybe not "*The*," just *Divine Obsession*. They rented a screening room in, I think, the Paramount Building. 10:30 one weekday morning. I'd never seen hardcore pornography before. Alice noticed, because it was mostly men there. They were all sitting with their legs crossed. When it was over, thank God it was over, his wife, especially, thanked us for coming. What do you say? What do you say in response to this movie? "I had a very nice time?" What I said was it was a very well-made, well-crafted movie.

Segaloff: The sort of thing you tell an actor backstage after a terrible play when you have to say something and don't want to lie.

Maltin: Anyway, he offered me this chance to do a screenplay, and I thought, well, who am I to turn down an adventure like that? He was going to pay me $1,000. What queered the deal, to use an old-fashioned expression, was that it was going to be in fourteen installments.

Segaloff: Fourteen? Sorry to laugh in your face.

Maltin: I don't know what a Writers Guild contract looks like.

Segaloff: Somewhat higher.

Maltin: First draft, second draft, notes, and all that kind of thing. Just the absurdity of that, really, that did it in. They made that film, and I don't know how hard it will be to research this, but my recollection is that the Loew's State Theater, where *Star Wars* or *Empire Strikes Back* played, had a very big marquee, just off Broadway, just west of Broadway. When UA pulled *Heaven's Gate* from distribution, the film that they booked was *Squeeze Play!* Another bullet dodged.

Segaloff: Okay, now here's a bullet you took: "Will the real Leonard Maltin please stand up."[*]

Maltin: I think I was at NYU. This was the later syndicated version of *To Tell the Truth* hosted by Garry Moore as opposed to the long-running network show with Bud Collyer. They taped five a day. It was a memorable day for several reasons. I remembered that Garry Moore was a fan of Buster Keaton, and he used to have him on his show, his daytime show especially, with some regularity. At one point, Garry Moore came to get a cup of coffee from the coffee urn. I approached him and said, "Tell me about working with Buster Keaton." He did, and I went and scribbled all that down and used it in my book, *The Great Movie Comedians*. I scored there. One of the guests on another episode they were taping that day was the photographer, Inge Morath. I got to meet and shake hands with her husband, Arthur Miller. There's no more to the story than that, but I shook hands with Arthur Miller! I realized I have got lot of those where all I did was say hello.

Segaloff: Like Rube Goldberg, you meet people, but in your case you knew who they were, which is something that I'm sure a lot of people in your age group didn't.

Maltin: I also spent a day at *MAD Magazine*.

Segaloff: With the usual gang of idiots?

Maltin: Yes, with Al Feldstein, the editor, who was extremely nice. Everyone I met there was nice. They gave me a souvenir bottle of Moxie.[†] Real Moxie, which I kept for a long, long time. Sorry, I don't have it anymore, but I spent a day at *MAD Magazine*.

Segaloff: You mentioned before that a lot of these people were simply in the Manhattan phone book.

Maltin: Oh, yes.

---

[*] The catchline for the reveal in the Goodson-Todman game show *To Tell the Truth*.

[†] A popular soft drink created in 1876 as a "nerve medicine" with an indescribable taste, supposedly gentian root extract, that you either liked or hated. The name came to mean "courage," which is what you needed to get through a bottle if you didn't appreciate the flavor. It was bought by the Coca-Cola company in 2018.

Segaloff: Did they think it was all unusual that somebody of your young years would know who they were?

Maltin: No one ever put it that way. I was a big fan of Roger Price. Do you remember Roger Price?

Segaloff: Do I! I am also a Grump.*

Maltin: I wrote him. I remember this. One night on the Jimmy Dean variety show, Rowlf† made his first appearance, and I loved it. I wrote to Roger Price, care of ABC Television's *Jimmy Dean Show*, and it got to him. He wrote back and drew a Droodle.‡

Segaloff: He had a short-lived magazine called *Grump*.

Maltin: You don't need to tell me. He commissioned me to write a piece for the debut issue and I mistakenly believed he had accepted it and was going to publish it, so for months I wore a Grump lapel pin, which I still have. Then the issue came out, and the article was not in it, because the problem that I couldn't solve was he wanted a 12- or 13-year-old voice. I was trying to write a humor piece that a grownup would write. But we were friendly for quite a while. Fade out, fade in spring of 1982, summer, I've now been sort-of hired by *Entertainment Tonight*. I still don't have a contract, but they're paying me scale which was $500. I would travel out here and spend a week here on my own and then fly home. Alice started coming out with me every third trip or so, because we didn't want to be apart. One night I'm working into the evening at our office which was then in Merv Griffin's building on Vine Street. I'm chatting with our receptionist, a sweet girl named Claudia, and Claudia says, "You won't see me for a couple of weeks. I'm traveling to the Far East with my father." "Oh, really? How's that?" "He's going on business, and I'm going to keep him company." I said, "What's your father do?" "Oh, he's in publishing." I said, "Really? What's his name?" Claudia Sloan was her name. Her father was Larry Sloan. I said, "Sloan, as

---

* *Grump* was a satirical magazine that featured articles by celebrity curmudgeons who took positions on life's frustrations. It lasted two years and, when Price folded it, he gave the mailing list to publisher Lyle Stuart who fulfilled Price's subscribers' subscriptions with his equally personal newsletter, *The Independent*.

† Rowlf, a large dog Muppet, was Jim Henson's network breakthrough in 1963.

‡ Droodles were simple, abstract drawings that made no sense until one read the description, and even then not everybody got them.

in Price/Stern/Sloan?" "Yes." She put me back in touch with Roger, who was then living out here, and he came to our New Year's Eve party. Imagine catching up with Roger as a grown up. I remember Price's law: "If everybody doesn't want it, nobody gets it." I asked him once after he was described in an article in *TV Guide* or something, as "cartoonist Roger Price." I said, "That doesn't really say it right. How would you describe yourself?" He said, "A cultural opportunist." Isn't that wonderful?

Segaloff: He's also known for *Mad Libs*,* which is one of the greatest inventions that will outlive everybody we know. It seems so basic, but didn't it grow out of an actual party game?

Maltin: I think so. He developed it with his longtime publishing partner Leonard Stern. And if I recall correctly, Steve Allen fell in love with it and plugged it on his show.

Segaloff: Among other celebrities, they say that Tommy Lee Jones is a tough interview, but how did you engage him?

Maltin: The first time I talked to him was for the Oliver Stone movie, *Heaven and Earth*. We were at the Four Seasons Hotel. Nobody warned me about him. He was in an upholstered winged chair, with his arms on the arms of the chair. I could see sometimes his grip was tightening. He was answering my questions. I liked the film, and I liked him in it. I said, "Do you think that acting is instinctual with you?" He bit my head off. He said, "I don't think anything is instinctual," blah, blah, blah. "Animals do things instinctually. I don't think that—." I said, "What would you call it? Ten days after you graduated from college, you were doing an off-Broadway show with no training. How would you describe that?" I saw his grip loosen. He considered that an intelligent question, and he answered me. Then I was full of praise for the Larry McMurtry mini-series, *Lonesome Dove,* and he loved *Lonesome Dove*. He was very fond of it, so that played well. We had a successful interview for *E.T.* Then when he was shooting in MacArthur Park for the movie *Volcano*, we went down there to talk to him and also Don Cheadle. They were both shooting that day. I talked to Tommy, and he was not in a bad mood that day. When we wrapped, that was his wrap for the day. He went to his trailer and got out of his movie wardrobe and put on his street clothes. Before he left the area, he came over and slapped me

---

* Innocuous narratives printed on pads with blanks that specify "noun," "verb," "adjective" etc. that party guests shout out without knowing the contest. When read back, hilarity ensues.

on the back, said, "See you again." Our sound man said, "As long as he's a star, you've got a job," because he's just a very difficult man.

They did a double junket for the John Grisham movie that he did with Tom Cruise, *The Firm,* and *Blown Away,* where Lloyd Bridges played Jeff's father in that, but Tommy's in that, too. He's a villain. I said, "Actors tend to say that they like playing villains better than heroes. Do you agree with that?" He said, "Yes. In fact, I would say that's stating the obvious." I said, "We specialize in that at *Entertainment Tonight.*" We went on. At the end of that interview, we said goodbye, and the publicist said, "Gee, you got the best interview all day."

He directed a film called *The Homesman,* which barely got released, but it was shown at Telluride. I interviewed him on stage after the screening. We met him and his wife backstage in the green room. Jessie was there. It's a tough film. The version we saw was apparently pulled back from the extremes that he shot. Meryl Streep agreed to be in it in a supporting role out of her fondness for him, or respect for him, but he's just pissy. I don't know why. I always remember that sound man.

Segaloff: Was Gene Autry one of your childhood heroes?

Maltin: Not really, I was a Roy Rogers guy. I came to appreciate Gene later, as an adult. I like his singing voice, and I like listening to his Melody Ranch radio show. Then I got to meet him and he was very nice to me.

Segaloff: He's a pretty fair businessman, too.*

Maltin: Yes. The authorized biography that his widow, Jackie, commissioned is very good. It's a really interesting book, because it's candid.† Warts and all. Alice and I were producing a video documentary special called "Cliffhangers" for A&E. That's why we shot Gene, because he starred in *The Phantom Empire.*‡

---

* Among Gene Autry properties was the Los Angeles Angels baseball team, which later became the Anaheim Angels.
† *Public Cowboy #1: The Life and Times of Gene Autry,* by Holly George-Warren (Oxford, 2009).
‡ A 1935 serial with Autry and Frankie Darro involving cowboys and the scientific city of Murania that happens to have sunk eons ago beneath Autry's Radio Ranch.

Segaloff: Oh, my favorite serial. Every Saturday morning in front of the TV.

Maltin: Jackie Autry was very nice. Not only did she set it up, but she said, "He's not doing too well today. We just came back from the Baseball Owners Association in the Midwest. If you can wait until next week, I think you'll get a better interview." We did. Then for Clayton Moore's eightieth birthday, which they did as a dinner in the Rotunda at the Autry Museum, I sat right next to Gene. I told him I was about to go on a book promotion tour. He said, "Really?" He says, "Have you got an advance man?" I said, "Not really." He said, "Well, here's what you do." He says, "You want to get there first thing in the morning and have the mayor give you the key to the city or something like that. You've got to do that early enough so it gets on the evening news and the late afternoon newspaper. Then you want to go to the Children's Hospital and visit the kids in the ward." He gave me step by step how to do a tour— if you happened to be a huge star. I also heard him use the F-bomb, referring to baseball players' salaries.

Segaloff: Oh, well, of course. Of course.

Maltin: That museum was willed into existence by him and his second wife, Jackie, who had been his banker in Palm Springs, and with Joanne Hale and her husband, Monte Hale, who was the last of the Republic singing cowboys. They were quite a foursome. We went to a lot of events in the early days of that museum's existence. I have a lingering fondness for the place. They changed the name. It was called the Gene Autry Museum. They changed the name to the Autry Museum of the American West, to sound more serious and to separate it in people's minds from what was then the Roy Rogers Museum out in Palmdale, which was really all about Roy's career.

Segaloff: Now comes your neighbor, Philip Carey. Why am I not placing that name?

Maltin: You'd know him if you saw him. Good-looking, tall, blonde hair. People out here knew him from a series of commercials he did for Granny Goose potato chips. It was a Stan Freberg-like campaign of having this serious, handsome guy say, "Hi, I'm Granny Goose. I guarantee these potato chips are more tasty." He was an up-and-coming, leading man type in the early '50s whose career had several ups and downs, some of them self-inflicted, apparently. We had a neighbor down the hall on 79th Street who was a performer, Gail

Matthius. She was on one season of *Saturday Night Live* and then moved out to L.A. to seek her fame and fortune. She told Alice that she had sublet to an actor, and that if we saw him, we should say hello and welcome him and all that. One day, Alice is taking garbage out to the chute. We were on one end of the hall. The garbage chute was in the middle. She sees this tall guy, and the lighting isn't very good. As he comes closer, she says, "Oh, you must be Gail's new sublet." "Yes. Hi. My name is Phil Carey." She knew him right away. He's in *The Long Gray Line*.

Segaloff: Sort of a Henry Fonda lite.

Maltin: We had dinner together several times. He came to New York to play what they were calling the daytime version of J. R. Ewing on *The Young and the Restless*.

He found newfound fame on the soap. Had a baby. Had a second family, young wife. When I tried to ask him movie questions, he was sort of unresponsive, but things came up spontaneously that were great. Alice was always self-critical of her cooking when having some people over. I said, "Honey, stop frowning. You look like Iron Eyes Cody." He said, "Iron Eyes Cody? What a son of a bitch." Something like that. "Now, Jay Silverheels, *there* was a nice guy." Out of the blue would come such utterances. He was just an ornery cuss. He played hooky on *The Long Gray Line* and went to New York City for the weekend, surreptitiously, he thought. When he came back to West Point, Ford put him in a swimming pool scene where the lights were very hot. He was never to go in the water. He was to be on the sidelines all day, broiling. That was his Fordian punishment.

Segaloff: I guess if you're going to be punished, it might as well be by John Ford.

Maltin: He talked about how he and Merv Griffin were both under contract to Warners in the early '50s, which is true. He said he didn't play up to the right people. He could have been nicer to Merv Griffin, and that might have repaid him. He could have been nicer to Aaron Spelling, another young actor working the same rounds as he. It was just an incidental episode in our lives. Alice and I look back over it. We've been married fifty years. I've experienced so much.

Segaloff: You must have tried your hand at many things and been involved with some interesting characters.

Maltin: Had so many episodes, I guess you call them, vignettes, episodes. A guy contacted me who was working with Gannett Newspapers, who had a scheme to dial a movie review. Call this 1-800 number and press four if you want a review of *Back to the Future*. Press five if you want a review of—

Segaloff: Sounds like MovieFone.*

Maltin: A cousin to MovieFone. I did samples, and it was going to be promoted by Gannett. The debut date had been set and announced, but I wasn't seeing anything in *USA Today*, the national newspaper published by Gannett. I finally called the guy. I was going to get five cents per call, something like that. No money up front. I said to my agent, "Nothing up front? No signing bonus? No, nothing like that?" "No." He said, "It's worth a flyer." "Okay." Then I called this guy, and I said, "Why have I seen nothing in *USA Today*? We're starting next week." Well, he says, "Their movie critic was a little bent out of shape that he wasn't doing it." I called my agent, and I said, "This man is a liar." *USA Today*'s movie critic is my old friend Mike Clark. Mike would have said something to me. We're old friends, and I don't think he would hold a grudge; if he had one, he would tell me. That was bullshit. There was another guy from AT&T, or purported to be from AT&T, that had another more elaborate plan. We spent lots of money on our lawyer. Our lawyer doesn't charge every time he picks up the phone and says hello, but he had to spend so much time negotiating this contract with the guy from AT&T that it cost us money, only to find out that he was a con artist. He was a total con man. We got one payment from him, but that one payment bought us a Peter Ellenshaw oil painting, so we have something to show for it.

Segaloff: We haven't talked about Freddie Bartholomew. He was alive, I suppose, at the time.

Maltin: He lived not far from me in North Jersey. I did call once. He was in the phone book, but his wife put me off. "Fred doesn't like to talk about those days." There was a fellow who took my animation class repeatedly at the New School who worked on a soap opera. Fred was, I think, the ad agency rep for that soap. The fellow said, "We work with him every day. He's a very nice man." I said, "I can't get past his wife." Well, in the last year or so of his life, he was living in

---

* MovieFone was a dial-in system for showtimes and theatre locations that died the instant the internet was invented.

Florida. I don't remember how I got the connection. Roddy McDowall figures in this. Roddy got him to talk on camera for *MGM: When the Lion and Roars*, that overblown documentary series. I got him on the phone repeatedly and did not record him, unfortunately. We had brief but nice conversations which I hoped would lead to a formal interview. I was using the pen name Henry Armetta, as my handle. Well, he worked with Henry Armetta.

Segaloff: Of course, at Metro.

Maltin: Said, "Oh, what a lovely man he was." He said, "How about Herbert Mundin?" I said, "Herbert Mundin is in *David Copperfield*." He played Barkus. Fred couldn't have been more delightful to chat with, but I didn't get the interview. It's always the ones got away. Somewhere in the deep recesses of my mind—I have to go into a hypnotic trance—I was pursuing Hedy Lamarr. I don't remember the particulars, but she was in Florida, too.

Segaloff: I saved the best for last because there's no other way to put it. That is your experience of driving Adolph Green and Isaac Asimov to Brooklyn.

Maltin: Our matchmaker, Herb Graff, got friendly with Walter Kerr. Walter, of course, saw every Broadway opening, but was given two tickets. His wife, Jean, was tired of coming in from Westchester to see bad shows, mediocre shows, so Herb was his date. Herb was his plus-one. Herb worked in the *schmatte* business, but he was also a film aficionado and collector. When you're seen with Walter Kerr and you can talk about show business and spin anecdotes, and he was a good spieler, people assume you're in the business. Through Walter, he became friendly with Adolph Green. That's how I got to meet Adolph, who was just a charming, lovely man who signed my published copy of the *Singin' in the Rain* screenplay. Herb also started going to the Dutch Treat Club, which was a luncheon society of mostly successful men, who gathered once a month at a hotel in Midtown New York for lunch and had a guest speaker. Herb was the guest speaker one time, and then they invited him to join. Lowell Thomas was the longtime chair of that, and I got him to get Lowell Thomas to sign one of his books for me. That's where he met Isaac Asimov. Herb's son was being bar mitzvah'd in Brooklyn, and he knew I was coming, and I drove. I said, "Would you mind driving Adolph Green and Isaac Asimov?" I said, "No." I only wish I'd had a little tape recorder. They were dining on each other's stories. All I remember of it was they both loved operettas, it turns out. Adolph had written faux operettas, and one of them was *Gamboling on the Green.* That's one of those experiences you want to be able to put into a little wallet or purse and be able to open that up and have it come back to life so you can share it with other people. Just to state the bare facts of it is not inherently interesting, but the fact that I got to do it was deeply rewarding.

THE FUTURE OF NOSTALGIA

Segaloff: I want to go back to the way the industry has changed. People would go to the movies once or twice a week, yet now it's an event. From fifty films a year per studio, now you're lucky if they release eight. It's a blockbuster mentality, mergers of film companies, loss of art house films, focus groups versus the gut instinct…

Maltin: As I pointed out before, the French film *Diva* played in the Paris Cinema in Manhattan for a year. They just kept renewing it, and renewing it, and renewing it. Such a thing couldn't happen today. It was unusual then, but not out of the question that a film could linger. When we were first married, I remember the Lina Wertmüller films being brought overseas by Don Rugoff.* He was the one who distributed *Swept Away* followed by *Seven Beauties*. It's all anyone was talking about. It defined the zeitgeist of the moment, at least in New York, and New Yorkers think that New York is the whole world. They're not entirely wrong. I remember as a kid, in Teaneck, I was still living at home, the summer that *Blow-Up* (1966) came out. Again, that's all anyone could talk about was, "Why was there no tennis ball?"† There are certain scenes, certain movies that had the ability to capture seemingly an entire country in a way that we don't see much today.

Segaloff: They became cultural references. You didn't have to say anything except "the black monolith" and everybody knew it was *2001*.

Maltin: Right. I have a memory, just came into my head like a flashback. I remember seeing the window card in our butcher shop. We lived on Grayson Place in Teaneck, up a hill from Teaneck Road. Down the hill were a block of four or five business establishments: a candy store, as we used to call it; they'd sell newspapers, magazines, that's where I bought my comics, where I bought *Famous Monsters*, *Mad Magazine*, and Bazooka bubble gum. Next to that was the butcher shop. His name was Bill Hasse, the Bill Hasse Butcher Shop, and then dry cleaners. That was that block. In the butcher shop

---

* Donald Rugoff (1927-1998) owned Cinema V (a.k.a. Cinema 5), the American distribution company of such landmark art films as *Putney Swope*, *Z*, *The Endless Summer*, *Monty Python and the Holy Grail*, and the aforementioned Lina Wertmuller films. He also owned showcase theatres in Manhattan. The film *Searching for Mr. Rugoff* (2019) by Rugoff's former employee Ira Deutchman is a fascinating portrait of this eccentric man.
† Spoiler: the last image in Antonioni's film is a tennis game played with no ball.

window, I remember seeing this hypnotic window card for *The List of Adrian Messenger*[*] with pictures of the five big, big movie stars who are all in that film in disguise. It captured my imagination and is the only time I can remember that a poster—of any size—got to me that way. I had to see that film and I did.

These window cards had the space on top where the theater owner could take a crayon, or a Magic Marker, and write, "Tue-Wed," or "Starts Monday." The idea that some theater in Podunk got shipments three times a week—these were 35mm prints in heavy cans, but they had a system, and it worked. They had a system of exchanges around the country. A friend of mine in Cleveland has cited chapter and verse for me about how it worked in Cleveland. Friday didn't used to be opening day.

Segaloff: Right, it used to be Wednesday.

Maltin: Wednesday. On Tuesday night, there was this massive machinery that went into overdrive to pick up the previous show, for which the projectionist would have had to make sure everything was rewound, or maybe they didn't want to rewind for inspection purposes. In later years, when platters came in, there's a lot of splicing and unsplicing to do, but these cans would be left in the lobby, and messengers would come who had a key to get in the lobby and take these heavy cans, and then bring these dozens and dozens of cans to the exchange, having switched out the next week's programming, or the next day's programming. It could be for one day.

Segaloff: You would see on the shipping exchange floor the cans lined up like soldiers.

Maltin: Yes. And they were bicycle prints. Oh, there's some wild stories about the bicycle prints.[†]

---

[*] John Huston's 1963 period mystery in which Robert Mitchum, Frank Sinatra, Burt Lancaster, Kirk Douglas, and Tony Curtis appeared under such elaborate makeup that they could not be recognized until the final reveal, "That's the end of the picture, but it's not the end of the mystery"

[†] Before platters, when films were on four or five separate twenty-minute reels, unscrupulous exhibitors would have an usher on a bicycle taking a reel from one theater to another, and then back again, to allow two theaters to show the same print. It went on all day, every day, and if the usher was waylaid by traffic, there was an impromptu intermission. The object was to show a film on two screens but only tell the studio about one screen.

Segaloff: By the way, did your friend tell you why they changed the opening to Friday from Wednesday?

Maltin: No.

Segaloff: That's so the reviews would be buried in Saturday's paper, which is the least-read issue of the week, and so if you wanted to hide a review, you would open a film on Friday. Also, the advertising would only be needed Thursday and Friday pre-opening, you wouldn't have to advertise Tuesday and Wednesday too. There was also showmanship in the presentation of a film. You would never show a blank screen—until General Cinema and Showcase Cinemas. You would always throw the image on the curtain and then open it grandly.

Maltin: Right, right, right. The Teaneck theater still exists in Teaneck, New Jersey on Cedar Lane. It's an okay theater, nothing special about it, nothing fancy, but it had something that I've never seen before or since, an illuminated clock perched right next to the screen and above it a little bit on the right-hand side. You couldn't help be distracted by it, but being compulsive by nature, I ascertained that no Disney movie ever ran more than 90 minutes. I think that's true. The animated features were always short, but I'm talking about *Son of Flubber*.

Segaloff: What was your favorite candy at the concession stand?

Maltin: I won't answer your question right away. I liked my popcorn drenched in butter, soggy with butter. I broke that habit pretty easily in adulthood. However, I remember when Roger Ebert got on a high horse about popcorn and so they started air-popping.[*] It tasted like Styrofoam. There was nothing appealing about that. I like Sno-Caps, and I like Raisinets. Those are my two favorite movie candies.

Segaloff: Did you ever sit on a row with a light on the end so you could see what color Juicy Fruits you were eating?

Maltin: No.

Segaloff: Oh, you missed out.

---

[*] Most movie theaters used to pop their corn in coconut oil, which is 92 percent saturated fat, and the "butter" they pumped onto it was not always real butter, it was hydrogenated soybean oil.

Maltin: Roger Ebert told my wife that Good & Plenty was either his favorite, or he liked it because it filled you up. There was one theater, the Rialto in Ridgefield Park, New Jersey, that had a popcorn dispensing machine. You put in twenty-five cents or whatever, and you held the bag under a chute, and it was engineered to dispense just the right amount.

Segaloff: I remember they had the Butter Cup, which was the brand name for this large waxed paper cup in which they put about a quart of popcorn. If the person behind the stand liked you, they'd stop halfway up, pump in a layer of butter, then go all the way up and put more butter on top.

Maltin: When we moved out here, David Shepard introduced us to popcorn laced with M&M's.

Segaloff: Oh, deadly.

Maltin: Deadly.

Segaloff: Like the gimmicks of William Castle, that's what they called showmanship in those days, and not just the inherent nature of the business, but also the press books would tell you, "Hey, Mr. Exhibitor, here's how do you do it."

Maltin: Do we know if anybody ever followed those tips?

Segaloff: Only if one of the exchange managers was coming to town or something. I once had to pay one of our cleaning crew to dress up as Henry VIII and stand in front of the theater showing *Carry On Henry VIII* (1971).

Maltin: You actually did that?

Segaloff: It was entirely useless. You did ballyhoo so that the newspapers would cover it. We pulled a stunt when I was working for theaters. During the Watergate hearings in 1974 there were two films, *The Mad Adventures of Rabbi Jacob* and *Bring Me the Head of Alfredo Garcia*. They were both playing at the same multiplex. One night the theater manager and I changed the letters to *Bring Me the Head of Richard Nixon* and *The Mad Adventures of Rabbi Korff* (Korff was a notorious Nixon supporter.) I phoned the newspapers anonymously the next morning to say, "Did you see what somebody did at the such-and-such Theater in Boston?" hoping they'd send a photographer. Instead, I got a call back from the newspaper's sales department an hour later, because I was the publicity director for the theater chain, "Nat, we saw what somebody did, but because you're such a big advertiser, we're not going to embarrass you." I never knew if he was onto me or corrupt; probably both.

HAS HIS WRITING CHANGED OVER THE YEARS?

Maltin: My writing has become more conversational. For starters, when I wrote my first two audition reviews for *Entertainment Tonight*, I think the reason that they played as well as they did is that I was reading my own copy aloud, so I knew the inflections. But I didn't understand writing for the ear. It took time.

Segaloff: Explain that.

Maltin: When you're writing to be *heard* as opposed to writing to be *read*, parenthetical phrases don't work, and other forms of syntax just are not user-friendly for a listener. Also, I became less formal. The guy I admire/envy is Roger Ebert, who I never read growing up because I had no opportunity. The *Bergen Record* didn't take his stuff, and no New York paper, I think, printed his reviews. I came to them online. Roger was an early adopter of computers in general and new technology. He decided to post his reviews online, so I started looking at them and consulting them. He was able to write in the first person and weave elements of his life into his reviews without seeming awkward or arbitrary. A certain subject would come into a review and it flowed naturally. I have a harder time. I'm still journalistic. Don't use that first person.

Segaloff: One avoids the use of one's name. It can be awkward unless there are ways around it. Of course, one should write in a linear manner for exactly the reasons you've said.

Maltin: Another one who did that was Andrew Sarris, who was also able to write an essay about the auteur theory.

Segaloff: I noticed something in a review you posted today (*Conclave*). At the end, you said how you and Alice differed in your opinions. I can't recall you having quoted anybody else in a review before.

Maltin: I've done it now and then, not often, but I thought it was worthy of inclusion. The punchline of the story is that they name, for Pope, a guy who has a slight skeleton in his closet.[*] The characters in the film consider it a triumph. Alice said that the news would come out in a matter of days so this is no conclusion. She felt that it negated the whole story. I didn't think that, but because it's a film that hinges on leading to a satisfying finale, that's why I thought I should acknowledge it.

---

[*] *Conclave* (2024) is a drama about the College of Cardinals choosing a new pope.

Segaloff: I agree. A film that reverses or does something like that at the end risks telling the audience, "We've been fooling you all along." *Fight Club* was like that to me, but not *The Sixth Sense*, which is interesting. Both involved huge reveals.

Maltin: I watched *Fight Club* a second time because I showed it in my class; that tends to be the only way I see a film twice. If I've seen it at a film festival or press screening, and then I run it at USC, and I'll sit and watch it with the class again. I don't think *Fight Club* adds up; *Sixth Sense* does. I think *Fight Club* plays fast and loose.

Segaloff: One of the reasons I mentioned your citing Alice at the end of it is it reminds me of something Pauline Kael always used to do, which is if there was an opinion she thought would make her look bad, and I'm reading a lot into this, she always laid it off on a friend who came to see the movie with her. "I had this friend who felt this way." I guess she had a lot of friends.

Maltin: One day I picked up the phone in our apartment; maybe Alice answered the phone. It was Pauline Kael, who had a surprisingly sweet voice, a very soothing, gentle voice. She was calling to talk about Harry Ritz, of the Ritz brothers. We had a nice chat for a little while, and that's the only time I ever had any contact with her. I don't remember if there was a question that I answered for her, but somehow that happened.

Segaloff: On the one hand, she called *2001: A Space Odyssey* monumentally unimaginative. On the other hand, because of her, everybody read film critics, and she was a magnificent force in spreading the word about what we do.

Maltin: No rose-colored glasses are necessary to recall that time when Kael and Andrew Sarris were leading the pack of people writing about film and stimulating a lot of conversation, literal conversation, figurative conversation about films. It was cool. It was exciting. I remember because my family got *The New York Times* every day. I remember Bosley Crowther's implosion over *Bonnie and Clyde* and how he wrote himself out of a career and a lifelong reputation through his stubbornness. It was fascinating to me that such a thing could happen over one movie.

Segaloff: He did it twice, and that's what killed him. He did it from the Montreal film festival, and then he did it when it opened. Jonathan Demme, who began as a publicist, talked about speaking with all of the other publicists at all of the studios, and how they would anticipate the new Fellini, they would anticipate the new Antonioni. Everybody was together in their thinking. The literati in New York, I'm sure, would go to the Fine Art or the Paris and see wherever the newest of the new wave were. It was a society.

Maltin: During my annual book tours, I came to be aware that in certain cities there was a given film critic had the power to make or break a movie the way they used to say *The New York Times* could make or break a Broadway play. Gary Arnold in Washington. Who in Boston?

Segaloff: Well, Kevin Kelly, sort of. He knew so little about movies that he didn't hold that much sway, so there was really nobody who could do that. For a time, it was Deac Rossell of *Boston After Dark*, then Janet Maslin, who went on to the *New York Times*.

Maltin: In Seattle, Bill Arnold, I think. If you were an indie or foreign film distributor, you really needed that to be a good review because if it was, people would come, and if it wasn't — my old friend, Gary Meyer, told me that it was imperative to open a film in New York and get a pull quote from, preferably, *The New York Times* before sending it out to the rest of the country because that's what sold the movie. "The performance of the year" — *New York Times*.

Segaloff: Did you ever write to be quoted?

Maltin: I'm not a good quote writer. I don't give good quotes. It's not because I don't want to, my mind doesn't work that way somehow. I'm good doing book blurbs. I'm proud of my book blurbs. I just blurbed Robert Bader's book on Zeppo Marx.* I used the word *unflinching*, and he really liked that. I gave that real thought because it's a no-holds-barred book, really a revelatory book. I had this experience, however, early in my run at *E.T.* when I was still commuting coast to coast. I flew home on a Friday afternoon and picked up the Friday *Los Angeles Times* Calendar section, their entertainment section the weekend that they opened *Eddie and the Cruisers* with Michael Paré. What I said on the air was, "Michael Paré seems all right, but I'll have to see more of his work before I'll buy this hype that he's the new James Dean." In the ad,

---

* *Zeppo, the Reluctant Marx Brother* (New York: Applause Books, 2024)

they quoted me, "...the new James Dean." It was a Friday, and I was on a plane, so I couldn't lodge a complaint. When I looked it Monday, the film had already died over the weekend, so it was a moot point.

Segaloff: Have you ever been burned out?

Maltin: Yes. It happened during my first year at *Entertainment Tonight*, this is '82, '83. Now when we look back, it seems like there were a lot of good movies. '83, '84, somewhere in there I remember seeing *Romancing the Stone* and being underwhelmed by that film. That's the word I want to use to describe it because already had been hyped to me. I thought, "This is okay, but it's not great." I was feeling a certain malaise. Then I went to a double feature at the Regency on Broadway in 67th Street. We saw a double feature of vintage Hollywood movies, and I said, "No, it's not me, it's the films." That gave me a good course correction moment. I said, "No, no, my antennae are still sharp."

Segaloff: You've done so many things. Is there anything that you want to do but didn't?

Maltin: Unrealized projects. There are very few, but I've been wanting to write a definitive article about Hugo Haas* for years and years and years. I have been seeking out people who knew him, people who worked with him, watching the films, making notes. It's all in my head and I've never sat down to do it because I always feel I'm still not fully prepared. I've got to see more.

Segaloff: That speaks to your methodology.

Maltin: Did I tell you the *Vanity Fair* story? One of my favorite things to do is to go to the special collections branch of the USC Cinema Library. They keep moving this special branch into fouler neighborhoods; I don't know how they find them. They have the Warner Bros. production files. This is my idea of fun. I went down for a day of research, and one of the things I wanted to see was if there was a paper trail that explained how the studio came to audition John Barrymore for the leading role in *The Man Who came to Dinner*. This

---

* Hugo Haas (1901-1968) was a Czech actor who left Europe when Hitler invaded, came to America, and became a writer-producer-director. His independence and personal drive distinguished him, but he always lived at the margins of Hollywood, never earning the success to match his ambition.

hearkened back to my stint at MoMA when I went through every file card and found that they had a nitrate reel of a screen test Barrymore made for that film.

Segaloff: Wow.

Maltin: As I recall, it's just him on screen, no one else. This was toward the end of his life, 1941. He's too mean. The tongue dipped in acid was a hundred proof, but it was really interesting to see. I wanted to learn if there were internal memos at Warner Bros. about filming Barrymore because the Warner Bros. had made their bones with John Barrymore in the '20s.

Segaloff: Sure. *Don Juan.*

Maltin: Even before *Don Juan.* They bought themselves prestige by hiring the number one matinee idol in the theater. There actually wasn't very much said who about who directed the test and that kind of thing. Then I found some interesting notes. They told me that one night, Jack Warner and his wife Ann went to dinner with Orson Welles and his girlfriend of the day, Dolores del Rio. *Citizen Kane* had not been released yet. They talked about Orson playing Sheridan Whiteside in the movie version of *The Man Who Came to Dinner*, and maybe he could direct it too. Jack Warner scribbled, I think on the back of an envelope or something. Salary was discussed: $150,000. I think he got more for starring than directing, but it was all there, in black and white. Then Orson went back East with Dolores del Rio, I think perhaps for the opening of *Citizen Kane.* J.L. [Warner] said, "Regards to Dolores." They obviously had a social evening that went well and drifted into business discussion of this juicy part and a juicy play that Warner Bros. had bought the rights to. You have to stop and think, "What if…?" If he had made that movie, it could have changed his entire life. He would've been in a mainstream Hollywood movie. That would've been his introduction to the public, not Charles Foster Kane. He would have a credential as a director of a major Hollywood studio movie. So much could have come from that. I don't remember why it petered out. I said, "This is the find of the century. What am I going to do with it?" I had photocopies made of the good stuff.

I made a cold call to Graydon Carter at *Vanity Fair.* I got his voicemail. I don't think it was his secretary; I think it was his voicemail. He returned the call, and I pitched this to him, and he said, "Yes." He said, "You'll be talking to my managing editor." I said, "Great." They sent me a contract for this piece. He was going to pay me $20,000. This is about twenty-three or twenty-four years ago. I was flabbergasted. I sat down and wrote the article and sent it in, and didn't hear anything for a little while. You're always waiting for the judgment of your editor when you're a freelancer. The clock was ticking. The calendar pages were flying through the air. Finally, I did talk to that managing editor again. He was my point person now, and he said, "We just published a piece this month about something, and it mentioned Orson Welles, and we thought it was redundant." They killed the article and paid me my full fee, not a kill fee,* and he gave me the rights back. I remember very clearly talking about it at the dinner table and trying to explain to Jessie, who was quite young then, "Honey, I know you won't understand this, but I would almost give them back the $20,000 if they put this in their Hollywood issue."

Segaloff: It's an iconic issue of an iconic magazine.

Maltin: Yes, and that byline would've meant the world to me, or so I thought.

Segaloff: *Vanity Fair* made its own gravy, so to speak, and it did have a certain respect when he was running it, certainly.

Maltin: What he did was, he made me invent a new newsletter publication for the express purpose of printing that article, and that's how *Leonard Maltin's Movie Crazy* came about.

Segaloff: Which I still have in my filing cabinet.

Maltin: I did it for ten years. I wrote every word. I didn't want contributors. I wanted this to be me. It became a vehicle for publishing stuff that I had in my trunk, in the proverbial writer's trunk, and an impetus to do new interviews with people, and an excuse to use my movie stills and collectibles. It was great fun, but hard work. The last couple of years it got to be feeling like a chore, and that was the death knell: when it started feeling like a drag. But along the way I had a chance to publish interviews that were just gathering dust, like the one I did with Robert Young.

Segaloff: Authors, I think, are buoyed with the adventure of writing and of finishing, but that's almost the easy part. When you start going over copy edits and drafts and proofreading and stills and captions, I think it takes away some of the joy

---

* A "kill fee" is paid when a publication decides not to run a freelance writer's article. The writer is usually paid half of the original fee and is given the rights back to sell the piece elsewhere.

of what you're actually supposed to do for a living, not the other stuff.

Maltin: Bernard Slade wrote a play, *Tribute* (1978) which Jack Lemmon starred in on Broadway. The first scene, he brings his date home to his apartment. She looks at him and says, "Nice place. What did you say you did for a living?" He says, "I'm a writer." She says, "Do you like doing it?" He said, "No, but I like *having done* it."

Alice Maltin joins us. She has been in the other room attending to business.

Segaloff: You're known as Alice and Leonard, or Leonard and Alice. In other words, you're a collective, and you are as well-known as Leonard is in a lot of ways.

Alice: I don't really think so.

Segaloff: You're the closer, you're known for your management.

Alice: Yes, I'm the one who stands next to the great. I'm the near-great.

Segaloff: You are very much your own personality.

Alice: Barbara and Frank, as they say.*

Maltin: When we were young and living in New York, we wanted to be Lee and Farrah.

Alice: Lee Majors and Farrah Fawcett because they were so gorgeous. We decided if we could be Lee and Farrah, that would be great.

Segaloff: Are you still starstruck?

Alice: Only certain people, I must tell you. Most of them, I really don't care.

Segaloff: Let's put it this way: Having dinner with Warren Beatty.

---

* Barbara and Frank Sinatra.

Alice: Yes. We had a co-op in Malibu. When Jessie said to me, "Mom, there was a guy on the phone who said he was Warren Beatty. Was he Warren Beatty?" I said, "Yes, he was Warren Beatty." Warren Beatty coming to the house, that meant something to me.

Segaloff: That disaster at the Academy Awards didn't do him any good, nor did his last film.*

Alice: The thing at the Academy Awards, that was unforgivable that they left them struggling like that.† I don't understand certain things. I'm starstruck for certain people. I don't really care much about the new crowd. I love Tom Hanks. Why? Because he probably reminds me of Jimmy Stewart.

Segaloff: They make two films and they're a star as opposed to making twenty films and then you have something to talk about.

Alice: I don't just want to be some silly woman who comes up and says, "Oh, I've just always loved you." I had a chance to meet Ginger Rogers. When we were staying at this hotel in New York, the door opened and there she was. Gorgeous. It was a small, private hotel. She was lovely and she complimented me. Jessie was in the stroller. She said, "What a beautiful little girl." In the hotel that we stayed in, the Wyndham, Jessica Tandy and Hume Cronyn had an apartment. One time I'm backing out of the elevator with the stroller. There's a voice that says, "Hello, little girl." It was Hume Cronyn. Things like that. I'm still reeling.

Segaloff: How has your relationship with Leonard changed over the fifty years that we're talking about?

Alice: We're very patient with each other. I can tell him anything. He can tell me anything. We appreciate each other. We enjoy what we can enjoy. There are things we can't do and things, financially, we've lost along the way, which is too bad. We know that we love each other no matter what.

---

* *Rules Don't Apply* (2016) which he directed, co-wrote, and in which he played Howard Hughes, the fulfillment of a lifelong ambition.
† At the 2017 Oscars, Beatty and Faye Dunaway announced the wrong winner of Best Picture: *La La Land* instead of *Moonlight*. They had apparently been handed the wrong envelope.

Maltin: At the beginning of Covid lockdown [in 2020], one night I turned to Alice. I said, "Isn't it nice that we still like being together? How lucky are we? We're going to be stuck."

Alice: We didn't know how long we were going to be stuck, but it didn't really matter.

Segaloff: You have to like each other, then you can love each other.

Alice: You have to care about each other. There are couples who don't care. It's hard to be with couples who don't care. I've got my problems. He's got his problems. The problems we had were outside problems that affected us. My pregnancies, my miscarriages, sick parents. His parents got sick. My father died. My mother fell in Florida. It's written in the Talmud that, when you're a widow, you have to move to Florida if you live in the Bronx. My mother was there and she was very happy. but she fell and broke her hip. I went to see what was going on in the hospital. She was in this really dark room with this other bed. I was always pushy. I said to the nurse, "Is there another room?" She said, "We have private rooms up on the tenth floor. Beautiful, overlooking, the bay and all that." I said, "What do they cost?" She said, "They're something like $25 a day. I said, "We want one." I got my mother out of there in a hurry. Right away, as soon as she was in this nice room with sun and everything by herself, she was doing better. I was there for two weeks. I knew that I had to bring her out. I said, "Honey," I came back to Leonard. I said, "Here's the situation. We bring her here or I spend half the year in Florida."

Maltin: Flying back and forth.

Alice: He's the first Jewish saint. He said, "Yes, bring her here," which I think kills your parents that my mother was living with us. His parents always had the idea that somehow they would have all a big house and live together. They really did. In Jersey, by the way.

Maltin: In Jersey. They visualized.

Alice: My mother, she had a good time. We took her to screenings. She got, of course, sicker and sicker. The last three years, I had full-time care in the house for her. I'm talking 24/7. You want to know what it cost me? It cost more than private school, and Jessie was in private school, but I wasn't going to put her in a home.

Maltin: Fortunately, I was making a really good living then and we could do it. People would say, "Why don't you put her in a nursing home?" No.

Segaloff: It's hard to do anything in this industry, which is run by jealousy and hatred, and be liked as universally as Leonard is. He's not insipid, but he's liked and respected. How does he do it? You tell me. You've been here for all of it.

Alice: He's just a good person. People would say to me, "What's he really like?" I'd say, "What you're looking at, that's what he's really like." I would wait for the dark side to emerge. It never happened. Leonard is a very good person. He loves what he does. He respects people. He's not threatened by people. I'm very proud of him. I get annoyed sometimes, but I'm very proud of him because when we're with other people and they'll ask a question, he'll come up with a fact. I'll go, "Where'd that come from?" He'll say, "I don't know." He's always modest. Very few people did what he did and remain modest.

Segaloff: Does he ever get moody or ill-tempered?

Alice: Yes. The Parkinson's has been fun.* Of course, he does. He had to deal with a lot of crap at *Entertainment Tonight*. That was very hard. The nature of things changing in the industry. He's basically a very level person. A very good person. That's the way he remains. I think that no matter what goes on in this town, people know that. They know he's the real thing. A lot of people say, "I'm an expert." He really is. He will never tell you that. People come up to him all the time and thank him for his books, for the videos that he did. They're in the business because of him. That's all ages. I think it's wonderful.

Segaloff: Leonard, is it still fun?

Leonard: The most fun is not knowing.

Segaloff: Not knowing?

---

* In July 2015 Leonard was diagnosed with Parkinson's Disease. He wrote about it in *Starstruck*.

Leonard: What's coming around the corner or what might be coming around the corner.

Segaloff: That's optimistic.

Leonard: Well, maybe nothing is coming around the corner. Freelancing, to me, is, to quote Mr. Dickens, the best of times and the worst of times. The optimist in me says, like the song from *West Side Story*, "Something's coming," and you never know.

Segaloff: How do you keep your spirits up?

Leonard: By writing something, by posting something on my website, which Jessie has to do, because I don't know how to do any of that.

Segaloff: But you've survived.

Leonard: The thing that makes me happiest is when a younger person recognizes me. Last Friday, I spoke at the Walk of Fame ceremony for Juanita Moore.* They do one posthumous star every year. They still want their $55,000. Her nephew is her only surviving family. He's been working on this with a guy that I met at the Orenda Theater, which is now a nonprofit in George Lucas country. A nice fellow named Derek asked if I would speak about Juanita's career and her significance, which I was happy to do. They had a nice turnout. Debbie Allen hosted it, and Loretta Devine was there, and Jayne Kennedy. It was lovely and I was pleased to represent the audience, in a way. I didn't know her personally, but I enjoyed and appreciated her work. And I was happy to participate.

People stop me, wherever I go, and the nicest thing I hear is, "You got me interested in movies" or "I lived by your annual book." I have even been told this by successful writers and producers. I never know what to say in return except to point to my heart and tell them how much it means to me. Harry Dean Stanton used to respond to a compliment by saying, "Thank you… that's very nourishing."

I never set out to inspire anybody. I just pursued something I cared about and was fortunate enough to make a living at it. To know that I have steered some people to become immersed in the world of film, and even work in this field,

---

* Juanita Moore (1914–2014) was a highly honored African American actress. She played Annie Johnson in *Imitation of Life* (1959).

is truly humbling. If I can borrow the title of Bing Crosby's autobiography, "Call Me Lucky."

APPENDIX A:
MENTIONED IN PASSING

Leonard's website www.leonardmaltin.com not only posts reviews and news, it gives him the forum to post appreciations of people he has met, admired, and lost. Here is a selection of some that have meant a great deal to him.

Remembering David Lynch (1946–2025)

Some forty years ago I first met David Lynch in a setting that could have come from an episode of *Twin Peaks:* the now-defunct Studio City branch of DuPar's, an all-American coffee shop where he had come to enjoy a well-crafted chocolate milk shake. He seemed to appreciate my enjoyment of seeing him at the cashier's counter.

Our next meeting was more productive, as *Entertainment Tonight* had sent me to the press junket for *The Straight Story*. My first interview was with its costar, Sissy Spacek. Trying to be cool, I said, "I'll bet it isn't every day you get a phone call from David Lynch." She replied, "Actually, yes it is. He and my husband Jack Fisk are close friends." Boy, did I feel foolish—and underinformed. In fact, Fisk was the production designer on *The Straight Story.*

It had been arranged for me to show the film to my class at USC, and I mustered up the courage to ask David Lynch if he would come down to campus the following week. He hesitated before answering and I thought perhaps I had disrupted the protocol of corralling guests. Then he said, "Can I smoke?"

I said, "Absolutely," having no authority to do so. With that, he agreed. On the night of the screening, I tried to prepare my twenty-somethings, who had so loved *Blue Velvet*, by explaining that this would be a very different experience... yet still "Lynchian." Just as he was devoted to DuPar's milkshakes he was enamored of what I'll call Americana, for want of a better term.

If you haven't seen it, *The Straight Story* is a charming, low-key story about a man named Alvin Straight (played by the wonderful Richard Farnsworth) who's getting on in years. When he learns that his long-estranged brother (Harry Dean Stanton) has had a stroke, he decides to visit him while he still can. He's going to make the journey, hundreds of miles away, on his gas-powered lawn mower. This leads to a series of amusing, surprising, sometimes poignant vignettes.

The class responded well to the movie, and to our guest. After I asked one or two questions he blurted out, "You said I could smoke." "Yes, I did," I responded, and he took out a cigarette and lighter. I trust that the statute of limitations has run out on my misdeed. And how ironic that smoking took down the quixotic filmmaker, who issued anti-smoking statements in the later part of his life.

Here is a p.s. to this story. In 2017, Harry Dean Stanton's longtime assistant Logan Sparks cowrote a disarming character portrait called *Lucky*. He got the talented actor John Carroll Lynch to direct and used Harry Dean's Rolodex to cast all the supporting roles with old friends: Ed Begley, Jr., Ron Livingston, Tom Skerritt, Barry Shebaka Henley, James Darren, Beth Grant et al. One scene at a local hangout required a "regular" to stop in and deliver a long, angry speech to anyone who would listen. The scene is a standout in a film full of wonderful moments and the man who delivered the screed was David Lynch. An actor of long experience would have considered memorizing this dialogue a challenge, but Lynch nailed it; I believe he did two takes altogether.

So few people saw *Lucky* (which is readily available online) that his appearance has now been eclipsed by his cameo as John Ford, of all people, in Steven Spielberg's *The Fabelmans*, where once again he strikes just the right note.

Anyone who wants to pigeonhole David Lynch is welcome to try, but they will be missing the big picture. He was many things to many people.

A Candid Chat with Robert Young (1907–1998)

After spending an afternoon with Robert Young and his wife Betty one day in 1986, I came home and told my wife, "That was the most candid and interesting interview I've ever done." I never published it until I launched my newsletter Leonard Maltin's Movie Crazy *in 2001.*

Robert Young was a ubiquitous figure in American life for six decades—in movies, on radio, and most successfully on television, in two hugely popular, long-running shows, Father Knows Best *and* Marcus Welby, M.D. *and in an equally durable series of commercials for Sanka. (There was also a short-lived series in between his two hits,* Window on Main Street.*)*

A mutual friend put me in touch with the actor, who wasn't enthusiastic about doing an interview. "After all, I'm retired," he told me on the telephone. "Usually, you do this sort of thing when you have a movie or a TV show to promote." He listed other reasons why he didn't want to talk about his career, but I kept my mouth shut, and before long he said he supposed if I really wanted to, I could come out to see him at his home in Westlake Village.

He and his wife Betty couldn't have been more gracious, although I will admit he was crustier than I expected. It didn't take long for me to see that he had harbored deep insecurities throughout his career. I asked if it was exciting to travel to England to make films in the mid-1930s and he responded that he thought he was being exiled. He told me how he sweated out the annual pickup of his contract at MGM—for fifteen years—always certain that he was going to be dropped. (After a number of years, he finally asked studio executive Eddie Mannix why they prolonged his agony by waiting until the last night of the year to send notice of his renewal. Mannix said, in all seriousness, that if they didn't protect themselves that way, they could be left holding the bag if an actor got into some sort of scandal during those last few weeks!)

He had already "gone public" about his longtime battle with alcoholism, which seemed to dovetail with the self-doubts he discussed in our interview. It was some years later that he spoke about his bouts of depression and the chemical imbalance that led to a suicide attempt in 1991.

None of that was on my agenda. I wanted to seize the opportunity to talk about his career, which he'd rarely discussed in any detail. His wife Betty not only participated in our conversation; she asked more questions than I did! She enjoyed drawing him out on certain subjects and correcting *some of the details in his stories. They had met in high school and were married fifty-three years at the time of our meeting.*

Incidentally, Young did not spend the rest of his days in retirement. He made several movies for television, including Mercy or Murder? *(1987), in which he played Roswell Gilbert, a real-life senior citizen who put his wife out of her suffering and stood trial for murder as a result. It was exactly the kind of meaty, three-dimensional dramatic role he coveted for so much of his career.*

Our conversation consumed several hours' time yet only began to scratch the surface of his résumé. I wish I'd had a chance to go back and ask about the many films we didn't get to discuss. But I hope you will agree that, in the famous words of Spencer Tracy in Pat and Mike, *"what's there is cherce." We began by discussing his salad days as a contract player at MGM, where he began working in 1931.*

ROBERT YOUNG: I got this call: Mr. Mayer wanted to see me. Well, gee, if he wants to see you, it means one of two things: either he's going to tell you you're doing a great job, which is very, very unlikely, or you were going to get fired. Or there's something wrong. You know you're in big trouble, you're going to face a cut, or something. So I was really shaking, literally shaking. And they had an interesting technique. He'd let you sit out in the waiting room for twenty or thirty minutes. You'd just fry out there, have a heart attack. And the woman that he had as his personal secretary, Ida Koverman, she wasn't even looking at me. She was cold as a chunk of ice. So you sit there and die forty thousand times. Finally the word comes and you get up and you almost fall flat on your face. Now, in the office, it's a half hour walk from the door to the desk, you know. There's a little figure sitting behind the desk. You get there and you don't sit down until you're told to sit down. "Bob," he says, "I've been thinking about you, and watching your work." I wait for what follows—nothing, no comment. He says, "A couple of things I think that you should do, for your career, and for us." Well, I came right up to the edge of my seat. This was interesting. Always eager to learn, always wanted to improve. He said, "Put on a little weight and get more sex."

I said, "Mr. Mayer, I don't know how to do either one of those!" I'd been trying to put on weight for years and years and years. I weighed the same for, I don't know, twenty years. Built like Jimmy Stewart, you know. "And as far as getting more sex is concerned, how do you do that?" "Well," he said, "You live at home, don't you?" And I said yes. "With your mother?" I said yes. He said, "I think you should have your own apartment. And then I think you should get your-self a valet. You know, a houseboy." I said, "Who needs a houseboy?" He said, "That's a front; you need that kind of thing. Japanese preferably. White coat, black trousers." I said, "What would I do with it?" He said, "He could greet the people at the door and serve the drinks." I said, "That's not gaining any weight," and he said "No, but it's a front, it's what the [reporters and columnists] see. The front. Also, you should go out to Mocambo and Ciro's and take a different girl each night. We've got a whole stable of girls here. Mary Carlisle, Madge Evans..." Golly, I can't even remember. It sounds so funny now as I tell it. You think, oh, it could never have been like that, but seriously, it was. This was his idea. I don't say that there was anything particularly wrong with it. The more macho image, God knows Clark Gable came right through the screen. This is what they wanted. And I repre-sented, I don't know what, the boy next door or something.

Betty Young: You did all right. Whatever it was you had.

Robert: Yes, by the grace of God.

Betty: Don't knock it.

Robert: I'm not. But that's what they wanted. I think the ulti-mate extreme was when they hired [Robert] Taylor, who was perfectly capable as an actor, but he was so damn handsome, that he, like Tyrone Power, looked almost feminine. He was what you might call a beautiful man. Not a handsome man, but a beautiful man. He was a wonderful, wonderful person. And a good actor too. But they were also looking for the, you know, the Clark Gables and the Spencer Tracys and that sort of thing. And I was somewhere in the middle there some-where. I was neither one nor the other. I think most of the time they were trying to figure what the hell I was, because casting is a big thing with them. And they just followed you might say the public's taste, as it were, in typecasting. If they responded to you as a nice guy, you could be the worst shit in the world, and from that time on, that's what you're going to play: nice guys. You could bellyache and squawk and say, you know, I have to exercise my talent, I have to stretch as an actor, it was a lot of crap. And they knew it was, but that's what you played. Or you make a hell of a hit like Bogart did in *The Petrified Forest*, and from that time on he was never without a gun in his hand, you know?

Leonard Maltin: So what was it like being a contract player? Did you feel like an indentured servant?

Robert: Well, I didn't know any differently. It was, like the saying goes, the only game in town. You couldn't freelance. You could freelance if you wanted to be independent and free of that kind of control and starve to death. So I got the apartment. Little Japanese houseboy. Whole bit. Followed the front. To the letter. I said, "Betty, I won't be able to see you for awhile. Just weekends." She said, "Oh? How's that?" So I told her about this situation with Mr. Mayer. She said, "That's very interesting. When this has all blown over, if it ever does, give me a ring. But in the meantime..." I said, "Wait a minute, this is for my career, I'm just doing this for my career. By orders of God. And you're telling me to defy this person and say no, I won't do it? Just for us? Why don't you understand? This is my whole goddamn career that's at stake." She said, "That's your problem. You won't get me to play that kind of a game. That's the way you want to go, that's up to you." Well, I sweated that out for about a week. And finally—

Betty: You tried it for six weeks.

Robert: Did I? Really?

Betty: He finally went into Mayer, and somehow or other he said, "I can't see that this kind of life is going to improve my acting. I'll just have to take my chances on my talent, not on how I live daily."

Robert: So it was, in a way, a good thing because we realized that we had to make a decision: Which way is it going to go, their way or our way? Not that ours was so defiant. But anytime that the two collided, we had to go our way because, as far as we were concerned, our whole future life depended on it.

Maltin: It seems as if the minute MGM signed you, they loaned you out.

Robert: After I'd left [Metro], somebody in publicity, a friend of ours, got curious and decided to tabulate the number of films I'd worked in, in those fifteen years. And it came out seventy-eight. That was a hell of a lot of films in that length of time. Thirty eight of the seventy-eight were off the lot. They always ask ten times more than they paid you, so I figured they've made money. It didn't cost them anything. But it was all right because all of it basically was training.

Maltin: And you did some good pictures off the lot.

Robert: Also, at Metro I was considered a socalled "featured player." That's a question of which side of the title your name goes on. When I was loaned out, to Paramount, for example, to work on a picture with Claudette Colbert and Melvyn Douglas, they put my name above the title, along with Colbert's and Melvyn Douglas'.

Maltin: Someone who worked within the studio system—but maintained his independence—was King Vidor. Tell me about working with him on *H.M. Pulham, Esq.*

Robert: Oh, he was wonderful. He was the nicest man. King did something that I didn't know about till after it was all over. I had a lot of respect for him as a director, for his accomplishments, *The Crowd* and God knows how many others. [When] I was given a part in *H.M. Pulham, Esq.* [it] threw me for awhile. And I pored over [the book by J. P.] Marquand for weeks and weeks and weeks, trying to figure out what the hell he was writing about. I got more and more caught up in the character and the more I did, the more I realized what a remarkable role this was for me. I mean, not only in length, but in dimension, different levels, going from a young man in World War One to a middle-aged, white-haired man... a big challenge, a hell of a challenge. And King Vidor, oh my God. I thought, what am I going to do?
        What I was told was that he stood against the entire studio. It was his choice that I play the role. And everybody got in the act. Those that had some say all lined up, literally, and said no. And he said, "Well then, I won't do it." They didn't want to say too many derogatory things about me, but they said, "You can get this one, you can get that one..."

Betty: They kept saying you were too young, you looked too young.

Robert: ... anything they could think of that would somehow diminish my attractiveness to King. King had his mind made up. I don't know why he did it, to tell you the truth. I was baffled when I was told about it. I said, "Oh, you're just telling me that to make me feel good." [And someone said] "Go ask King if you don't believe me." So I finally muscled up enough courage to ask him. I went to King and I said, "I've been told that you put up a pretty good fight for me to play the role," and he said, "That's right." I said, "Did you ever have any regrets?" He said, "Not once." I said, "What do you think about the end result?" He said, "Just exactly the way I thought it would." Well, it was nice to hear.

Maltin: It's such a mature film. As you said, it's so much more intelligent and mature than most of the stuff that was being made.

RY: Well, yes, I hadn't played anything like that since I'd left the stage. All I was playing was these flip, light comedy [parts], that kind of thing. I'd been playing things like *Married Before Breakfast*, and *The Bride Wore Red*, these brilliant things. It was a really great challenge to an actor; some of them were unbelievable. I often said to Betty, if I could make anything out of this, I deserve an Oscar.

Betty: He played a football player and a baseball player. He damn near got killed playing the USC football team.

Robert: Oh yes, my athletic days. Never threw a baseball, never threw a football. Of all the people in the world, they cast in that picture, *Navy Blue and Gold,* Jimmy Stewart and me and Tom Brown. I said, "You'll never get this released. The first day it plays, the laughter you'll be able to hear for twenty-five city blocks. And the exhibitor's going to pull the film out of the projector and that'll be the end of it." That damn thing is still playing and people come up to me; they say, "I saw you the other night in *Navy Blue and Gold.* Boy, was that some picture. You'd think they were Annapolis graduates.

Betty: Ray Bradbury has seen it nineteen or twenty times. He said that he played hooky from school to see it.

Robert: Yeah, it was down at the Wiltern theater. It was an awful joke to me; I used to look at Betty and I'd think, either these people are fruity or I am. There's something wrong here. Until finally it kind of dawned on me, gradually: that's the magic. They didn't see that I was 135 pounds; I was a lunging, crushing, fullback. It took me a long time to realize that it wasn't the actors so much, or the script, or the camerawork, or the director, it was the audience. The audience made the magic, made it possible. Of course, granted, all these mechanics of it made it possible to give the audience the opportunity.

Maltin: You worked with King Vidor again on another great film, *Northwest Passage*, and so much of the action seems real. Was it?

Robert: Yes. We shot at McCall, Idaho. We weren't wearing buckskin, we were wearing suede, or something like that, to approximate buckskin. We grew our beards. We weren't allowed to wash our clothes, and we went through mud and slime and, oh, unbelievable. It kept getting worse, and then we'd hang these things out at night, and they would turn sour. If you got on the downwind side, you couldn't stand it; you'd faint. [It would] make you throw up, it was so bad. There were about seventy-five or eighty of us, plus another hundred townspeople that they dressed up.

Maltin: What about that incredible sequence crossing the river?

Robert: The human chain?

Maltin: Yes.

Robert: They did it by cuts. They never did show that human chain all in one chunk, clear across the river. I don't think anyone's particularly aware of it. That's what I call the magic. They showed the establishment of it, coming from the other side, and leaving the shore and so forth, then a different angle; it linked up with that side like Hands Across America, not seeing that this wasn't hooked up to anything. And in the audience's mind, they supplied the picture of the total human chain across the river. But true, there were certain reality in the sense that we were in the terrain which was not unlike the Hudson River Valley, where it was supposed to have taken place. The clothes we wore were real, the muskets we carried were authentic—I don't think anyone ever fired one, probably would have blown his head off if he had—but they were genuine muskets that they used in that period.

Maltin: Do you think that that comes through in terms of your performance? Do you react differently being in the real surroundings?

Robert: Oh sure.

Maltin: What was it like working with Spencer Tracy?

Robert: He was marvelous; I liked him very much. He was a little bit quiet; we didn't have a backslapping, howling with laughter kind of relationship, [but] he was very friendly. He was a lovely, lovely man. He endeared himself to my heart the first day we were there. We were in this renovated camp which had been unused for about twenty years, so you can imagine what kind of shape it was in, right on the shore of Lake Thea, in McCall, Idaho. They stuck up a service tent and the caterer brought the tables and chairs and the stove and everything else in there. Well, we went to breakfast, or whatever the hell the first meal was that we had there, and Spence stood up and threw the plate clear across the tent.

Betty: They had powdered eggs.

Robert: Oh, it was awful. He went right to the unit manager [and] said, "When you correct the situation, I'll be back. I'll be on the set. Otherwise, don't bother me. Don't even talk to me." Well, you don't think the telephone wires didn't get hot the next day. I don't know the hell they produced it that quickly, but the next day there was a new unit manager. It was the most incredible transformation you ever saw. Overnight, there was a complete transformation; we had the most divine food. We were eating like Spago's, choice steak—

Betty: They didn't have frozen food in those days.

Robert: No. Beautiful steaks, fresh vegetables, so I went to this guy, his name was Charlie something, and I said, "How in the hell did you manage this?" And he kind of smiled. He said, "I was a road manager for a circus for about twenty years." I said, "But how did you get this done?" He said, "I called Salt Lake City. I said, you got a good chef there? Yep? Send him up. Metro-Goldwyn-Mayer, that's the magic word."

Maltin: But it took Tracy to do it.

All Tracy said was fix this and then I'll be back. And walked out. No shouting. I watched him and I thought to myself, man that's great. That's power.

Betty: Like Norma Shearer.

Robert: Oh, Norma Shearer used to break me up. She always smiled. And it wasn't a false smile; it was a lovely, sweet, gentle smile. They would ask her something, "Miss Shearer," or "Mrs. Thalberg," something they wanted done, and she would just smile and say no. And that was all. And you could just feel the other person [thinking], there's nothing you can do. What do you do, argue? She just smiled, and said no. And that was it. Bingo. Took care of the whole thing.

Maltin: People talk about how you could never see Tracy's technique, and that was his magic. What was your observation?

Robert: It might be easily covered with one word in quotes: "natural." He was very intuitive, and whatever he did, he just always came out right. Directors never talked to him I mean, what's the point in talking to him? Tracy, sort of, almost unconsciously, knew more about how that scene should be played than the director did. And that's one of the reasons I think he and Katie [Hepburn] got along so well. I think she acts very much that same way. She just acts from something inside, that's intuitive, instinctive, whatever you want to call it.

Maltin: When you worked with her it was very early in her screen career, and she was thought kind of odd at that point.

Robert: She was. But even then, you could feel, you could sense that she was her own person. In those days, they all came out of the same drama school. Not Katie. There was no mistaking that this was a very unique personality.

Betty: Anybody that's original is criticized as much as praised.

Robert: They broke the mold when they made her. Same way with Tracy. I think that were ideally cast together. As I think Reagan is ideally cast as the President. Best role he's ever had in his life. It beats George Gipp.

Maltin: Did Marie Dressler make an impression on you when you made *Tugboat Annie*?

Robert: Couldn't help it. She was really lovely, a wonderful person. She'd come up the long hard way, and she was very, very grateful. And she wouldn't take any nonsense from this baboon, Wallace Beery. [Dressler had worked with Beery before, in the 1930 hit *Min and Bill*.]

Betty: When you're doing a scene and [the other actor is] off-camera, he's supposed to be quiet. Well, [Beery] was always doing movement.

Robert: Anything to distract you. She straightened him out the first day. She said, "Look, you silly shit, you pull one more thing like that on me and I'll have your head on a platter like John the Baptist, with a personal note to L. B. Mayer." And she was so huge, she looked like she could do it. He said OK, he got very cowed, and then he was like a little boy being very careful that mommy didn't catch him with his hand in the cookie jar. No, he really behaved himself on that one. I realize that his other thing was just an act: anything to destroy the other actor, anything to spoil it for them. But he couldn't do that with Marie.

Betty: She was sort of protective of you, too.

Robert: Oh, she was wonderful. She wouldn't let him do that to the crew members, anybody. [As for Beery] I developed a loathing for this man that almost ended my career. I was always ending my career. And Betty again came to the rescue. I came back to the hotel room one night after doing a scene and I said, "This is as far as I can go. I just have to phone my resignation."

Betty: He had to hug and love him.

Robert: He played my father. It was called *West Point of the Air*. I was supposed to be a young cadet in the Army air corps, and he was a mechanic, just a grease monkey. And there was some kind of a conflict, I've forgotten what it was, but anyway, there was a very emotional scene. The boy had to cry a little bit and plead with his father and so forth. When [Beery] couldn't think of a line, he rubbed his face and went, "Awww-mmmmm." After the two-shot, which went miserably—it was horrible, just little pieces of it were usable—the director then went to the overshoulder shots. [Beery has] got his script [but] he drops it on the ground and when he picks it up, he goes to the wrong page, and for my cue he's not reading the right line. I'm supposed to be standing there crying. And I was building up on the inside; the pressure was so enormous I thought, I'm going to scream any second. I'm going to say, "You shit, you ignominious dumb bastard," every name I could think of. He was the most insensitive, the most inhumane—[That night] I said to Betty, "Honey, I can't, I won't. Life is too short. Why should I screw around with that baboon? I can't work with him." She said, "Do you suppose Metro-Goldwyn-Mayer is going to have superimposed on a frame a sentence which says, 'Mr. Young's performance was due to the fact that he lost his temper because of Mr. Beery's behavior?' Who's going to explain that performance of yours? Because you're the one that's up there on the screen, and you're not looking like your heart is breaking for your old father. That's going to show." If there's one thing about the camera, it sits out there and says, "Don't get cute. Don't get fancy. Don't think that you can play a scene with your mind down at Vons Market." Because they can see it right in your eye.

Maltin: So you survived it.

Robert: I survived it, again, with Betty helping. I got back on the set the next day and I thought, my best way of getting even is to give a performance that's better than his.

Betty: The studio tried to get in the radio business, and they had a show called *Good News*, which was an hour show that had everybody on it. Meredith Willson was the orchestra [leader], and they tried everybody to be master of ceremonies, and nobody could do it, but Mister Young, and he got it.

Maltin: Talk to me about radio a little.

Robert: Well, I loved it.

Betty: He had a show with Frank Morgan and Fanny Brice.

Robert: At least they both had stage experience. But some of the screen actors were dreadful, just dreadful. They didn't know what the hell to do with their voice; they'd never acted with their voice before, as an instrument, so they tried to do it with their face. Well, can you see anything over the air with a radio broadcast? As a result, it was just absolutely nothing. So then we'd work with radio actors, who were trained; they could do nine dialects in fifteen seconds, and [the movie people] looked like jerks, absolute jerks; it was an embarrassment.

Betty: Don't forget, too, that this was live. Radio was live and with an audience. When Joan [Crawford] did a show with Bobby, she finally took her shoes off, and then she took her clothes off, she didn't want any makeup, then she had the audience cancelled. Do you remember?

Robert: She couldn't stand the presence of the audience there because she would be performing in front of an audience, and she had never done that before. Even though she was facing a microphone, and she wasn't doing a play, she couldn't stand it, so she had the audience dismissed. They sent the audience home.

Betty: Gable couldn't do it.

Robert: Their voices would quake, they would get so nervous. The first show I did, when I got this *Good News* assignment on a kind of a trial basis, they ran every contract player they had through it to see who was going to end up with it. And I ended up with the job. Soon as I started on kind of a steady basis, I was very much aware of the skill of the radio actor.

Betty: And you had terrific training too.

Robert: I thought to myself, I'd better be very, very careful because these are sharp cookies. I don't want to make too big a fool of myself; I'd better watch what they do. Or listen to what they do and try to catch on.

Betty: The movie stars overacted a lot on radio.

Robert: They're so used to working in front of a camera. Now they're working in front of a microphone. A microphone can't see a goddamn thing.

Betty: But you had terrific voice training, and Bobby has a God-given voice to begin with. I know about it. We were all working to place our voices, and Bobby would get up and speak, and that was it. He just was born with it.

Robert: You have to use your voice like a musical instrument on radio, you see? You've got to use it just exactly like a musical instrument.

Maltin: So you just took to radio.

Robert: I loved it. Of course, I loved acting. It didn't make any difference to me whether I was on the street corner, or in somebody's basement, or in front of a camera, or up on the stage, or in front of a microphone. As long as I was performing or playing a role, I was happy as a clam. It didn't make any difference; I could do it in the living room all by myself. So it was just another medium to me. It was exciting. I think I would have had a wonderful time in a circus, as a clown.

Remembering Clayton Moore (1914–1999)

I remember the first time I met Clayton Moore: it was in New York City in 1979 at a so-called nostalgia convention. Spanky McFarland was there along with other icons of popular culture. Clayton was just leaving the main room as I arrived, and we said hello, but more importantly, I got to see him in action. He'd just finished an hour-long autograph session and was about to take a well-earned rest. A young boy and his father strode over to him and beseeched him for one more snapshot. Looking magnificent in his Lone Ranger garb, Clayton never hesitated for an instant. He happily posed with the youngster, and a moment before the flash went off, raised his shoulders and arms so it would be an "action" shot!

That told me almost everything I needed to know about Clayton Moore. He loved his fans and would do anything rather than let them down, even if it meant summoning an ounce of energy at a moment when he'd just as soon have relaxed.

In later years, I got to know the man better and often thought how accurate that first impression had been. As he got older, it became more difficult to summon those bursts of energy, but nonetheless, he always did. Toward the end, rather than ever let his fans see the Lone Ranger as anything but virile and strong, he refused all offers for public appearances.

Although I grew up watching him on television, I didn't know very much about Clayton Moore until I became a diehard old-movie buff. That's when I became familiar with his work in Republic Pictures' Saturday matinee serials of the 1940s. You couldn't ask for a more dashing hero. He even played villains from time to time in Westerns and seemed to relish every moment. Some of my favorite Ranger episodes involve the Masked Man taking on a disguise, which enable Clayton to ham it up as a grizzled prospector or some other salty Western character.

When it came time to pen his autobiography, Clayton needed prodding. He wasn't one to dwell on the past, nor was he a raconteur by nature; he was a hard-working actor who did his job. But when his daughter Dawn screened some of the Republic serials for him, they stirred up a string of fond memories, and author Frank Thompson was able to continue the process and produced a delightful book.

Much was written upon his death about the way Clayton Moore possessed the role of the Lone Ranger, and vice versa. I fear that some people may have misread this as borderline lunacy. Rest assured, Clayton never thought of himself as the masked rider of the early west; this was no victim of Sunset

Boulevard-like delusion. What he did realize was how lucky he had been to inhabit a role that meant so much to millions of people, young and old. And as a public figure, he understood how important it was to embody the spirit and values that character represented. He made a commitment to embrace those values in his own life.

At his memorial service last December, friends and family spoke of him and the Lone Ranger in the same breath. This was no contradiction; Clayton Moore was a good and decent man. No wonder he became so indelibly associated with the character he played.

Remembering Dale Evans (1912–2001)

When I was asked to write an official obituary for Dale, I added some of my own words, and information, to material Cheryl Rogers had already gathered at the Museum. I don't feel it's right to take full credit for it.

But I can add a few thoughts that are strictly my own. Like so many of you, I grew up watching and loving Roy Rogers and Dale Evans. I never dreamed that I would get to meet them, as I did in recent years, first at the Golden Boot Awards, then for several television interviews. Upon Roy's death, my family and I paid a condolence call at her home, and that is when we got to know Dale a little better; my wife, daughter, and I all came away impressed.

What impressed us most was her directness; Dale didn't mince words. She was a deeply religious woman, but unlike some people one thinks of as pious, she also had a hearty sense of humor. It was that combination of qualities that made her unique, and lovable.

My daughter Jessie, twelve years old at the time, fell into a long conversation with Dale when we first visited her home and told her that she would be having a Bat Mitzvah the following June. Dale replied that she had never been to a Bar or Bat Mitzvah, although she had been to Israel several times, and had great respect for the Jewish people. Jessie, as direct as Dale, immediately invited her to the ceremony... and Dale happily accepted.

Sure enough, the following year, Dale attended my daughter's Bat Mitzvah in Los Angeles, which of course floored many of our friends.

Two of them, married freelance writers and researchers Rob Edelman and Audrey Kupferberg, had come from upstate New York. When we saw them later that year they told us they'd never had such a successful summer, and they knew the reason why: Dale had blessed them when they met in June.

I'm sure they're not the only ones who felt that way. Dale Evans was a remarkable woman. She was guided and inspired by her faith, not only in God but in the goodness of people... and people felt better just for being in her presence.

At her funeral, a reporter asked me what set Dale and Roy apart from other stars of their generation. I realized that part of the answer was that they not only allowed, but encouraged, the line between real life and make-believe to blur: the people we saw on screen were a lot like the people who got married and raised a family together. Like other Western stars, they didn't isolate themselves in Hollywood; they went on the road and met their fans up-close, creating a bond that never existed between moviegoers and such idols as Clark Gable or Bette Davis.

Movie, radio and television audiences felt as if they really knew Roy and Dale. Those of us who were lucky enough to take that relationship one step closer loved them all the more.

Dale Evans, whose sunny presence in twenty-seven movies and scores of television appearances with her husband, Roy Rogers, earned her the title "Queen of the West," died at her home in Apple Valley, California today, of congestive heart failure. She was 88. Better known in recent years for her appearances on the Trinity Broadcast Network and a series of inspirational books, Evans also wrote a number of songs, including "Aha, San Antone," featured in John Ford's film *Rio Grande*, "The Bible Tells Me So," and "Happy Trails," which served as the signature tune for her and her husband for several decades. *TV Guide* recently cited it among the most popular television theme songs of all time.

Dale was born Frances Octavia Smith on October 31, 1912, in Uvalde, Texas. At age fourteen, she eloped with her high school sweetheart, but the union was short-lived. A year later, she found herself in Memphis, Tennessee a single parent, determined to make a living in the music field. She landed a job with local radio stations (WMC and WREC) singing and playing piano, using her married name, Frances Fox. During a brief stint at WHAS, the station manager renamed her Dale Evans, after a silent-film star he admired, Dale Winter. The teenager reportedly balked at first, because she thought Dale was a boy's name.

As Dale Evans, she made her way to Chicago and found steady work singing at such nightspots as the Blackstone Hotel, the Sherman House (where she worked alongside "Fats" Waller), the Drake, and the Chez Paree supper club. Anson Weeks hired her as vocalist for his orchestra just as they began a major tour to the west coast. After a two-month stand at The Coconut Grove, Dale left the Orchestra and returned to Chicago where she was hired by WBBM, the local CBS affiliate. Talent scouts from Paramount Studios discovered her and arranged a screen test in Hollywood for the movie *Holiday Inn*, starring Fred Astaire and Bing Crosby. She didn't get the job, but her agent showed her screen test to 20th Century Fox, where she was signed to a one-year contract. This resulted in small parts in two pictures, *Orchestra Wives* and *Girl Trouble*.

She was then hired as vocalist on the popular *Chase and Sanborn Show* on NBC radio starring Edgar Bergen and Charlie McCarthy, where she sang every week with Ray Noble and his Orchestra. This exposure led to an offer from Republic Pictures, where she made her debut in *Swing Your Partner*, and pleased studio executive Herbert J. Yates enough for him to exercise his option for a one-year contract. Her early films there include *Hoosier Holiday, In Old Oklahoma* (with John Wayne), *Here Comes Elmer, Casanova in Burlesque* (with Joe E. Brown), and *The West Side Kid*.

Inspired by the enormous success of Rodgers and Hammerstein's Broadway musical *Oklahoma!*, Yates decided to put his number one cowboy star, Roy Rogers, into a series of musical Westerns that would be more lavish than the ordinary Saturday matinee entries. With her singing talents, Dale was an obvious choice to costar in *The Cowboy and the Senorita* (1944), the first of twenty-seven films she and Rogers would make together.

This onscreen team became an offscreen team on New Year's Eve, 1947. They were married on the Flying L Ranch in Davis, Oklahoma, where they had just completed filming *Home in Oklahoma*. The owner of the ranch, when he learned they were to be married, offered the ranch as a wedding site.

An instant family was formed. Dale had her son, Tom, and Roy had an adopted daughter, Cheryl, and birth children Linda Lou and Roy Rogers, Jr., known as Dusty, from his first wife, Arline, who had died after Dusty's birth. Roy and Dale had one child together, Robin, whose death from complications associated with Down's syndrome inspired Dale to write the first of her inspirational books, *Angel Unaware*. The family swelled with the addition of Mary Little Doe (Dodie), of Native American heritage; John David (Sandy), a battered child from an orphanage in Kentucky; Marion (Mimi), their foster child from Scotland; and Debbie, a Korean War orphan whose father was a G.I. of Puerto Rican ancestry.

The family lost three of the children in tragic circumstances: Robin in infancy, Debbie in a church bus accident when she was twelve, and Sandy in an accident while serving with the military in Germany.

In 1950, Roy and Dale formed their own production company to produce a weekly half-hour television series, *The Roy Rogers Show*, which ran until 1957, and then in reruns for years to follow. Their enormous popularity as a team led to personal appearances in every major arena in the world; they toured from New York City (Madison Square Garden) to Houston's Fat Stock Show to Toronto's Canadian National Exposition. Every summer they would take their children along as they swept the United States playing state fairs and rodeos.

Among Dale's many honors were California Mother of the Year in 1967, The Texas Press Association's Texan of the Year in 1970, The Golden Boot Award in 1988, Cowgirl Hall of Fame in 1995, Cardinal Terrence Cook Humanities Award in 1995, and three stars on the Hollywood Walk of Fame.

Roy Rogers and Dale Evans headlined their own television variety series and appeared as guests on network shows throughout the 1960s, '70s, and '80s. A series of health setbacks plagued Evans in recent years, but she rebounded each time, continuing her series *A Date with Dale* for Trinity Broadcasting Network, and writing steadily. Her most recent book, *Rainbow on a Hard Trail*, was published in 1999, a year after the death of her husband.

Evans also made special effort to attend an annual fundraising gala for the Roy Rogers-Dale Evans Museum in Victorville, California, not far from her home, and traveled to cheer on three of her granddaughters (Mindy Petersen, Candie Halberg, and Julie Ashley) who perform as The Rogers Legacy, and her grandson Rob Johnson who sings with his band Heritage. Evans could boast of fifteen grandchildren and thirty-six great-grandchildren and six great-great-grandchildren at the time of her death.

Perhaps the Dixie Chicks put it best when they named their debut album "Thank Heavens for Dale Evans."

Remembering Diane Disney Miller (1933–2013)

Every time I chatted with Diane Disney Miller I had to pinch myself, realizing that I was talking to Walt Disney's daughter. Now I have to come to terms with a different reality following her sudden and untimely death. I mourn for her large, loving family—her husband Ron, seven children, thirteen grandchildren, and one great-grandchild—as well as the extended family she fostered while mounting a series of tributes to her dad, culminating in the opening of the Walt Disney Family Museum in San Francisco.

Walt Disney was a very public figure, but Diane did her best to avoid the spotlight until she realized that her father's centennial year was approaching in 2001. She worried that people didn't know who he was any more. The once-familiar face and voice from years of television exposure was fading into the shadows. If people recognized the name, it was as a corporate entity and no longer associated with a real, live person. She made up her mind to reverse that process, even if it meant having to sacrifice some of her own privacy.

Our first meeting took place, fittingly enough, at Disneyland, where I moderated a panel about Walt Disney for a crowd of fans and devotees. She was reticent about public speaking but gamely agreed to participate. Everyone who attended—including me—found her to be sincere, self-effacing, and most of all, down-to-earth. This was no Hollywood princess, even though she had every right to be. When, toward the end of the lively discussion, I asked what misconceptions about her father she'd most like to set straight, she could barely be heard over the chatter of the other panelists as she replied, "Well, he isn't frozen!" I asked her to repeat that statement so everyone could hear. I knew it would get a big response, and it did.

That night I brought along my worn copy of the 1957 paperback book called *The Story of Walt Disney* on which her byline appears. She expressed embarrassment as the book was actually written by *Saturday Evening Post* contributor Pete Martin, but she was kind enough to sign it all the same. That small gesture was typical of her.

We got to know each other better year by year as I participated in early meetings about her proposed museum and interviewed her at the centennial tribute to Walt Disney at the Academy of Motion Picture Arts and Sciences. When, at the end of the program, I asked how she liked to remember him, she disarmed the crowd by saying, "He was just my Dad," or words to that effect. That's the Walt Disney she knew best, and the one she wanted us to know better.

Diane took any attack on her father as a personal sting and couldn't understand why so many people seemed to thrive on wildly false accusations and name-calling. She knew he wasn't perfect and came to accept the idea that her Museum timeline wouldn't be complete without an examination of the Disney studio's painful labor strike of 1941. (Diane had her own childhood perspective of that watershed event: she recalled some of her father's leading animators swimming in her family pool on weekends during happier times in the 1930s. That casual camaraderie faded after the strike.) No father—or mother, for that matter—ever had a stronger advocate.

Diane Disney Miller leaves behind her own legacy, including a world-class museum, Los Angeles' Walt Disney Concert Hall (for which she heroically campaigned at a crucial moment in its gestation) and many cherished friendships. My family and I will miss her and her great spirit. Our only consolation is knowing that she is reunited with her sister Sharon and her beloved parents.

Remembering Dick Jones: The Voice of Pinocchio (1927–2014)

Some years ago I showed the 1939 classic *Destry Rides Again* to my class at USC; most of the students had never seen it. Following the screening I introduced Dick Jones, who appeared in the film and was featured in the penultimate scene with James Stewart. We talked about the fact that he worked with Stewart that same year in *Mr. Smith Goes to Washington* and also spent some time at the Walt Disney studio recording the dialogue for Pinocchio. I turned to the class and said, pointedly, "He was the voice of Pinocchio." This was greeted by a chorus of oohs and ahhs and immediately changed the tenor of the evening.

Pinocchio gave Dick a kind of immortality, but if it affected him, he certainly never showed it. He was gracious and self-effacing, proud of the work he did in show business but not one to live in the past. When jobs became scarce, he moved on, obtained a real estate license, and made a good living, specializing in appraisals. Or as he liked to say, "I didn't retire from the motion picture business; I'm just an actor without a job right now."

My wife was tongue-tied when she first met him, as she had a crush on Dickie, as he was then known, from his days on early television as the sidekick to Jock Mahoney on *The Range Rider* and the star of his own series, *Buffalo Bill, Jr.* The fact that he was so warm and likable made it all the more rewarding to know him and his cheerful wife Betty.

I think one reason Dick remained down-to-earth is that he'd been through so much in his life. Earning prizes as a champion horseback rider in Texas rodeos at the age of 3, relocating to Hollywood, going out on auditions, winning some parts and losing others, serving in the Army during World War II, then coming home and not finding any jobs—and so much more.

After the war he wanted to get married and start a family. Unable to find work in movies, he took a job at a gas station. "Then I started working as a carpenter; I worked apprentice to get a journeyman's on that, and I was doing pretty good. I was making $35 dollars a week if it didn't rain. We had [our first child] Melody and paid for it out of $35 dollars a week. Boy, you can't have a baby today at that price. I worked all kinds of jobs 'cause I had a sexy brunette wife and babies to feed. I stood in the unemployment line one time and that was so degrading, I said, 'No way! I am healthy, I'm not going to do this; I'm going to earn my keep.' And I never did stand in line again. Then getting that job with Gene Autry—I don't know what happened, but right after that I got all kinds of calls." Autry cast him in some of his Westerns, then put him to work with Jock Mahoney on *The Range Rider*, which showed off Dick's remarkable agility and horsemanship.

He and "Jocko," one of Hollywood's most talented stuntmen, got on famously and devised their own elaborate action scenes for the half-hour series, which was filmed at a breakneck pace. "Oh, man, we had so much fun," Dick recalled. "We'd stay up at night and conjure up things and say, 'Well, has this ever been done?' 'No, but we're gonna figure out [how] it can be done.' We did stuff that's never been on television before. Our timing was identical. We could say, 'OK, one, two, three' and walk around the block and come back and we'd still be on the same count."

Yet he was a man of quiet contradictions. Although he was once billed as The World's Youngest Trick Rider and Trick Roper, he confessed to me that he never liked horses and didn't own one. And while he was happy to be identified as the voice of Pinocchio, he admitted that it was one of his toughest assignments because he always felt claustrophobic indoors. "Most of the time they'd have to spend half an hour trying to find me 'cause I'd be around the studio somewhere."

Yet it's that credential more than any other that will keep Dick Jones' name alive in movie history.

Our condolences go out to Dick's wife and family. He lived a full, rich 87 years, but we'll miss him just the same.

Remembering Esther Williams (1921–2013)

Long after she retired from public life, Esther Williams had a needlepoint pillow on her sofa that bore the legend, "Yes, I still swim." That says a lot about the woman who smiled and swam her way through so many glossy MGM musicals: she had a sense of humor about herself. It was only after the death of her husband (and former costar) Fernando Lamas that she returned to the limelight, giving Barbara Walters a long and candid prime-time interview. After that, Esther became a familiar sight at Hollywood gatherings, and I got to know her a bit. She was fun to be with, always candid and colorful.

What struck me most was that she retained the mindset of a champion athlete. She started swimming seriously when she was eight. "We didn't have any money to go to swimming pools," she told me, "and the Pacific Ocean was my pool. That's where my sister taught me how to ride waves and how to swim. I had such fun with that the rest of my life. I'd go swimming way far out in the ocean, and boys would follow me when I was a teenager in high school. I said, 'You'd better not follow me, 'cause I can get back and you may not be able to.' Even at twelve and thirteen and fourteen, I knew what boys were all about."

She wasn't intimidated by Louis B. Mayer or anyone else she encountered in her accidental climb to movie stardom. She told me that in her eyes, "L. B. Mayer was only a man, a little immigrant that came across the big Atlantic Ocean, and he wanted so to be American. I could empathize with him, even though I was only eighteen, and it worked." Early in her tenure at the studio he shouted at her, and she said, "Mr. Mayer, please don't ever yell at me." He said, "Why not? I yell at everybody." And she replied, "Because you can't get to the end of the pool first." Looking back at that moment decades later, she admitted, "I don't know where it came from, but I stopped him from yelling and he said, 'I can't do what?'" I said, "You can make movies, but you can't get to the end of the pool first, so you can't yell at me till you can.' And my relationship from then on was one where on the lot, he would see me walking and call to me, 'I can't get to the what?' and I'd say, "Let me know when you can make it.'"

She credited producer Joe Pasternak with making her a star in the frothy musical *Thrill of a Romance*, of which she later wisecracked, "Just the title could give you diabetes. But it was Van Johnson, and he was the fifth most popular actor in the [top] ten, and we were just cute as a button together—two rosy-faced, wholesome people. That made me the Girl Next Door and it gave me twenty-six movies instead of just one." She even introduced a song standard, "Baby, It's Cold Outside," in the 1949 movie *Neptune's Daughter*, with Ricardo Montalban.

Some people I've spoken to don't understand how a swimmer could have become a movie star (leaving aside for the moment Buster Crabbe and Johnny Weissmuller), but there was a precedent: in the silent film era, Australian-born swimming champ Annette Kellerman was a vaudeville and movie headliner. Esther later portrayed her in the 1952 movie *Million Dollar Mermaid*. Then, in the 1930s, Olympic skating champion Sonja Henie—who could neither sing nor dance— became a box-office star at 20th Century Fox. All MGM had to do, according to Esther, was "melt the ice and toss a girl in." There was much more to it, of course, including constructing an underwater tank with portholes, developing special cameras and waterproof makeup, and devising precision water ballets—in Technicolor, no less. Audiences responded with great enthusiasm.

Esther's movies were sheer escapism and didn't pretend to be anything more. She never disparaged her years at MGM, but I think she was prouder of her achievements as a swimmer. She regretted missing out on the 1940 Olympic Games, which were canceled because of the war in Europe, but she never lacked for confidence. As she explained, "the champion spirit isn't anything that goes away." It held her in good stead to the very end of her life.

Remembering Harry Carey, Jr. (1921–2012)

The last survivor of John Ford's stock company has left us. Harry Carey, Jr. died peacefully the day after Christmas at the age of 91. Everyone who was lucky enough to spend time with Carey—whose lifelong nickname was Dobe—basked in the glow of his wonderful stories. Thank goodness he set so many of them down in a book, *Company of Heroes*, and made himself available to interviewers and historians over the years.

As a baby boomer, I first knew him as Bill Burnett on *Spin and Marty*, the serial that was such a popular part of Walt Disney's daily television show *The Mickey Mouse Club*. It was only later that I realized what an extraordinary life and career he had.

His father was John Ford's first star and collaborator, Harry Carey, and his mother Olive Golden Carey was also an actress, first in silent films during the teens, then later as a character woman in the 1950s and '60s. Dobe married the daughter of another prominent character actor, Paul Fix. It was quite a family. His father and Ford had a falling-out which was never fully explained or understood. Toward the end of Harry Senior's life, he told his son that after he died, the Old Man would most likely look after Junior and cast him in a film—and that's exactly what happened. Dobe was given a costarring role with John Wayne and Pedro Armendariz in Ford's beautiful production *Three Godfathers* and came through with flying colors. Ford even dedicated the film to Harry Carey, Sr.

That didn't stop the famously quixotic director from needling young Dobe or making his life as difficult as any other actor in his troupe. Dobe once wrote, "John Ford could see, in detail, something going on two hundred yards away and probably hear every word, even though he said 'What?' all the time. He never missed a thing. He knew what was going on behind him and we never caught him looking. When he was very old, he did have a cataract removed from his left eye and wore a patch over it afterwards because he said it was overly sensitive to light. But most of us believed it was because it was the ham in him that caused him to wear it. I loved him like a father and so did the rest of his gang, but we all felt that he was playing his role a lot of the time. He always wore dark glasses, though, so you could never see where he was looking. His daughter Barbara always said, 'He didn't want you to see those soft, kindly eyes.'"

If you want to give yourself a real treat, get ahold of Warner Home Video's DVD release of *Wagon Master* (1950). One of John Ford's personal favorites among his films, *Wagon*

Master is a film of modest ambition and enormous charm. It afforded the director an opportunity to showcase two of his "discoveries," wrangler-turned-actor Ben Johnson and Dobe. They are perfectly cast (in tailor-made roles) as carefree young men who are persuaded to help a wagon train of Mormons make their way to their new homestead. All the emblematic ingredients of a Ford Western are here, from the majestic scenery of Moab, Utah to spirited scenes of folk-dancing. Four of Stan Jones' evocative songs are beautifully sung on the soundtrack by the Sons of the Pioneers, while Richard Hageman's score extends those themes and makes fine use of other Americana. The cast is full of familiar Ford faces like Ward Bond, Jane Darwell, Hank Worden, Russell Simpson, and the director's brother Francis Ford, along with such newcomers as Kathleen O'Malley and young James Arness.

But the real treat, especially for film buffs who already know the picture—aside from having such a beautiful copy as this—is a commentary track featuring director Peter Bogdanovich and Dobe Carey. Bogdanovich aptly describes the director's work here as silent picture-making (every shot—without calling attention to itself—is perfectly framed, and wonderfully descriptive, a credit to veteran cameraman Bert Glennon), and shares generous excerpts from his audio interview with Ford from 1966. Carey has vivid memories of making this film and gives us a wonderful sense of being there, whether recalling one of his costars or complaining that "Uncle Jack" placed his hat on his head for one scene in a way that made him feel like the Village Idiot—but one dared not touch an article of clothing that the boss had arranged to his liking.

Being with Dobe and his loving wife Marilyn (who survives him) was never dull. He loved telling stories, especially to an appreciative audience, whether it was over dinner or in front of a camera. One night my wife and I ran into him and Marilyn at a local restaurant after I'd read a biography of William Mulholland which told the horrifying story of the 1927 dam break that flooded Harry Carey, Sr.'s ranch in Saugus, not far from William S. Hart's property. I asked Dobe if he had any memories of the incident, and indeed he did: he was six years old, and although he and his mother were in New York at the time of the tragedy, he vividly recalled its aftermath. He especially felt terrible losing his friends among the ranch hands who died in the flood. How many other people could I discuss this with seventy years after it took place?

I feel awfully lucky to have known him.

Remembering Janet Waldo (1919–2016)

When Janet Waldo passed away on June 12 at the age of 96, most of the obituaries spotlighted the fact that she was the voice of Judy Jetson on the long-running Hanna-Barbera animated series The Jetsons. *But that was just one facet of the actress' long and colorful career. I interviewed her for my* Movie Crazy *newsletter in 2004 and thought it would be worthwhile reprinting that conversation now in tribute to this lovely lady.*

As an adolescent in Seattle, Washington, Janet dreamed of performing on the Broadway stage. Instead, fate (and the fine hand of Bing Crosby) brought her to Hollywood. For many another attractive teenager this might have led to stardom, or at least starlet-dom, but she never felt comfortable in front of the camera and, as she readily admits, the studio didn't seem to know what to do with her.

Waldo did build a rewarding career, however: she discovered radio at a time when the major networks were operating in high gear on the West Coast and jobs were plentiful. She established herself as the preeminent teenage actress in the situation comedy field, working on all the top shows with everyone from Orson Welles to Frank Sinatra, starring in Meet Corliss Archer, *and playing opposite many of the biggest stars in movies.*

Like many of her colleagues, she did a fair amount of television work as radio drama faded from the scene (she and Richard Crenna, longtime friend and fellow radio juvenile, played teenagers in a memorable I Love Lucy *episode of 1952 called "The Young Fans") but this was never her forte.*

Fate smiled again when she agreed to audition to play the daughter in a new Hanna-Barbera cartoon series called The Jetsons *in 1962. Doing the voice of Judy Jetson has brought her a kind of immortality. It also opened up an entirely new career which kept her busy for decades: contributing voices to scores of television cartoons, including the lead role in* Josie and the Pussycats *and assorted other characters on* The Smurfs, Wacky Races, The New Adventures of Superman, *and other series right up through* King of the Hill.

Waldo enjoyed another perspective on show-business as the wife of Robert E. Lee, whom she met when he and his partner Jerome Lawrence were prolific radio hyphenates—writing, directing, and producing a variety of shows ranging from Favorite Story, *a dramatic anthology hosted by Ronald Colman, to* The Railroad Hour, *a series of condensed musicals and operettas starring Gordon MacRae. Lawrence and Lee later gained greater fame as playwrights, with such enduring successes as* Auntie Mame, Inherit the Wind, *and* First Monday in October *to their credits.*

More recently, Waldo was active in California Artists' Radio Theatre, founded by actress Peggy Webber, and played a wide variety of parts including a starring role opposite Robert Rockwell in her late husband's two-character play The Lost Letters of Robert E. Lee. *Listening to this poignant drama, one can hear time stand still, as the actress sounds just as girlishly endearing as she did on network radio in the 1940s. (Tapes and CDs of CART productions can be purchased at www.cartradio.com)*

Janet Waldo was dismissive of her movie career, yet her experiences in Hollywood were as rich and varied as anyone's in show business. I think her natural charm and enthusiasm comes through in this interview.

Leonard Maltin: When I called you today on the phone you said, "You must have worked in radio, you're so punctual." Was that one of the first lessons you learned?

Janet Waldo: Oh, was that ever a lesson! When I first started in radio, of course, it was live, and I lived quite close to CBS. I got a call because the ingénue that was playing a role opposite Kirk Douglas on a *Silver Theatre* had panicked. She just panicked, she couldn't go on, and they said, "Can you get here in fifteen minutes?" I had just gotten my license, and I got in my car and I sped; I was going so fast and a policeman stopped me and he said, "Young lady, you're speeding," and I said, "But I'm late! I'm late! It's radio, I have to be there on time, they're going to go on the air without me, I have to be there" and he said, "Oh! I'll escort you." So he blew his siren, escorted me to the studio, and I got there and did the show without having seen it at all. I can't believe I wasn't terribly nervous, but I wasn't. And opposite Kirk Douglas, you know. It went beautifully. In fact, Harriet Nelson heard it and she said, "That's the way you should sound all the time," 'cause I did Emmy Lou on her show as a teenager. The policeman stayed and watched the show and after we finished he said, "Gee, that was great, I really enjoyed that. I just want to thank you. And here's your ticket."

I even I remember my husband Bob chewing out an actress who was five minutes late. He said, "You won't work in radio if you're late. You can't do that." That's why I really can tell people who've worked in radio; they're never late.

Maltin: Where did you grow up and how did you get started in show business?

Janet: You really want to hear that? OK. I was born in Yakima Valley, Washington, and I went to a little country school in a little town called Parker. My father was a railroad man, and we moved from place to place to place. My parents were very concerned because my sister was a genius at the violin, and my father used to say, "I don't want my girls to grow up and marry some guy who's gonna take the eggs to market. I want them to have a good education." They had owned a ranch which they traded for a house in Seattle, Washington and my sister and I got to go to school in Seattle. Then I got very interested in drama, all phases of drama. As a little girl we'd come home from someplace and they'd put the headlights of the car on, and I'd perform. I was doing a play and Bing Crosby had a publicity gimmick going where he was [doing] a sort of talent hunt. His scouts saw this play and they said, "We want you to enter a contest." I was fourteen, [and] I was scared of contests. My mother and my sister said, "You're going to do it," and I won it! They brought me to California with my mother, and Paramount put me under contract, but the problem was they did not know what to do with me. I was very young, and I was trying to compete with all of the glamour girls. To this day I know how to pose for a bathing suit picture because, you know, you stand on your toes, you don't ever let your heels go down. They taught me a lot of things like that.

Maltin: So you were being groomed as a starlet at Paramount?

Janet: Well, [I had] what they called a stock contract.

Maltin: Who else was there at that time?

Janet: Susan Hayward. She had been under stock contract. Let's see, who else was there? Interestingly enough, not much has happened to any of the girls who were there with me, but they were all gorgeous. They were all models, but they couldn't act. And I could act, because I had had really good experience in Seattle and I had done play after play after play. I was very comfortable acting, and they didn't know how to act. They used to say that I was the best actress on the lot, but they didn't know what to do with me. They used to call me the little girl with the little boy's figure.

Leonard: Did they give you bits in movies?

Janet: Oh, yes, they gave me bits. I got to work with some wonderful people. I remember working with Fred MacMurray and they had me be a hat check girl. I remember

I was in a little outfit; he picked up his hat and gave me a tip. And I thought, being an actress, how can I make them notice me? So I did a double take on the tip. And they made a little bit more to do because they would like me to be inventive. But I wasn't glamorous and I wasn't sophisticated in any sense. They used to say to my mother when she brought me down, "Be careful of the wolves," and she didn't know what they meant. She thought they meant a wolf at the door. My mother was more naïve than I was, 'cause my parents were right out of Dickens, they were so sweet and so naïve and so gentle and totally unsophisticated. A lot of people said, "Were you approached, did people try anything?" Actually, a couple of them did, but (*laughs*) I was so dumb and so young that I didn't know what [was going on.] One young man, you probably know him, I don't dare mention his name, a big, big producer in the business took me in his office, locked the door and—you've heard "chasing around the desk?"—that's literally what he did. I didn't know what his problem was! (*laugh*) And he was a very, very big producer. You see, I was so dumb that I didn't know what they wanted of me, and I didn't think I could deliver it. One producer said, "I have a part for you coming up in a picture, but you have to show me that you can kiss passionately." And I'd say, "I don't know how to kiss passionately!" And he'd say, "Well, do you want to try it?" And I'd say, "No!" I didn't get the part.

Maltin: Would you show up for work every day? Would they have things for you to do?

Janet: What you did was what we called glorified atmosphere, just background stuff, and once in a while, they'd give me a little break. I was pretty fortunate, but I was miserable. And that's why I have never felt comfortable doing on-camera [work], even though I've done a lot of on-camera and was working on a show when I got the cartoon. But I just have felt inhibited. I remember I would get so nervous doing on-camera stuff. That's why when I discovered radio, it was like a beautiful coming home to me. I'd done a little theatre, never radio, but I loved it, I felt secure and I enjoyed it thoroughly.

Maltin: How did it come about?

Janet: Well, my option was dropped. I had an agent; actually Larry Crosby sort of took my under his wing. Bing was so sweet and wonderful to me; he'd give me a lot of little bits in his pictures, but Bing knew that I was not a happy person in front of the camera. His brother Larry would take me to his show, *Kraft Music Hall,* and my mother and I would walk to the studio and they would arrange for us to sit right down front, and I just thought, "This is the most wonderful thing in the world, 'cause they had scripts, they didn't have to worry about lines and they were so relaxed; this is so great." As time went on, I got to work with Bing in radio and in fact, one of the shows that I got—I wanted to play the lead in it—they were auditioning for it and they auditioned ninety girls. Now, in radio days, that was a lot. But my mother and I knew the title of the script that they were doing. We knew that it was an old Alice Faye movie. My mother went down to Los Angeles with me to one of the faraway places where they showed old movies in those days, and I watched Alice Faye and I imitated her. I picked up every nuance that she had, I would take a little piece of paper with me in the theatre and write down her lines and then I would listen until I heard it in my own head. I auditioned and I got the part.

Bing was wonderful to me and very sweet. I worked with him several times [and once it was with] Charles Boyer. I have a picture of us together. Bing and Charles Boyer were standing and while we were waiting for them to take the picture, Charles Boyer said, "I'll wear mine if you wear yours." And Bing said, "Well, I'll wear mine if you wear yours." I had no idea what they were talking about, and it was their toupees.

Maltin: Great! So at this point did you start going out on open auditions?

Janet: Oh yes, and I was more aggressive in radio; I was so laid back in films, I would hide in the ladies room, you know, rather than run into somebody that I should meet and should say hello to. In radio, I would go to the lobby of CBS and sit around with all the other actors and wait for the directors to come by and say, "Hi! I'm Janet Waldo and I'd just love to work for you!" (*laughs*) Then they'd say, "Well OK, come on, I'll give you a chance, I'll have you audition." But the real break came [because] my sister knew a man who was very close friends with Edward G. Robinson. The next thing I knew, Tommy Freebairn-Smith [the director] gave me a call to be on the show, not an audition. I was confident, because I knew acting, I knew theatre and I loved radio. So, they gave me the script.

Maltin: This would be on Robinson's show *Big Town*?

Janet: On *Big Town.* And it was [the role of] a very emotional, very dramatic young girl. I read it and I realized later Lurene

Tuttle was sitting right beside me and they were just going to let me try it. I was called for the job, but they were prepared to replace me in the event I couldn't deal with it. I remember hearing Eddie say, "She'll be fine. She'll be just fine." And he called me many, many times after that and I got to do wonderful roles in *Big Town*. It was a wonderful experience because he was so wise as an actor and as a performer. He would rehearse all day long and I learned so much from working with him. He would give direction but he was great, he'd give you wonderful ideas. That really got me started in radio, because then I was kind of a biggie, because I'd worked on Eddie Robinson's show. After I did *Big Town*, I started getting lots of calls and then, very early in my career I got the call to audition for *Meet Corliss Archer*. I didn't want to do a teenager because I always wanted to be a Broadway actress and theatre was what I really loved, next to radio. And I thought, "I want to be the world's greatest actress," and I thought "just a teenager?" That was too easy. I [auditioned] and they chose me and I did it for ten years.

Maltin: The original show that introduced *Corliss Archer, Kiss and Tell*, had been a success on Broadway, right?

Janet: Yes.

Maltin: Was the playwright F. Hugh Herbert involved in the radio show at all?

Janet: Yes, he was my mentor. I just loved that man, he was so good to me. He wanted me and no matter what I did, it was perfect as far as he was concerned. He was the most sentimental and adorable man and his family; his daughters, I always felt, resented me because they wanted to play Corliss. Hugh was wonderful. He hired my husband—who was not my husband then—to do ghost-writing of a couple of scripts. Bob never liked to admit to this (*laughs*); he'd be mad at me for telling. In fact, on the *Meet Corliss Archer* show he invented the fact that Dexter had an old jalopy car, and they got more gags with that car doing all the different sound effects; Bob invented that. Hugh liked Bob very much and encouraged him. He was just a wonderful man. I think he considered me like one of his daughters. I had a fan club, and he let me have my whole fan club come out and have a pool party at his place; they had a beautiful home up in Bel Air, which Casey Kasem bought later. But doing *Corliss* was both good and bad for me; it was easy for me, I just loved doing it, but there was no challenge as far as acting.

I also did Emmy Lou on *Ozzie and Harriet*. As much as I loved *Corliss*, there was no teenager written as well as Emmy Lou. Sherwood Schwartz wrote most of the spots; they were little cameos, and they were always after the first act. Emmy Lou, their little girl who lived next door, would come breezing in and say, "Yoo hoo, Mr. Nelson! Hi, Mr. Nelson!" and then she'd come in and do this little bit with him and she would have an imagination that would just go crazy and then Ozzie would connect with her imagination, and he would get all steamed up and then she'd say, "Well, goodbye Mr. Nelson!" and she'd go. It was just a little gem; it was just the most fun to do. In fact, Bing Crosby wanted me to do a radio show of his and he wanted me to do the squeals which I invented—well, Ozzie and I invented—on *Ozzie and Harriet*. I was very gullible and very naïve; Ozzie would tease me all the time and I never knew when he was teasing or when he was real. I said, "Bing wants me to do this Emmy Lou character in his show and we'd have to go to San Francisco to do it." He said, "I don't know about that, Janet. Well, if he wants you to do the squeals, he has to say, 'squeals courtesy of Ozzie Nelson'." I believed him and I said to Bing, "Ozzie Nelson thinks that I shouldn't do the squeals unless you can give him billing," and Bing says, "Well, I'll give him billing, what the heck?"

Maltin: Who directed the *Corliss Archer* show?

Janet: Tom McAvity was the original director. Later on, his wife Helen Mack directed it and, later on, Edna Best directed it. When Edna Best directed it, it was the only time that Corliss (using accent) was just a little teeny bit British because Betsy would say, "Janet, darling, you're not sounding quite right in that line, now you'd better just give it a little more oomph, you know?" And I'd say, "OK!" and I was just a tinge British as Corliss, during that phase.

Maltin: Very funny. Was she a good director?

Janet: Wonderful director. Edna Best was a very good friend, and her husband, Nat Wolf, was an agent and was my husband's agent. Her daughter, Sarah Marshall, is still very much around. She was also a very fine actress.

Maltin: Tell me about Helen Mack.

Janet: I loved her dearly. She was a pixie. Very much of a pixie, a very cute little lady who was always playing sort of the little girl. She was always the little girl, and I should know about that, but she was a wonderful director for *Corliss*, very easy, very relaxed. A beautiful lady.

Maltin: Of course, I only know her as an actress in 1930s movies like *The Son of Kong*.

Janet: She was beautiful, but she liked to direct, and she had one of her first chances with *Corliss Archer*. I think she also directed *Date with Judy* on occasion. She was excellent, and she had a great sense of humor and timing.

Maltin: What other roles did you enjoy performing on radio?

Janet: Bob, my husband, did *Favorite Story* and he really saved the day for me in radio because he cast me in all sorts of wonderful acting roles. I met Bob in the halls of CBS and he cast me as Cathy in *Wuthering Heights* with Bill Conrad, which was one of my favorite roles of all time. He cast me as Roxanne in *Cyrano De Bergerac* opposite Ronald Colman. Then later he had me do it again opposite Howard Duff. He also cast me as the Bird Woman in *Green Mansions,* which is one of my favorite roles of all time; he gave me wonderful opportunities. And I'll tell you a story: shortly after we were married, I did *Green Mansions* for him. It was three days after we had been married, and I came to rehearsal and, of course, this was very exciting for me, and he said, "Jan darling, you're sounding a little too much like Corliss Archer." Oooh, I was angry. I was furious. I thought, "How dare you say that to me!" and an old-time actor, Norman Field, who worked in radio a lot, said, "Come here, I want to talk to you a minute. Janet, you want to keep a happy marriage?" And I said, "Oh yeah." And he said, "When he's your director, you're an actor; never let your marriage or your relationship with him interfere with your job. You do your job and you don't get personal about it." I never forgot that lesson. And actually, it was one of the best jobs I ever did, because I didn't sound like Corliss Archer!

Maltin: Was there any other downside to doing a long-running show?

Janet: You could get lazy because it [became] routine. The trick in radio was to try to come up with something interesting with an uninteresting or rather dry piece of material. I remember one time with Bob Hope—I don't know whether it was a Bob Hope show or another show that he was on—I was supposed to be selling Girl Scout cookies. I had to give this big pitch to Bob Hope and I decided, instead of saying, "Hello Mr. Hope, I have these cookies and I hope you'll be interested," I did the whole thing really bored. I talked very fast, like I'd said it a thousand times, and it just went beautifully and it was a different approach. But if you get lazy and think, "oh, well I'll just read what's here," it doesn't work. The real challenge in radio for me was working in front of an audience. Because the audience literally times things for you. I miss that now so much because you would know how to play to the audience.

[Also, in radio] you have to play it opposite each other, that's what makes it so real. You can't do radio if you aren't real and if you don't listen. Listening is the most important thing that we did in radio; we had to, because [there was so little rehearsal]. And we were all very good friends; everybody helped everybody. I remember when I first started in radio, I was very nervous and scared, and Elliott Lewis was on a show, we were doing a *Silver Theatre* or something and he just said, "You know what you do? Go and put your hand against the wall and it'll steady you," 'cause I was really shaky. I put my hand against the wall and he'd sort of lean up against me and say, "You can do it, you can do it, kid. You can do it." They were just so helpful to each other and if I couldn't do a part, I would always say I'm not free to do it, but why don't you call so-and-so? We all did that for each other.

Maltin: Today there are professional cartoon voice-over performers, but in the first generation of television cartoons everybody came out of radio.

Janet: I was so thrilled when I discovered cartoons because I was doing an on-camera show with Tony Franciosa and I had never done a cartoon. My agent sent me to audition for *The Jetsons* and I thought, "Oh, cartoons." And when I started working, I knew most of them from radio: Daws Butler, Don Messick, Casey Kasem. Mel Blanc, of course, I had worked with in radio. He was a very good actor.

Maltin: But people don't often realize just how good they were as actors.

Janet: Daws was born teacher and if you worked on a show with him, he could hardly resist teaching. In my case, it was very gratefully received. He'd say, "Hey Janet, you don't want to just make that an ordinary character. Give it a little something extra." And he'd give me some ideas. He taught many of the current people in cartoons. Nancy Cartwright [who plays

Bart on *The Simpsons*] studied with Daws and gives him full credit for her ability as a radio actress, certainly. By the way, Nancy and I did *Little Women* for Peggy Webber's California Artists Radio Theater (CART); I played Amy and Nancy played Beth. That's one thing [about] cartoons: you have to have a different voice and that's what I thought was such fun. Joe Barbera would always say, "Now that's a good voice Janet, but can you sustain it? Can you hold it? Can you remember what you did?" And that is the real challenge, because you can come up with something on the spur of the moment. I remember I did a character from "Good Cavekeeping Magazine." Her name was Hedda Rocker, and she was sort of a blustery lady. I did it and he said, "Mmm-hmm, well that's OK, but now can you do it again?" And sometimes he would have me do it again to just be sure before he would let me have the part.

Maltin: Very interesting. Very canny, too.

Janet: Joe was a wonderful director.

Maltin: Who did you most enjoy working with in radio?

Janet: Bing. 'Cause I loved Bing and he changed my life. You know, if it hadn't been for Bing, I would never have come to Hollywood. Even though he was a very reserved and, some people think, cold man and hard to get to talk, I felt such gratitude to him.

Maltin: Why do you think some movie stars were so nervous when they appeared on radio?

Janet: I think that movie actors were intimidated by the fact that "this is now," and live. [When tape came in] they all relaxed a lot more and they blew [lines] like crazy. But in live radio shows, they couldn't afford to blow; they knew that and they were feeling that their life was at stake, that they could ruin their career by being really bad. I worked with Clark Gable and he was terrified. He was trembling, his whole body was just trembling when he was doing it. I couldn't believe that this brilliant Rhett Butler was that scared. It just fascinated me 'cause I thought, what does he have to be scared about? He's Rhett Butler! I worked with Abbott and Costello and that was a time that I was mortified because I made a boo-boo. They talked so fast, you never could keep track of how fast they talked, and I was just reading; we'd had maybe one read-through, and they had given so many instructions to the audience about "when we want you to laugh," he would take his pant leg and jiggle it, you know? I was playing a very young girl who was talking to them and saying, "Oh yes, Mr. Abbott, Mr. Costello," and there was this silence. It was my cue, but it was dead air—well, forever is ten seconds, five seconds, but I hadn't realized they'd gotten to that place that fast. That was pretty mortifying to me.

Oh, so many stars that we worked with. And we learned from them. You know, working in radio, that was a thrill. You could work with these big stars and you could see what they did right and what they did wrong. And you could see why they were stars. Claudette Colbert was just wonderful, brilliant, a very good radio actress. She wasn't intimidated by it at all. I played her daughter on *Secret Heart*.

Maltin: Did you work with Bette Davis?

Janet: Yes. She was not temperamental, very nice, very businesslike. You know, it was very short; I mean, we didn't have a lot of time together. I worked with Laurence Olivier and Vivien Leigh, and Laurence Olivier said to Vivien, "Darling, that line, you're reading it a little wrong. That line should be read this way." And he read it and she looked at him and she said, "It's my line, dear."

Remembering Joe Franklin (1926–2015)

I can't accept the idea that Joe Franklin is dead. He seemed ageless, as much a part of the New York scene as the Brooklyn Bridge. If you didn't grow up in the New York City area his name might not resonate, unless you remember Billy Crystal's hilarious (and accurate) portrayal of Joe on *Saturday Night Live* in the 1970s. Crystal's affectionate impression was based on a lifetime of watching Joe. He was a fixture on local television from 1950 to 1993, hosting a daily talk show that was strangely endearing. Originally called *Joe Franklin's Memory Lane*, it featured old movie clips and records from his enormous collection, along with an array of studio guests. Having started out on radio in his teens, Joe was a smooth talker and a master spieler, but he also had an amazing knack for making gaffes and never realizing what he'd done.

He used to boast that future stars, from Barbra Streisand to Liza Minnelli, made their TV debuts on his program, but what made it unique was the unpredictable mix of people he had on his panels, and the way he insisted that they engage with one another. I remember the day he had director Frank Capra, musician Artie Shaw, and the owner of a local Greek restaurant on together. After awkwardly asking the great filmmaker why he hadn't used Shaw's wife Evelyn Keyes in any of his movies, he insisted that Capra shoot a scene for his next film at the Acropolis Restaurant on Eighth Avenue! Another time, the city Traffic Commissioner was sitting next to Buddy Rogers, who was there to promote a Mary Pickford film series. "Commissioner," said Joe with a straight face, "I want you to make all the streets in the city 'one way' so every car will go to the Beacon Theater for the Mary Pickford festival."

Joe built up unknowns, wannabes, and used-to-bes with the same enthusiasm he summoned when genuine stars stopped by. I know this first-hand because I made my television debut on his "live" morning show when I was 16. I met Joe the night I attended Raymond Rohauer's tribute to Ginger Rogers at the Huntington Hartford Museum. I was pretty nervy back then and pressed a copy of my *Film Fan Monthly* magazine into his hands as we were exiting the auditorium. Joe told me to call him the following Tuesday at 3pm and he would book me on his program. I did as instructed and he came through as promised. But having watched his show for so many years, I knew that when I turned up he would have no memory of my name or the magazine I'd given him. Many was the time I'd seen him introduce an unknown like me and expect him, on cue, to blurt out his name and save

Joe the trouble. Most of them would sit there for an awkward moment. That wasn't going to be me.

My friend Chris Steinbrunner, who worked as the film buyer at Joe's station, WOR, told me that I shouldn't expect Joe to show up until seconds before airtime. Sure enough, as I stood in the reception room at 1440 Broadway, surrounded by other guests for that day's 90-minute show, various publicists and handlers started pacing nervously and wondering where our host could be as a gigantic clock on the wall ticked away the minutes to 10:30. True to Chris' prediction, Joe calmly strode in at 10:29, greeted one and all, made his way into the studio as his opening theme music ("Twelfth Street Rag") was playing, and clipped a microphone to his tie just as the final image in his main-title montage dissolved to him behind his desk.

Since Joe hadn't ever written my name down, let alone the name of my fanzine, I was ready when my moment came and introduced myself to the television audience. I returned many times over the years, and each appearance was memorable in its own way. He gave every guest a generous plug for whatever he or she was promoting, but in return you had to pay close attention. One time Joe started out by mourning the people who had lost their lives in a tragic plane crash a few days earlier, including some recent guests. He turned to me and said, "Leonard, what do you think about these airline crashes?"

One time he called me at home on a Sunday evening and asked if I was free later on. I hesitated to answer, because with Joe this could lead to a supermarket opening or an appearance at a Chinese restaurant. Instead, he brought me along for a late-night appearance on *The Candy Jones Show* on WMCA Radio. That night he told New York's night owls that of all the people he'd introduced on his television show, he was proudest of me. I am certain he never made that particular statement again. Later, a listener phoned in to ask if Joe knew the name of the leading man in an early talkie. It was a very obscure title, but without missing a beat Joe responded, "It might be Conrad Nagel." My wife and I adopted that as an all-purpose catchphrase when we don't know the answer to any question, and we think of Joe whenever we utter it.

After his television show expired, Joe remained active on New York radio for a number of years. Over the course of time, it was inevitable that he would turn up, playing himself, in New York-centric movies like George Gallo's *29th Street* and Woody Allen's *Broadway Danny Rose*. In 1997 Joshua Brown made a wonderful documentary called *50,000,000 Joe Franklin Fans Can't Be Wrong*. It captures Joe in all his glory:

in his famously cluttered office, dealing with his many hangers-on, meeting fans, and broadcasting to the world. You can find it, in sections, on YouTube, along with many excerpts of Joe's television shows. They all make me smile, but I'm especially happy to revisit his interview with Bing Crosby, in which Joe's love of nostalgia meets its match, and segments from his trip to Hollywood for his 40th anniversary special, in which Bob Hope says, with real fondness, "Joe, you're a legend."

He was indeed — one of a kind.

Remembering Lauren Bacall (1924–2014)

Lauren Bacall was one of the last links to the golden age of Hollywood, yet she gracefully reinvented herself in later years, first on Broadway and then onscreen. She became a welcome presence as a character actress in such varied films as *Murder on the Orient Express, The Shootist* (with John Wayne), Lars von Trier's *Dogville*, and *Birth* (with Nicole Kidman). She contributed a fine voice performance to the American version of Hiyao Miyazaki's animated feature *Howl's Moving Castle* and earned an Oscar nomination playing Barbra Streisand's mother in *The Mirror Has Two Faces*.

She had nothing but praise for Streisand, who also directed the film. In fact, it was the first time Bacall had worked with a female director. "It's great to be directed by a woman who really knows what she wants," she told me, "and Barbra certainly does know what she wants. She has a vision and she knows how to realize that vision.

"She had a definite concept of me playing this part. The preconceptions of me by a lot of people that I'm always this glamorous figure—or whatever people think I am—she wanted me not to be like that. And I said, 'I don't want to be like that. We've had enough of that,'" she said with a laugh. "We have a kind of thread between us that connects us, and I felt it in the scenes when we were playing them."

She was a formidable woman—some might say intimidating—yet she professed to be insecure. It's not necessarily a contradiction. I had good experiences every time I interviewed her, but I was always conscious of being on my toes. You didn't want to hesitate, or waffle, when speaking with Miss Bacall. (In that regard she was not unlike her friend Katharine Hepburn.)

Whenever we spoke, I covered the immediate subject at hand and then "snuck in" some questions about friends and colleagues from Old Hollywood, from Peter Lorre ("Funny, very analytical. A very complicated, fascinating man") to Charles Boyer ("Adorable man, wonderful actor. He was a terrific chess player and an insomniac. He and Bogie used to play chess on the set when we were making that terrible movie that almost ruined my career, *Confidential Agent*."). I once told her how much I enjoyed her appearances with Humphrey Bogart on Jack Benny's radio show, and she smiled at the memory. "He was a genius at what he did," she said. "And he was so generous to his guests. He didn't try to hog the limelight all the time, which was, of course, very rare.

"He came to see me in *Applause* half a dozen times, at least. When he first saw me in the show in New York, he said,

'You have perfect timing.' My God, coming from Jack Benny, who had perfect timing, I was so flattered."

Ultimately, I think of Lauren Bacall as a survivor: a star in her debut movie, *To Have and Have Not*, when she was barely twenty, opposite the man who would become her husband, Humphrey Bogart, widowed in her early thirties, she moved from Hollywood back to her home town of New York and remarried. A year after divorcing her second husband (Jason Robards, Jr.) she made her Broadway debut and won a Tony Award for her performance as Margo Channing—a role created by her favorite actress, Bette Davis—in *Applause*. That opened the next chapter of her acting career, out of Bogart's shadow, and led to many fruitful years, culminating in an honorary Academy Award in 2010. That's a life, and a career, worth celebrating.

Remembering Robin Williams (1951–2014)

I felt lucky every time I got to chat with Robin Williams, but when I once said, "I'd love to get inside your brain," he replied, "Leonard, you don't want to go there." It's a sad fact that many people who possess great gifts are also greatly troubled. Some of them hide it from the world, while others can't. It's a crushing blow to learn that this wildly talented man took his own life. How sad for his family and friends, not to mention fans and admirers. We've been robbed of his presence and his talent.

The first time I met him was during a press junket for the 1990 drama *Awakenings*, in which he starred opposite Robert De Niro. At the time, *Entertainment Tonight*'s modus operandi was to roll tape the minute our interviewee walked in the door, and Robin didn't disappoint. We used up a 20-minute cassette and afterwards I told my boss that he could have (and should have) used the entire tape, start to finish. It wasn't just that he was funny; he riffed on everything around him, including me, but he also knew when and how to be serious. He could turn on a dime and change the air in the room.

Other comedians have turned out to be good dramatic actors, but when Williams revealed that facet of his talent it was surprising because his comedy was so manic and spontaneous. People either forgot, or didn't know, that he had studied at Juilliard under the imposing John Houseman before becoming a street performer in San Francisco. Beyond that, he clearly had a keen insight into human nature: the same observational skills that fueled his comedy enabled him to explore the serious, even darker, side of a character.

I like a lot of his films, from *The Fisher King* to *Aladdin*, but two of my favorite performances are in movies that didn't reach wide audiences. In *One Hour Photo* (2002) he plays a clerk at the photo-developing counter who takes more than casual interest in his favorite customers. He was so convincing that, as I left the theater, I kept thinking, "I know that guy." He also did exceptional work in Bobcat Goldthwait's dark comedy/satire *World's Greatest Dad* (2009) as a failed writer who seizes an opportunity to achieve notoriety following a family tragedy.

I feel crushed by the news of Robin Williams' death. What a loss it is for all of us who enjoyed him on television, stage, and film. I looked forward to every talk-show appearance he made, because he never let an audience down.

We'll always be able to see him, thank goodness, but now the experience will be bittersweet.

Remembering Roger Ebert (1942–2013) with his wife, Chaz

Roger Ebert and his wife Chaz were so linked, in my mind, that it's impossible for me to think of one without the other. Once people see Steve James' moving documentary *Life Itself*, which opens theatrically on Friday, they will surely understand why. Following a screening at USC this past Friday, I moderated a Q&A session with Chaz and asked her what surprised her most about people's reaction to the film thus far. Her answer: that audiences are so moved by their love story.

During Roger's lifetime, he and Chaz tried to keep their family life private. Anyone who encountered the couple at film festivals could see how they cared for each other—all the more so after Roger became ill. But in this surprisingly wide-ranging documentary, people will see how devoted Roger was, not only to Chaz but to the family he inherited when he married her. Home movies of their travels, and his interaction with his devoted children and grandchildren, reveal a side of Ebert that outsiders didn't see.

I never got to know Roger well, largely because he was based in Chicago and I was in Los Angeles. We enjoyed chatting when we'd run into each other at industry events and the annual Telluride Film Festival. But my wife Alice and I noticed a palpable change in him when he married Chaz, the brilliant and compassionate woman who became his soul mate. She was more than a partner; she was his Rock of Gibraltar.

Members of the audience at USC asked about their relationship and Chaz replied that, despite surface appearances, they were more alike than unalike. The only time she recalled a differing point of view based on race came when the O.J. Simpson verdict was delivered in 1994. Roger didn't understand why black people cheered at the news, and Chaz explained that it was a reaction to years of injustice, not merely one high-profile case. He said he hadn't considered that. When I first screened the film at the Sundance Film Festival in January, I had a highly emotional reaction, as my wife did the other night. Anyone who has gone through a difficult illness, or cared for someone who was dying, will certainly relate. What makes *Life Itself* so impressive is the way Roger and Chaz opened themselves up to filmmaker Steve James during Roger's penultimate hospital stay in Chicago and its aftermath. I told Chaz that I found it both brave and risky for her and Roger to expose themselves as they did, but she made light of that. They knew that James (who made his name with *Hoop Dreams* twenty years ago) believes all of his documentaries to be collaborative projects and would never include anything that his subjects found objectionable.

Yet this is no puff piece: the film paints a fascinating and rounded portrait of Ebert (and, of course, his longtime partner Gene Siskel), warts and all. I'll tell you more when I post my official review of the film later this week. For now, suffice it to say that *Life Itself* is more than the biography of a film critic: it is a story of talent, perseverance, luck, serendipity, sadness, and—yes—love.

Remembering Roger Mayer (1926–2015)

When Martin Scorsese presented him with the Jean Hersholt Humanitarian Award in 2005, I'm sure many people watching the Oscarcast around the world had no idea who Roger Mayer was. Hollywood insiders and the community of film archivists knew him well as a fair-minded business executive and a generous benefactor. I was lucky enough to call him a friend.

Roger suffered a heart attack on Tuesday at 89. He had a bout of health problems last year that had many of us worried, but he eventually rallied, so this news comes as a shock.

Roger belied his age for many years, chairing meetings with vigor and enthusiasm and raising funds for causes he cared about. My wife and I learned that it was difficult—nearly impossible—to say no when he hit you up for a contribution.

Even after he retired from Turner Entertainment, he remained active on the boards of the Academy of Motion Picture Arts and Sciences, Motion Picture and Television Fund, the National Film Preservation Foundation, the Los Angeles Chamber Orchestra, and the Library of Congress' National Film Registry, among others, giving of his time and expertise in countless ways. He was a master negotiator who understood the handling of delicate egos; he knew when to impose rules and when to bend them.

Trained as a lawyer, he broke into the movie business in the 1950s working for the irascible Harry Cohn at Columbia Pictures. Cohn respected Roger, but only to a point. When, after many years, Roger told him he'd gotten a better job offer, Cohn gruffly told him to take it. He did.

When I first met him in the 1980s, he was a Vice-President of MGM, which was still in its longtime home in Culver City. I asked if he was any relation to the legendary Louis B. Mayer and, with a sly smile, he said he wasn't—but never discouraged anyone from thinking otherwise if it accrued to his benefit.

Roger was largely responsible for MGM investing in its film library long before the age of home video, and saving thousands of 35mm negatives that might have otherwise disintegrated. He pooh-poohed the idea that he was a visionary and said it just made good business sense to protect a company's assets. He brought the same solid thinking to his long tenure as president of Turner Entertainment and even weathered the storm of controversy over his boss' endorsement of colorization. I'm sure I'm not the only friend who avoided the subject whenever possible.

Roger was of a generation that was taught to give back, and he set a standard we can only hope that younger movers and shakers in Hollywood will follow. He was a pragmatist but also had a big heart, and he genuinely cared about movies. Most of all, he was devoted to his family, especially his soul mate Pauline, a bright, positive woman who was always at his side during their sixty-two-year marriage. When he read that my *Movie Guide* was shutting down last fall, he and Pauline insisted on taking Alice and me to dinner, and we had a long, lovely evening together. I value it now all the more.

It's easy to mouth platitudes like "we will not see his like again" but in the case of Roger Mayer, the clichés seem valid. He leaves a void that will not be easy, or even possible, to fill: a kind, generous man whom I think of as irreplaceable.

Remembering Stan Freberg (1926–2015)

Stan Freberg was one of my heroes; he died on Tuesday at the age of 88. If you don't know his name, you should, and if you do a search online you may find yourself an instant fan.

When I was a kid, committing his comedy records to memory and eagerly awaiting his latest commercials, I never dreamed that I would meet him, let alone call him a friend someday. I can't overstate the influence he had on me during my adolescence; he helped shape my sense of humor and permanently planted his ideas, catchphrases, and voices into my consciousness. Say the name "Ben Franklin" and I think of that founding father uttering the words "life, liberty and the purfuit of happineff" from the album *Stan Freberg Presents The United States of America*. At odd moments his parody of Harry Belafonte's "Banana Boat (Day-O)" ("too piercing, man.") or his bow to radio censorship, "Elderly Man River," pop into my head. ("You're welcome, I'm sure.")

It's heartening to know that I'm not alone. When some friends of Stan's mounted a tribute to him last November at the Egyptian Theatre in Hollywood, notables ranging from Steven Spielberg to Weird Al Yankovic sang his praises. Everyone spoke from the heart and few could resist quoting their favorite Freberg lines.

I first met Stan when I got to interview him about his autobiography *It Only Hurts When I Laugh*, for *Entertainment Tonight* in 1988. When he told me he was about to embark on a book promotion tour, I asked if he'd ever done anything like that before. He said he hadn't, and I took the liberty of offering some advice, based on my experiences: always have something to eat with you for plane rides at inconvenient hours, take Vitamin C on a regular basis, etc. Two weeks later he called me from out of town to thank me and declared, "A book tour is the literary equivalent of the Bataan death march!"

Sometime later my wife Alice dubbed him an honorary Jew, which delighted him no end, as many people mistakenly thought he was part of our Tribe. In fact, he was the son of a Baptist minister. Our daughter Jessie soon became a Freberg fan as well, sputtering with laughter while listening to "Sh-boom" or "The Great Pretender."

Imagine, then, what it felt like to have him as a guest in our home. Our friends were amazed—even overwhelmed—to meet him. One night our party turned into an impromptu musicale. I worked up my courage and asked if he'd be willing to sing "Take an Indian to Lunch," from his *United States* album. He said yes without hesitation but asked who might accompany him on the piano. I said I would, if he could perform in the key of C. He did, and needless to say, he brought down the house.

As a lifelong fan, I thought I knew all there was to know about Stan as a radio, television, and recording artist, but it turns out he had more to do with movies—especially animated cartoons—than I realized when I was young. Because Mel Blanc was the only performer to receive credit on Warner Bros. cartoons, I never knew that Stan contributed a number of voices to Looney Tunes over the years, including Bertie of Hubie and Bertie, one of the Goofy Gophers, Pete Puma, and that unforgettable lunkhead Junyer Bear in Chuck Jones' Three Bears cartoons ("What's Brewin', Bruin?," "A Bear for Punishment," et al.). That alone would earn him a place in the pop culture hall of fame. He finally got the credit he deserved on Friz Freleng's "Three Little Bops" in 1957. He also provided the voice of the beaver in Walt Disney's *Lady and the Tramp* and George Pal's Yawning Man in *tom thumb*. He was even featured on-camera in a 1953 Republic feature called *Geraldine*, singing some of his parodies including the Johnny Ray send-up "Try." He not only appeared in *It's a Mad Mad Mad Mad World* but created the TV commercials for Stanley Kramer's mega-comedy.

I'm not sure the generations that followed the Baby Boomers recognized Stan and his genius as we did. This may have wounded his ego in recent years, but his admirers never lost sight of who he was or what he meant to us. His humor has worn well. and his voice work speaks for itself—pun intended. He was one of a kind.

His loss hits me hard, because he lives inside my head, and always has. I'll never forget him, nor will I forget the kindness he showed me and my family. Freberg forever!

Remembering Tony Martin (1913–2012)

Tony Martin had a golden voice, and even in his nineties exuded charm and class. I was thrilled when I first got to meet him and got an even bigger kick when I saw him and his wife at my synagogue's High Holy Days services! "This," I thought, "could only happen in Hollywood." Yes, Tony Martin was born Alvin Morris, or "Haim Avruch," as he once told me. It was 20th Century Fox chief Darryl F. Zanuck who renamed him and even went so far as to bill him as "Anthony Martin" a couple of times early in his screen career.

He never became an A-list movie star, but if you want to see him at his best, check out a cute Columbia B musical from 1940 called *Music in My Heart*, in which he stars with Rita Hayworth and a first-rate cast of character actors. It's an utterly formulaic and inconsequential film, but fun to watch, and Martin is effortlessly charming. Bob Wright and Chet Forrest wrote the tuneful score, and one of the songs that Martin introduced, "It's a Blue World," earned an Academy Award nomination that year.

And if you want to hear some of Jerome Kern and Oscar Hammerstein II's *Show Boat* melodies done to perfection, check out the condensed version of their classic work as MGM incorporated it into the Kern biography *Till the Clouds Roll By*. Martin makes an ideal Gaylord Ravenal opposite Kathryn Grayson.

His best overall film is the one he produced, with his agent Nat Goldstone, *Casbah* (1948). It took nerve to take on the role of the daring French rogue Pépé le Moko, created by Jean Gabin and immortalized for American audiences by Charles Boyer in *Algiers*, but he pulled it off quite well, especially with actors like Peter Lorre and Thomas Gomez to play against, and two beautiful leading ladies (Yvonne De Carlo and Marta Toren). But he was proudest of the fact that Harold Arlen and Leo Robin provided four exceptionally good songs ("For Every Man There's a Woman," "Hooray for Love," "It Was Written in the Stars," and "What's Good About Goodbye"), the first of which was nominated for an Oscar. He continued to sing them for the rest of his life. (In *The Two of Us*, the autobiography he co-authored with his wife Cyd Charisse, and Dick Kleiner, he ruefully tells the story of how *Casbah* came about and how he lost every cent he put into it. Sorry to say, this first-rate film directed by John Berry is not available on DVD.)

Typecast as a straight man to such comics as The Ritz Brothers and The Marx Brothers, Martin rarely got to show his own sense of humor. But there is a famous unused take from a 1940 recording session with Harry Sosnik and his Orchestra. Martin is smoothly singing the ballad but when he flubs a lyric, instead of stopping cold he continues, mimicking one of his heroes, the ultra-hammy Harry Richman, right to the end of the track. It's wonderful.

In 2004, my wife and I were delighted to see him perform, at age 90, at the Cinegrill in the Hollywood Roosevelt Hotel, which was then under the supervision of a major Martin fan and booster, Michael Feinstein (who later booked him at his nightclub in Manhattan). He still wore a tuxedo better than anyone I know; he even had a signature line of tux apparel with After Six years ago. His voice wasn't what it was decades ago—whose is?—but he still sang quite well, and more important, he knew how to sell a song. After going for the high note at the end of "All the Things You Are," he said with a smile, "That's the last time you're ever going to hear that note from me." He was unflappable, even when he forgot some lyrics (the only time it happened all night) to "How Do You Keep the Music Playing." Instead of trying to pretend there was nothing wrong, he joked about sometimes making up better words when he forgets the real ones.

When he played Catalina Jazz Club five years later, I went back and, while his voice had diminished, his warmth and ability to put over a song (at age 95!) had not.

He was devoted to his wife of sixty years, Cyd Charisse, and when I spoke with him a few years ago he was still devastated by her passing in 2008. He endured another tragedy when their only son, Tony Martin, Jr., died in 2011. Tony Jr.'s face used to light up when he spoke about his parents, especially when he described them casually rehearsing in the kitchen for an appearance together as recently as the year 2000.

I feel privileged to have spent just a little time with Tony Martin, and I know I will continue to enjoy his voice—and his presence on screen—for many years to come.

Appendix B:
Leonard Maltin Credits

As author

Movie Comedy Teams, NAL, 1970. Revised editions 1974, 1985.

Behind the Camera, NAL, 1971. Reissued as *The Art of the Cinematographer,* Dover, 1978.

The Great Movie Shorts, Crown, 1972. Reissued as *Selected Short Subjects,* Da Capo, 1983.

The Disney Films, Crown, 1973. Revised edition, 1985; 3rd edition, 1995 from Hyperion; 4th ed., 2000, Disney Editions.

Carole Lombard, Pyramid, 1976.

Our Gang: The Life and Times of the Little Rascals, co-author with Richard W. Bann, Crown, 1977. Revised and reissued as *The Little Rascals: The Life and Times of Our Gang,* 1992.

The Great Movie Comedians, Crown, 1978.

Of Mice and Magic: A History of American Animated Cartoons, NAL and McGraw Hill, 1980. Revised edition, 1987.

The Complete Guide to Home Video, co-author, Crown, 1981.

The Great American Broadcast: A Celebration of Radio's Golden Age, E.P. Dutton, 1997.

Leonard Maltin's Movie Crazy, M Press, 2008.

Leonard Maltin's 151 Best Movies You've Never Seen, Harper Studio, 2010.

Hooked On Hollywood: Experiences from a Lifetime of Film Fandom, GoodKnight Books, 2018.

Over The Moon: Illuminating The Journey, Titan Books, 2020.

Starstruck: My Unlikely Road To Hollywood, GoodKnight Books, 2021.

As editor

Leonard Maltin's Movie Guide (originally published as *TV Movies,* then *Leonard Maltin's Movie & Video Guide*), NAL/Penguin, 1969, 1974, 1978, 1980, 1982, 1984, 1986, 1987, published annually since 1988. Published in Dutch as *Speelfilm Encyclopedie,* Sweden as *Bonniers Stora Film & Video Guide,* Italian as *Guida Film.*

The Real Stars, Curtis, 1973.

The Real Stars #2, Curtis, 1974.

The Laurel And Hardy Book, Curtis, 1973.

Hollywood: The Movie Factory, Popular Library, 1976.

Hollywood Kids, Popular Library, 1978.

The Real Stars #3, Popular Library, 1979.

The Whole Film Sourcebook, NAL/Universe Books, 1983.

Leonard Maltin's Movie Encyclopedia, Dutton/Penguin, 1994.

Leonard Maltin's Family Film Guide, Dutton Signet, 1999.

As contributor

A Concise History of the Cinema, Tantivy/A.S. Barnes, 1971.

The Compleat Guide to Film Study, The National Council of Teachers of English, 1972.

The American Film Heritage, AFI/Acropolis Books, 1972.

Directors in Action, Bobbs Merrill, 1973.

The Encyclopedia of Jazz in the Seventies, Horizon, 1976.

The Movie Buff's Book 2, Pyramid, 1977.

The It's A Wonderful Life *Book*, Knopf, 1986.

The Complete Guide to American Film Schools, Penguin, 1994.

Private Screenings: Insiders Share a Century of Great Movie Moments, American Film Institute/Turner Publishing, 1995.

The Book Of Movie Lists, Contemporary Books, 1998.

American National Biography, Oxford University Press, 1999.

Charles M. Schulz: Conversations, University Press of Mississippi, 2000.

Citizen Sarris: American Film Critic, Scarecrow Press, 2001.

The Cartoon Music Book, A Cappella, 2002.

The World Almanac and Book of Facts 2005, World Almanac Books.

Disney Insider Yearbook: 2005 Year In Review, Disney Editions.

My Favorite Place On Earth, National Geographic, 2009.

As General Editor, Curtis Film Series

Preston Sturges by James Ursini (1973).

Hollywood Director by David Chierichetti (1973).

Karloff by Denis Gifford (1973).

B Movies by Don Miller (1973; reprinted by Ballantine, 1988).

Don Siegel, Director by Stuart M. Kaminsky (1974).

As General Editor, Popular Library Film Series

The Abbott And Costello Book by Jim Mulholland (1975).

Tex Avery, King of Cartoons by Joe Adamson (1975; reprinted by DaCapo, 1985).

Hollywood Corral by Don Miller (1975).

Stanley Kubrick: A Film Odyssey by Gene Phillips (1975).

Superman: From Serial To Cereal by Gary H. Grossman (1976).

Robert Altman: American Innovator by Judith M. Kass (1978).

Author of forewords

Let Me Entertain You by Jordan Young, Moonstone Press, 1988.

Walt Disney and Assorted Other Characters by Jack Kinney, Crown, 1989.

Chronicle Of The Movies, Crescent, 1991.

Justice For Disney by Bill Justice, Tomart Publications, 1992.

Superman: Archive Editions, Volume 4, D.C. Comics, 1994.

Animation: The Art of Friz Freleng, Donovan Publishing, 1994.

Listening To Movies: The Film Lovers Guide to Film Music by Fred Karlin, Schirmer, 1994.

Our Movie Heritage by Tom McGreevey and Joanne L. Yeck, Rutgers University Press, 1997.

Walt's Time by Robert B. Sherman and Richard M. Sherman, Camphor Tree, 1998.

Writers On Directors by Susan Gray, Watson Guptill, 1999.

I Have a Lady in the Balcony by George Ansbro, McFarland, 2000.

Sound and Vision: 60 Years Of Motion Picture Soundtracks by Jon Burlingame, Billboard Books, 2000.

My Life is in Your Hands/Take My Life: The Autobiographies of Eddie Cantor, Cooper Square Press, 2000.

Ub Iwerks: The Hand Behind The Mouse by John Kenworthy, Disney Editions, 2001.

The Barrymores: Hollywood's First Family by Carol Stein Hoffman, University of Kentucky Press, 2001.

Hans Conried by Suzanne Gargiulo, McFarland, 2002.

The Marx Brothers Encyclopedia by Glenn Mitchell, Reynolds And Hearn, 2003.

Monster Kid Memories by Bob Burns, Dinoship, 2003.

Dummy Days by Kelly Asbury, Angel City Press, 2003.

Moving Pictures and Classic Images by Samuel K. Rubin, McFarland, 2004.

Our Gang, Volume 1, Fantagraphics Press, 2006)

Mouse Tracks by Tim Hollis and Greg Ehrbar, University Press of Mississippi, 2006.

Old Jewish Comedians by Drew Friedman, Fantagraphics Press, 2006.

Gremlins by Roald Dahl, Dark Horse Comics, 2006.

Harlan Ellison's Watching, M Press, 2008.

Stooges Among Us, Bear Manor, 2008.

Did You Grow Up With Me, Too? The Autobiography of June Foray, Bear Manor, 2009.

Mister Magoo's Christmas Carol: The Making Of The First Animated Christmas Special by Darrell Van Citters, Oxberry Press, 2009.

100 Greatest Looney Tunes, Insight Editions, 2010.

Boris Karloff Tales of Mystery Archives, Volume 6, Dark Horse, 2011.

None Of The Above by Harlan Ellison, Edgeworks Abbey, 2012.

The Three Stooges: Hollywood Filming Locations by Jim Pauley, Santa Monica Press, 2012.

The Complete Peanuts, Volume 17, Fantagraphics, 2012.

Summer Movies by John Malahy, Running Press, 2021.

Laurel & Hardy On The Radio & On The Phone! by John Tefteller, Tefteller, 2018.

The Ultimate Droodles Compendium by Roger Price, Tallfellow Press.

The Total Filmmaker—Updated Edition by Jerry Lewis, Michael Wiese Productions, 2021.

Duke: The Official John Wayne Movie Book, Media Lab Books, 2022.

Hanna-Barbera: The Recorded History by Greg Ehrbar, University Press of Mississippi, 2024.

Collecting Laurel & Hardy by Danny Bacher and Bernie Hogya, Schiffer, 2024.

Maltin has written and/or produced, and/or hosted and/or consulted on countless documentaries, television specials, home video special features, commentary tracks, interviews, and anthologies for ABC-TV, CBS-TV, Turner Classic Movies, Turner Entertainment MGM/UA, A&E/Republic, Discovery, and the highly valued Walt Disney Treasures home video series.

NAT SEGALOFF BIOGRAPHY

Nat Segaloff is a writer-producer-journalist. He covered the film industry for *The Boston Herald* but has also been a studio publicist, college teacher, and broadcaster. He is the author of over thirty books including *Hurricane Billy: The Stormy Life and Films of William Friedkin, Arthur Penn: American Director* and *Final Cuts: The Last Films of 50 Great Directors* in addition to career monographs on Stirling Silliphant, Walon Green, Paul Mazursky and John Milius. His writing has appeared in such varied periodicals as *Film Comment, Sight and Sound, Written By, International Documentary, Animation Magazine, The Christian Science Monitor, MacWorld, Air Mail* and *American Movie Classics Magazine*.

As a TV writer-producer, Segaloff helped perfect the format and create episodes for A&E's flagship *Biography* series. His distinctive productions include episodes on John Belushi, Stan Lee, Larry King, Shari Lewis & Lamb Chop, and Darryl F. Zanuck. His extraterrestrial endeavors include the cheeky sequel to the Orson Welles *Invasion from Mars* radio hoax, "When Welles Collide," which featured a *Star Trek* cast. It was produced by L.A. Theatre Works and became a Halloween tradition on National Public Radio. In 1996 he formed the multi-media production company Alien Voices with actors Leonard Nimoy and John de Lancie with whom he produced and adapted five best-selling, fully dramatized audio plays for Simon & Schuster: *The Time Machine, Journey to the Center of the Earth, The Lost World, The Invisible Man* and *The First Men in the Moon*, all of which feature *Star Trek* casts. Additionally, his teleplay for *The First Men in the Moon* was the first-ever TV/Internet simulcast and was presented live by The Sci-Fi Channel.

Nat is the co-author of *The Waldorf Conference*, a comedy-drama about the secret 1947 meeting of studio moguls that began the Hollywood Blacklist. Other books include *More Fire! The Building of The Towering Inferno*, *Breaking the Code: Otto Preminger vs. Hollywood's Censors* (including the comedy *Code Blue* by Arnie Reisman and Segaloff), *The Exorcist Legacy: 50 Years of Fear* and *Say Hello to My Little Friend: A Century of Scarface*, and *The Naughty Bits: What the Censors Wouldn't Let You See in Hollywood's Most Famous Movies* (Sticking Place Books, *The Rambo Report*, and *Bogart and Huston: Their Lives, Their Adventures, and the Classic Movies They Made Together*. There will also be an expanded edition of *The Exorcist Legacy*.

Nat lives in Los Angeles waiting for his phone calls to be returned.

NAME INDEX

www.ingramcontent.com/pod-product-compliance
Lightning Source LLC
Chambersburg PA
CBHW060124130626
46556CB00006B/2227